LOTTIE,

018,

THE
WORLD ATLAS OF
STREET FOOD

THE WORLD ATLAS OF STREET FOOD

CAROL WILSON & SUE QUINN

Thames & Hudson

NORTH AMERICA

CENTRAL AND SOUTH AMERICA

EUROPE

CONTENTS

1 In Kashgar in remote western China, a vendor grills lamb kawap (kebab) before sprinkling the hot skewers with a mixture of cumin, white pepper, chilli and salt. The food in this oasis city on the historic Silk Road is influenced by the Uyghur – an ethnic group of Turkic-speaking Muslims.

INTRODUCTION

Street food is precisely what the words evoke – tasty, ready-to-eat food or drink that is available on the street at a market, fair, park, beach or other public place, sold by a vendor from a stall, cart or food truck. Often the food is cooked in front of you. The people you buy the food from are the chefs, owners and servers; consequently it is artisan cuisine at its best. This is a communal enterprise; in order to succeed, a variety of traders gather together to present an affordable, quick, lively alternative to conventional bricks-and-mortar food outlets.

Undeniably, street food is an international phenomenon that has revolutionized how we eat. Its growing popularity all over the world proves that this way to dine is not merely a fad, but is here to stay. Over two billion people now consume street food every day. There is no age bar to enjoying street food; it appeals to all levels of society and is an informal and pleasurable way to enjoy tasty cuisine, including gourmet dishes, with family and friends. Eating outdoors can be social, cheerful and spontaneous. Of course, street food is fresh, accessible and affordable. Another bonus is that people get to try food that they ordinarily would not, other than in a high-priced restaurant.

The cuisine found on the street is changing the way we engage with food as it becomes progressively more upmarket, attracting serious foodies, tourists and a daily lunch crowd all seeking tasty, good-value 'food on the go' made by authentic small producers. The whole experience is becoming more personal. Vendors are passionate about their creations and usually buy fresh seasonal ingredients locally, thus connecting their businesses directly with small-scale farms and growers. Farmers' markets in turn have helped popularize street food. The food truck movement – which started in California in about 2004, when catering trucks from Hollywood film sets were taken onto the streets – has grown considerably over the last few years; it brings the best in street food to many more areas and has the advantage of easily adapting to new food trends.

Globalization has also had a significant influence on street food. It is possible to find all types of street food in every major world city – from Thai food in London to Indian food in Vancouver. The different dishes available in each market are described in the individual market introductions of the book.

Live music and other entertainment often add to the ambience to offer a completely different dining experience with a great atmosphere. The whole buzz that street food creates of people eating and drinking together has a communal feel. Festivals, concerts and night markets are also gaining from the street food revolution as the range of quality food on offer at these events continues to evolve and grow.

Throughout the world, street food enterprises also play an important role in the economic development of many towns in developing countries. Eating on the street is part of everyday life and offers the least expensive and easiest means of obtaining a nutritious meal outside the home for many low-income people. In some countries, particularly in Asia, workers and students buy their first meal of the day from street food vendors.

Street food regulations and controls vary widely from one country to another – even among cities in the same country. International organizations such as WHO (World Health Organization) and FAO (Food and Agricultural Organization) are acting to update and modernize food safety legislation to ensure that street food is safe; measures include hygiene training, educational drives, licensing and regular inspections to safeguard the public. North America and Europe, in particular, enforce strict rules and regular inspections.

Street food, of course, is not a new phenomenon. The tradition of selling food on the streets dates back to the earliest civilizations when ready-made foods were sold from baskets, trays and movable stands. Throughout Europe, Central and South America, parts of Africa, the Middle East and Asia there is a long-standing, often ancient, tradition of street cuisine, using indigenous foods unique to their own cultural history. Later, as trade expanded, new ingredients were introduced, adding variations to many dishes. During the colonial periods in North America, Australia and New Zealand, vendors sold food from carts.

Street food may not be new, but there is no denying that it remains a huge trend. The cuisine found on the streets has become increasingly sophisticated and attracts a vast audience. Visitors can now take a tour of a city based on the street food they would like to try and in the locations they would like to experience it. Starting out in street food is a rising trend and some stalls have grown into prosperous business empires. Conversely, several high-end chefs have ventured onto the streets to get a piece of the action, selling restaurant-quality food from trucks. Other big-name food chains such as Taco Bell, KFC and Byron are rolling out food trucks at popular venues. Even the prestigious Michelin Guide has created a new street food category that should be more wallet friendly than most of its starred restaurants.

Organized geographically by continent, country and city, bringing together street food from all over the world and accompanied by stunning photographs of the food available, this book profiles the best street food markets and food trucks across the planet. Also included are listings of delicious local specialties to try and easy-to-follow recipes that enable you to recreate the standout dishes in your own home. This comprehensive and beautiful book highlights the best places to find the tastiest food-on-the go in the globe's major cities.

NORTH AMERICA

VANCOUVER MONTREAL SAN FRANCISCO
LOS ANGELES DALLAS AUSTIN
NEW ORLEANS CHICAGO BOSTON
NEW YORK WASHINGTON, DC

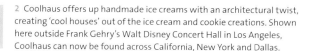

2 Coolhaus offers up handmade ice creams with an architectural twist, creating 'cool houses' out of the ice cream and cookie creations. Shown here outside Frank Gehry's Walt Disney Concert Hall in Los Angeles, Coolhaus can now be found across California, New York and Dallas.

The vast continent of North America encompasses an enormously diverse and complex cuisine. Early English, French and Dutch settlers – together with a multitude of immigrants, ethnic groups and indigenous cooking – established a pattern that gradually developed into a strong regional cuisine with countless new dishes and techniques. Immigrants tailored their own native dishes to the ingredients they found in their new homeland, and North America's street food now incorporates ethnic foods from every part of the world, reaching from the Mediterranean to Asia and from Mexico to South America. Chinese food is widely available, although often 'Americanized'. Japanese sushi, Vietnamese and Thai foods have also been adapted in recent years.

During the American colonial period from the late sixteenth century, street food included tripe, oysters, roasted corn ears, fruit and sweets. Tastes have changed over the years and, while there isn't one particular national dish, anything barbecued and all things grilled or smoked are definitely at the top of the list – along, of course, with the omnipresent hamburgers and hot dogs. Every region has its own distinct cuisine. For example, New Orleans has a unique melting pot of flavours due to French, African, Indian and Spanish influences. The Spanish influence via Mexico is also apparent in California. Early Spanish missionaries introduced almonds, fruits such as figs and grapes, cereals, chickpeas, chillies, wheat, chickens, cows, goats, sheep and domesticated turkeys, all of which still play a considerable role in local cooking. Early colonists boosted their food with game hunted by the Native Americans. Colonists brought wheat with them, but these strains were not easily cultivated in California, so they made corn tortillas until wheat became more plentiful. In addition, there was seafood from the north coast; fresh produce from the Central Valley; fruits and nuts from the San Joaquin Valley and the south; and meat from the state's cattle ranches.

Similar influences reached West Texas, with beef playing an important role. West Texans adopted beans from the Mexicans and consequently beef, beans and corn bread or tortillas became staple foods. Each of the five regions of Texas was settled by pioneers from different parts of the United States and Europe, all with their own unique food heritage. In north-eastern Texas the new settlers learned how to plant corn and use wild plants from the Native Americans; they supplemented native foods with produce grown from seeds they had brought with them. When wheat flour became cheap, corn bread gave way to biscuits (similar to British scones). Inhabitants of the lower southern United States settled in deep east Texas, and while some were poverty stricken, living on wild berries, fruits, plants and any game they could hunt, others were affluent plantation owners, who brought fine foods and southern hospitality to their Texas plantations. South Texas was also influenced by the cuisines of Mexico and Spain, and Mexican cooking, in particular, became widespread. Tacos, guacamole, tamales, enchiladas and tortillas became daily foods.

Chicago evolved as a major agricultural and industrial city. Towards the end of the nineteenth century, before the era of railways, Chicago became the meat capital of America, as the Chicago stockyards were a stopping-off point for cattle being driven from Texas and the Midwest to slaughter in the east.

New York's state fruit is the apple and the 'Big Apple' has steadily progressed from a Dutch village to today's cosmopolitan city, with an amazingly diverse cuisine. Fields, forests, farmlands, ocean and rivers all generated a glut of ingredients that were sold in the city's markets. As far back as 1691, the city began regulating street vendors selling from carts.

Canada's cuisine also differs greatly depending on the region and there is a wide variety of Chinese food throughout the country due to immigration. Generally, traditional Canadian cuisine has British influences, but there are American influences as well. Western provinces have clear German, British, Ukrainian, Italian, Scandinavian and Polish associations, while the regions of Ontario and Waterloo are predominantly German. French regions of Canada such as Quebec have strong French influences in their food. Poutine (French fries, Cheddar cheese curds and gravy) is arguably the country's national dish. It originated in Quebec, but is now found all over Canada. Quebec is also well known for Montreal smoked meat (large thick portions of smoked brisket piled on rye bread with mustard) and tourtiere, a French-Canadian meat pie.

Vancouver, like many large Canadian cities, is a food fusion capital due to the influence of Asian and European cultures. Vancouver's location is ideal to reap the fruits of the sea and seafood is very much a part of the city's food culture, as is locally made cheese and fresh produce. If there's one food item that's synonymous with Canada it must be the maple tree, whose leaf decorates the national flag. Maple syrup and maple products are prevalent throughout Canada and many families enjoy a visit in early spring to a maple sugar 'shack', where sap from maple trees is boiled in a large, open pan to make maple syrup.

Fast food and street food have helped define the cuisine of North America. Street food, especially from food trucks, is becoming ever more popular among foodies and some cities hold festivals to celebrate this new style of cooking and eating. Boston, for example, holds a popular Food Truck Festival, although Portland, Oregon, leads the country in the food truck category with a designated area where trucks congregate. Food trucks can be found in almost every city, selling everything from ethnic specialties to gourmet treats. From coast to coast, these food trucks are making their mark as the latest and greatest in cutting-edge American cuisine.

GRANVILLE ISLAND PUBLIC MARKET

VANCOUVER

Situated on what was once industrial wasteland, Granville Island is now a vibrant hub of activity. Technically a peninsula and not an island, it sits under Vancouver's iconic Granville Street Bridge, attracting more than ten million locals and visitors each year for its boutiques, studios and restaurants, as well as a microbrewery and distillery. But the heart and soul of Granville Island is its public market, a large indoor space that houses an array of food vendors.

Hungry visitors can fuel up at the food court, which sells a global selection of casual meals such as fish and chips, sushi and tacos. There's plenty of indoor seating, but on sunny days visitors are drawn to the outdoor area behind the market where they enjoy breathtaking views of False Creek and lively music from buskers.

This is also a place to stock up on fresh produce, meat and seafood, as well as abundant specialty food items. During the summer, there are berries and stone fruits in profusion, alongside seasonal vegetables such as tomatoes and green beans, shipped in fresh by local farmers. Vendors take pride in their enticing displays, carefully arranging produce by size and colour. Butchers offer kebabs, free-range chicken and ribeye steaks, while seafood shops stock West Coast salmon, spot prawns and oysters. Artisan food producers proffer drool-worthy homemade pasta, soups, gourmet chocolate, jam made with local fruit, and aromatic tea blends. Local crafts and artwork round out the goodies available. TL

Where: 1669 Johnston Street, Vancouver, BC V6H 3R9
When: Daily 9 a.m.–7 p.m.

SPOT PRAWN CEVICHE
A West Coast recipe combining sweet prawns, citrus and spice.

SERVES 8

Preparation: 15 minutes
  plus 4 hours marinating
Cooking: 3 minutes

900 g–1.3 kg/2–3 lb very fresh
  uncooked peeled spot prawns,
  heads reserved
Juice of 8 limes and 8 lemons
½ sweet onion, chopped
2 large tomatoes, chopped
1 bird's-eye chilli, finely sliced

3 tsp fish sauce
85 g/3 oz fresh coriander, finely
  chopped
3 tbsp cornflour, seasoned with salt
  and pepper
Vegetable oil, for deep-frying
2 large avocados, chopped
2 large cucumbers, peeled and
  chopped
Yuzu pepper sauce, or other hot sauce
Tortilla chips, to serve

- Cut the bodies of the prawns into 2.5-cm / 1-in. pieces and place in a large shallow bowl. Add the lime and lemon juice, cover with cling film and transfer to the fridge to marinate for two hours.
- Add the onion, tomatoes, chilli, fish sauce and fresh coriander to the prawns. Cover and return to the fridge for a further 2 hours.
- Toss the reserved prawn heads in the cornflour. Pour vegetable oil in a pan to come 10 cm / 4 in. up the side and heat to 190°C / 375°F. Fry the prawn heads for 2 to 3 minutes until crisp, then transfer to a plate with a slotted spoon.
- Just before serving, peel, stone and chop the avocados and add to the marinated prawns, along with the chopped cucumbers.
- Garnish the ceviche with the crispy fried prawn heads, add pepper or hot sauce to taste, and serve with tortilla chips on the side.

VENDOR SPOTLIGHT

Oyama Sausage Co. is a must for delicious charcuterie, cheeses, terrines and pâtés, as well as smoked sausages. During the barbecue season, up to forty different types of fresh sausages are available, such as bison with rocket and garlic. A fixture of the market for over thirty-five years, **Lee's Donuts** has developed a loyal following for some of the best doughnuts in the city: try honey dip, buttercrunch, peanut or iced maple varieties. Vegetarians and vegans celebrated when **CHAU VeggiExpress**, which also operates a branch in East Vancouver, opened a stall in the market, with a menu featuring Vietnamese-inspired favourites such as turmeric coconut curry soup, chock-full of vegetables and rice noodles. Local five-year-aged Cheddar, French Camembert and fresh curds can be found at **Benton Brothers Fine Cheese** (below). The company takes its cheese very seriously, sourcing from small artisan producers. **South China Seas** showcases the diversity of Vancouver's palate, with a plethora of spices, sauces and specialty foods.

1 Fresh oysters served up at La Boîte aux Huîtres. 2 Lobster tails being grilled in front of visitors' eyes. 3 Breaded scallops – another seafood highlight at Jean-Talon. 4 Crêpes, served in homage to Montreal's French roots.

JEAN-TALON MARKET MONTREAL

Although it is one of the biggest public markets in North America, Jean-Talon has always preserved its village vibe, attracting locals and tourists alike since its creation in 1933. Located on the site of an old lacrosse field in the heart of Petite Italie (Little Italy), it is home to more than 300 stalls, selling fresh local produce and a wide range of snacks and meals to eat on the spot. The market has been designed to operate in all seasons: during Montreal's harsh winters, walls are placed around the covered central section to keep temperatures comfortable, while in summer stalls are set up in the open-air arcades that surround the covered area.

Jean-Talon is the perfect place to get a good overview of French-Canadian cuisine. Poutine – an indulgent combination of French fries, gravy and cheese curds – is the signature dish of Quebec. Les Volailles et Gibiers du Marché makes several varieties, including a poutine au canard effiloché, which is covered with shredded duck confit. Another unmissable experience is the bison burger from Le Bison de la Petite Nation.

There is also a huge variety of seafood. The best place for raw and cooked fish is Les Délices de la Mer, who source their products from the Gaspé Peninsula on Quebec's westernmost tip. Try their breaded scallops, which are served with a tasty garlic dipping sauce. If the sun is out, head to La Boîte aux Huîtres for a few oysters at the counter. Those with a bigger appetite will enjoy their lobster rolls, which are filled with onions, celery, lettuce and mayonnaise.

If you're seeking something more exotic, spicy burritos, chorizo tortillas, samosas and Moroccan pastries all celebrate the cultural diversity of the city. El Rey del Taco – just opposite the market – offers authentic Mexican food. Their pork and pineapple tacos al pastor have gained a dedicated following in Montreal. Délices d'Asie serves up a huge range of spring rolls, for both vegetarians and meat-eaters. VL

Where: 7070 Avenue Henri-Julien, Montreal, Quebec H2S 3S3
When: Open daily 7 a.m.–6 p.m. except Thursday and Friday to 8 p.m. and Sunday to 5 p.m.

MAPLE SYRUP AND PECAN PIES
Sweet maple syrup balances nutty pecan in these indulgent pastries.

MAKES 12 SMALL PIES
Preparation: 40 minutes plus
  2 hours chilling
Cooking: 30 minutes
For the pastry:
250 g/9 oz plain flour
¾ tsp salt
2 tbsp sugar
225 g/8 oz cold unsalted butter
1 tbsp lemon juice

125 ml/4 fl oz cold water
For the filling:
225 g/8 oz light brown sugar
55 g/2 oz unsalted butter
2 eggs
175 ml/6 fl oz dark maple syrup
1 tbsp lemon juice
1 tsp vanilla extract
¼ tsp salt
175 g/6 oz roasted pecans

- Grease 12 tart or muffin tins.
- Using an electric mixer, beat together the flour, salt, sugar and butter. Add the lemon juice and the water and beat until the dough clumps together. Gather it into a ball, wrap in cling film and refrigerate for at least 2 hours.
- Preheat the oven to 200°C/400°F/gas mark 6.
- Flatten the dough into twelve 10-cm/4-in. discs and press them into the tins. Pierce the dough all over with a fork. Put in the oven.
- Melt the brown sugar and butter in a pan over a low heat until bubbles appear, then remove from the heat.
- In a separate bowl, whisk together the eggs, maple syrup, lemon juice, vanilla extract and salt. Still whisking, slowly pour the butter and brown sugar into the mixture.
- With the filling now made, take the pastry cases out of the oven, pour in the liquid mixture, then divide the pecans among them.
- Bake for 10 minutes, then reduce the heat to 190°C/375°F/gas mark 5 for 15 to 20 minutes. Cool in the tins for 10 minutes, then place on a wire rack to cool completely. Chill for 30 minutes before serving.

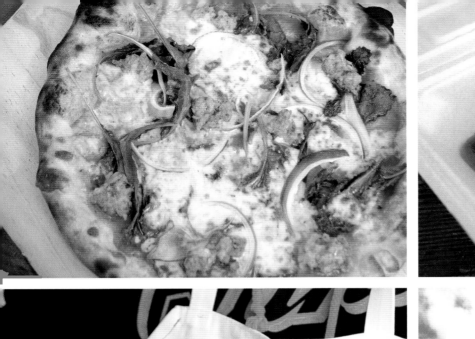

FERRY BUILDING MARKETPLACE SAN FRANCISCO

Opened in 1898, the San Francisco Ferry Building is – along with the Golden Gate Bridge and the Pan Am Building – one of the city's most famous landmarks. The building's imposing clock tower has been a reference point to travellers on the Bay for more than a century. Located on the Embarcadero by Market Street, the Ferry Building (FB) Marketplace is a treasure trove of food shops and eateries that applauds San Francisco's culinary and cultural diversity, and the abundance of artisan food of the Bay Area. After surviving two earthquakes (1906 and 1989), the building's recent redevelopment has seen 6,040 square metres (65,000 sq ft) of marketplace space created on the ground floor, with office space on two floors above.

Now, from famous restaurants to lunch counters, artisan cheeses and fancy mushrooms to confections and cappuccinos, the FB Marketplace offers almost everything your taste buds might crave. Three days a week, outside the building, the Ferry Plaza Farmers' Market – a favourite shopping place for San Francisco's chefs – adds to the cornucopia by offering glorious fresh produce as well as artisan foods and food kiosks. Street snacks include tacos, hot pastrami sandwiches, wood-fired pizza and grilled meats. Be sure to visit The Farmer's Wife stand on Thursdays and Saturdays. **MS**

Where: One Ferry Building, San Francisco, CA 94111
When: Vendor hours vary, but building opens Monday to Friday, 10 a.m.–7 p.m.; Saturday 8 a.m.–6 p.m.; Sunday 11 a.m.–5 p.m.

1 Neapolitan-style pizza from Pizza Politana. 2 Pastrami on rye – a classic. 3 Twists on Korean classics from Namu. 4 The Ferry Building stands tall. 5 Famed grilled cheese from The Farmer's Wife. 6 Check out Mexican eatery Tacolicious.

7–8 Chef Aaron displays a freshly made mariachi chicken sandwich from RoliRoti. 9 Barbecue aromas fill the market. 10 RoliRoti – every meat-lover's dream. 11 Sustainable, homegrown oysters sourced from Northern California at the Hog Island Oyster Co.

VENDOR SPOTLIGHT

Try a cappuccino from **Blue Bottle Coffee**, together with one of the fresh artisan breads from **Acme Bread Company** such as their sweet and sticky cinnamon currant bread. Swoon over iconic northern California Mt Tam cheese at **Cowgirl Creamery**, then grab a melty bite at their Cowgirl Sidekick food bar next door. Pop in to **Boulettes Larder** for Mediterranean farm-to-table breakfast or lunch, but also to buy ingredients and complete meals to go. **The Slanted Door** offers top-notch Vietnamese cuisine, but for a quick bite stop by their Out the Door lunch counter (try the excellent beef pho or lemongrass chicken with roasted chillies and peanuts). A dessert from **Miette** is a must, but so are the **S'mores Bites** (below) – fluffy vanilla bean marshmallows drenched in pure bittersweet chocolate from **Recchiuti Confections**. And when ice cream calls, **Humphry Slocombe** is your answer.

GRILLED CHEESE SANDWICH

Mushrooms, balsamic and caramelized onions elevate a humble snack.

SERVES 4
Preparation: 20 minutes
Cooking: 20 minutes

2 tbsp extra virgin olive oil
2 garlic cloves, peeled and halved
375 g/13 oz mushrooms, thinly sliced
Sea salt
Freshly ground black pepper

125 g/4½ oz butter
375 g/13 oz onions, thinly sliced
1 tsp caster sugar
3 tbsp good quality balsamic vinegar
8 slices bread cut from a crusty loaf
200 g/7 oz Mt Tam cheese (or any Brie-type cheese), thickly sliced
200 g/7 oz Emmental cheese, sliced

- Heat the oil in a pan with the garlic. Add the mushrooms, season with salt and pepper, reduce the heat, cover and cook for a few minutes until soft. Remove the lid, stir and raise the heat to medium-high for 2 minutes so the mushrooms colour and crisp a little. Remove from the heat and set aside.
- Heat 2 tablespoons of the butter in a pan, add the onions, season with salt and pepper and stir. Cook on a medium heat for a couple of minutes, then sprinkle with the sugar and stir. Add the balsamic vinegar and stir. Cook until tender and lightly caramelized. Remove from the heat and set aside.
- Melt the remaining butter in a small pan. Preheat a grill pan on medium. Brush both sides of the bread with the melted butter. Add the fillings on four of the slices in the following order: onions, Mt Tam/Brie, mushrooms, Emmental. Top with the other slices of bread and place on the grill pan, pressing down with a metal spatula. Toast without burning until the cheese melts. Flip and toast on the other side. Serve immediately.

LOS ANGELES

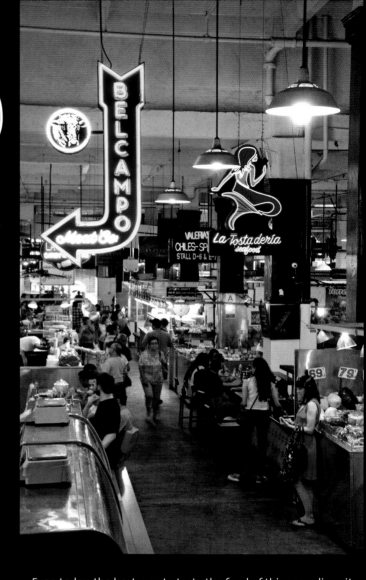

In the late nineteenth century, the onset of the Gold Rush, the arrival of the transcontinental railroad and California's newly realized statehood gave rise to the first street food in Los Angeles. Chinese and Mexican immigrants sold food from carts in the city's streets to satisfy the influx of newcomers, who wanted cheap, filling eats. By the mid-1920s, the street food scene was booming with vendors, many of them Mexican, selling their country's favourite dishes. By the 1930s, tacos were the most fashionable street food in Los Angeles. Chinese carts also offered produce and native snacks from their home country.

With the opening of downtown's Grand Central Market (see p.28) in 1917, stalls were established to house individual vendors and customers began buying their food from markets rather than carts. More street food vendors gradually appeared to take advantage of the city's rapid expansion, with hot dogs and sandwiches sold from mobile trucks from the early 1940s. Workers in offices and factories could grab lunch and street food sales rocketed. Today this lively market draws crowds of locals and tourists alike to enjoy the unique mix of traditional and fashionable foods on offer. There's a huge choice – everything from gourmet burgers to Chinese-American and, allegedly, the best Thai food in the whole of the United States. It becomes very busy at lunchtime and is a popular meeting place, so it is best to visit in the morning. The newest addition to the city's markets is 626 Night Market, held in the summer months. This is the largest Asian-themed night market in the country and it is something of a culinary sensation. Modelled on the night markets popular across Asia, the market brings ethnic food and retail to LA foodies.

Even today, the best way to taste the food of this sprawling city is from the countless markets, carts, stands and trucks that can be found all over Los Angeles. From Korean, Iranian, Guatemalan and Mexican to traditional American foods, there is a dizzying variety to choose from. Food trucks (see p.32) can be found across the city in parking lots, roads and parks, although dates and times are flexible. They offer a huge variety of food, from Korean kimchi quesadillas and Mexican suadero (Mexican brisket) to fresh crab rolls and New England clam chowder. The city's Street Vending Compliance Program is responsible for inspecting vendors who prepare and sell food and a numbered and dated sticker fixed to the truck or cart identifies them as approved and safe mobile food vendors.

There are several noteworthy markets within LA. A favourite is Abbot Kinney Boulevard in Venice, which is best to visit on the first Friday of the month when it's packed in the evening with food trucks and artisan stands selling a variety of popular dishes.

Highland Park, to the north-east of Los Angeles, teems with Mexican street food trucks and drive-throughs. El Mercado in Boyle Heights is another favourite haunt for Mexican food, with many small eateries serving first-rate food cooked to order. Alameda Swap Meet is an old school flea market that takes place on the first Sunday of every month. It offers an enormous variety

of ready-to-go food, especially Mexican. El Faro Plaza, across the way on South Alameda Street, also has some great food vendors offering fantastic street snacks, particularly delicious carnitas (slow-cooked pork). Stroll along Olvera Street opposite Union Station and you'll find windows and stands selling taquitos (small tortillas with a host of tasty fillings) and tortillas. Try the authentic beef taquitos with warm avocado sauce from Cielito Lindo, who have been operating their stand since 1934.

In South Los Angeles chicken reigns and along the train tracks you will find many vendors cooking chickens over charcoal. Look out for juicy chicken marinated in citrus and spices, then grilled and served with beans, rice and salsa in a tortilla.

GRAND CENTRAL MARKET

LOS ANGELES

In the heart of downtown Los Angeles, Grand Central Market is where city workers jostle for lunch with culture vultures or hang out for cocktails after office hours. Built as the city's first food arcade in 1917, European immigrants kept the market busy, but as they moved west, Grand Central became the preserve of the large Latino population of East LA. After a period in the doldrums, when it declined to a bargain-basement bazaar, Grand Market was bought by a developer with a vision of revitalizing LA's fading downtown, faith borne out with the arrival of spectacular new art museums. In 2013 a new wave of vendors arrived to complement long-time presences such as Tacos Tumbras and Chiles Secos, widen the range of offerings and provide a perch for the hungry to dine at as well as take home eclectic purchases not available elsewhere.

Now the market — an orderly, square indoor space with a dining patio — is more ethnically diverse than ever, with Mexican and Salvadoran joined by German, Italian, Jewish, Japanese, Thai and Chinese vendors, not to mention chefs like Mark Peel, a founder of Californian cuisine. There is also a specialty baker, a cheesemonger, a microbrewer and teams of mixologists and coffee roasters. What's to eat? You can find everything from raw oysters and sea urchins to falafel and currywurst, artisanal ice cream and single origin coffee. Vegans are catered for on many stands, but Texas BBQ has managed to establish a presence to please those who find all that healthy Californian food just too damn clean. AG

Where: 317 South Broadway, Los Angeles, CA 90013
When: Daily 8 a.m.–10 p.m.

1–2 Wexler's Deli uses old-school methods to handcraft smoked meats and fish. The O.G. pastrami mustard on rye is a mouth-watering example. 3 A Mexican dish of meat and beans. 4 Wexler's Deli cook, Geo Sandy, slices pastrami.

VENDOR SPOTLIGHT

Eggslut, once a wildly popular food truck, attracts an early crowd with every version of the quintessential brunch staple, notably its signature coddled egg layered with smooth potato purée or its Fairfax sandwich – soft scrambled eggs and chives, Cheddar cheese and caramelized onions in a warm brioche bun (below). Lunchers fall on the home-smoked pastrami sandwiches from **Wexler's**, which has brought Jewish deli back to Grand Central after decades, while the nostalgic sit down to won ton soup at **China Café**, a market fixture since the 1950s. Newcomer **Bar Moruno** attracts spice lovers with cumin-spiked kebabs evoking the markets of North Africa, and German visitors may be surprised to find an authentic taste of home at **Berlin Currywurst**. After picking up a fresh-baked loaf from **Clark Street Bread** to enjoy with regional handmade dairy delights from **DTLA Cheese**, few manage to leave without dessert from **McConnell's Fine Ice Creams**. The artisanal maker tempts with eclectic flavours such as whisky and pecan pralines and eureka lemon with marionberries, as well as the more traditional vanilla.

BAR MORUNO'S ROASTED BUTTERNUT SQUASH WITH DUKKAH
A dish inspired by the warm, vibrant flavours of Spain and North Africa.

SERVES 8 (as a side dish)
Preparation: 30 minutes
Cooking: 1 hour 20 minutes
For the dukkah:
340 g/11¾ oz raw cashew nuts
70 g/2½ oz sesame seeds
1 tbsp nigella seeds
1 tbsp cumin seeds
2 tbsp coriander seeds
55 g/2 oz butter

1½ tsp Aleppo pepper
Salt
For the butternut squash:
1 butternut squash, halved
   lengthwise and seeds removed
55 g/2 oz butter, softened
Salt
Prepared dukkah
2 tbsp browned butter
2–4 tbsp runny honey

- Preheat the oven to 160°C/325°F/gas mark 3. To make the dukkah, toast the cashews on a baking sheet until lightly golden and fragrant, 8 to 10 minutes.
- Combine the sesame and nigella seeds and toast in the oven until fragrant, 4 to 6 minutes.
- Roughly chop the cashews and roughly crush the cumin and coriander. In a sauté pan, melt the butter until it begins to brown. Add the crushed cumin and coriander seeds and toast until fragrant, about 2 minutes, then add the cashews and toast for a further 2 minutes until they begin to brown. Stir in the sesame and nigella seeds, along with the Aleppo pepper and salt. Remove the dukkah from the heat and set aside.
- Heat the oven to 230°C/450°F/gas mark 8. Score the flesh of each squash half in a crosshatch pattern, cover generously with softened butter and salt.
- Roast cut side up until the squash is soft and the outside caramelized, 40 to 60 minutes, checking every 10 minutes until soft enough to pierce with a knife. Serve drizzled with dukkah, browned butter and honey.

LOS ANGELES
FOOD TRUCKS

Food trucks have been a feature of the Los Angeles streetscape for decades, but they have only recently evolved beyond *loncherias* (snack bars) dispensing strictly Mexican fare. Now 5,000 trucks cover the metropolis, offering a wide range of gourmet fare. Mexican food remains a favourite, but Angelenos have other passions, too. Check out locations at roaminghunger.com, which updates the food truck calendar weekly.

Border Grill offers a sophisticated, modern take on Mexican staples such as quesadillas and tamales, while tickling French fries with coriander and adding Cuban treats like chicken with roasted tomatillos. They may love spicy, but Angelenos also crave the simplicity of grilled cheese sandwiches, which can be found wherever a food truck convoy gathers. **The Grilled Cheese** serves the classic version, along with variations including Brie and pear, French onion and caprese with basil and mozzarella.

For Californians, what is really exotic is fresh lobster caught on the East Coast, and **Cousins Maine Lobster** has been meeting these cravings since 2012. They offer lobster rolls, tacos and tails; don't miss the guilty pleasure of tater tots (deep-fried grated potato) with lobster chunks and salsa. There's even lobster ice cream!

Canter's is the original LA deli, so unreconstructed that hit television show *Mad Men* used the restaurant as a backdrop. However, fourth-generation rock chick Bonnie Bloomgarden has dragged the 1931 outfit into the twenty-first century with a truck dispensing Reubens (hot corned beef sandwiches), potato pancakes, matzo ball soup and other deli favourites. They hit the Westside streets when not catering for studio shoots and bar mitzvahs.

Coolhaus (a play on the name of Dutch architect Rem Koolhaas) is the brainchild of architect Natasha Case. It dispenses ice-cream sandwiches named for equally famous colleagues such as Frank Gehry. A California fixture since 2009 – when the original van was the first food truck to serve the Coachella music festival – it is renowned for its signature Tahitian vanilla bean flavour as well as crazier options including fried chicken and waffle. **AG**

POBLANO QUESADILLAS WITH CHIPOTLE SAUCE

These quesadillas, inspired by the popular food truck Border Grill, have a wonderful depth of flavour thanks to a mix of Latin cheeses.

SERVES 6
Preparation: 30 minutes
Cooking: 10 minutes

4 poblano or large jalapeño chillies
350 g/12 oz Mexican manchego cheese, grated
220 g/8 oz panela cheese, grated
115 g/4 oz cotija cheese, grated
6 flour tortillas
75 ml/2½ fl oz good-quality bottled chipotle salsa
30 g/1 oz unsalted butter, melted
Sour cream, to serve

- Roast the fresh chillies over a gas flame or under the grill. Keep turning so that the skin is evenly charred, without burning the flesh. Transfer the charred chillies to a closed plastic bag and steam for 10 to 15 minutes. Pull off the charred skin by hand and dip briefly in water to remove blackened bits. Once peeled, cut away the stems, seeds and veins and dice the flesh.
- In a bowl, mix together the cheeses.
- Divide the cheese mixture into six portions and spread over half of each tortilla. Sprinkle 1 tablespoon of chipotle salsa over each. Arrange the diced chillies evenly over the cheese. Fold over and brush with butter.
- Heat a frying pan and cook the tortillas buttered side down until lightly golden, about 3 to 4 minutes. Brush the uncoated side with butter and flip over.
- Continue to cook until the cheese begins to ooze. Serve hot with extra chipotle salsa and sour cream.

DALLAS FARMERS' MARKET

DALLAS

The hub of good food in Dallas for decades now, the Farmers' Market has continued to thrive thanks to its dedication to giving the city's foodies exactly what they want – excellent fresh produce. The market is committed to helping to educate the local community to live in a healthy and natural way when it comes to food, aiming to promote a more sustainable, nutritional lifestyle among its customers and, by doing so, make a wider social impact. With roots in the community dating back to the late nineteenth century, it started as a humble horse-and-wagon wholesale business for local farmers and traders. As the city expanded, so did business and by 1941 the site was officially sanctioned as a municipally owned and operated market.

The most recent incarnation of the market has seen the event split into 'The Shed' for local farmers and producers and 'The Market' for more than twenty different vendors offering Cajun, Caribbean, tapas and banh mi together with a whole host of others, serving seven days a week for anything up to twelve hours a day at the busiest of times. Covering 2,415 square metres (26,000 sq ft), the hall also includes four anchored restaurants as well as arts and craft stalls selling artworks and antiques. Reconfirming its commitment to education and the promotion of healthy living, the market also offers school tours, chefs' demonstrations and even yoga classes, as well as hosting a nighttime wholesale market open to chefs and the public from May to November, 8 p.m. to 8 a.m. **JW**

Where: 920 South Harwood Street, Dallas, TX 75201
When: The Market: Open daily 11 a.m. – 7 p.m.; Friday 11 a.m. – 8 p.m.; The Shed: Friday 10 a.m. – 3 p.m.; Saturday 9 a.m. – 5 p.m.; Sunday 10 a.m. – 5 p.m.

VENDOR SPOTLIGHT

The food vendors at Dallas Farmers' Market offer an excellent range of sweet and savoury, so you'll be sure to find not only a nutritious but a delicious selection for a day's eating of diverse cuisines. **Cajun Tailgators** offers Louisiana-style delicacies such as fried catfish (below) or alligator po'boys alongside classic gumbo and jambalaya. Taqueria La Ventana mixes authentic Mexican tacos with a modern Texas sensibility, while **Rex's Seafood at the Market** presents a remarkable selection of fish in a variety of styles – crawfish hushpuppies, blackened tilapia, ceviche, even good old fish and chips. For those with a sweet tooth, **Palmieri Café** serves delectable pastries like pasticciotto (a delicious custard-filled cake), inspired by owner Corrado Palmieri's southern Italian heritage, and **Chelles Macarons** is a local bakery that specializes in the tasty little French delicacy.

PASTICCIOTTI

These delectable custard-filled pastries are originally from Puglia in Italy.

MAKES 10 INDIVIDUAL PASTRIES	2 egg yolks
Preparation: 45 minutes	**For the custard:**
Cooking: 25 minutes	500 ml/18 fl oz milk
For the pastry:	½ vanilla pod, split and seeds
250 g/9 oz plain flour	removed, or a little lemon zest
1 tsp baking powder	125 g/4½ oz caster sugar
125 g/4½ oz unsalted butter	50 g/1¾ oz cornflour
125 g/4½ oz caster sugar	4 egg yolks plus extra
Pinch of salt	for glazing

- For the pastry, mix together the flour, baking powder, butter, sugar and salt until the mixture is the consistency of a crumble. Add the egg yolks and stir together until the mixture is combined. Wrap in cling film and refrigerate for 30 minutes.
- Preheat the oven to 200°C/400°F/gas mark 6.
- For the custard, place the milk in a small pan with the vanilla pod or lemon zest and warm gently. Remove from the heat and leave to infuse.
- Mix together the sugar and cornflour, then beat in the egg yolks.
- Add the mixture slowly and gradually to the hot milk, stirring constantly. Put the mixture on a low heat and allow to thicken by boiling, stirring continuously.
- Roll out the pastry to a thickness of 5 mm / ¼ in. and cut out twenty ovals to fit the moulds. Line ten moulds with a pastry oval.
- Fill with the custard cream and cover with the remaining pastry ovals.
- Brush with egg yolk and bake for 25 minutes. Remove from the oven and serve warm.

1–3 The food at East Side King tastes even better than it looks: Poor Qui's Buns stuffed with roasted pork belly and fried Brussels sprout salad.   4 Poutine from Baton Creole.   5 No Bull Brisket – a vegan spin on the Texas staple.   6 Deep-fried jambalaya on a stick.

AUSTIN
FOOD TRUCKS

Austin in Texas has over 1,000 food trucks, with more opening daily. **BBQ Revolution** offers a vegan spin on the Texas staple. With dishes such as the No Bull Brisket made from local wheat roast, tempeh ribs and smoky soy curls alongside classics like gluten-free coleslaw, baked beans and Cajun corn, this will be among the healthiest trucks you'll find – as tasty as the 'real' thing.

East Side King was created by local chefs Paul Qui and Motoyasu Utsunomiya as a side project for them to have some fun and creative freedom with their cooking. It is Asian fusion in the American South at its best. The psychedelic artwork that adorns both the outside and inside of the truck, by Japanese punk rocker artist Peelander Yellow, is every bit as much a part of the experience as the Thai Chicken Karaage, Poor Qui's Buns or the fried Brussels sprouts salad.

Hey!...You Gonna Eat Or What? is a bright red truck where you must love meat slapped between two pieces of bread. Known for its sarcastic slogans, sometimes the food comes sassy as this place has a (friendly, self-appointed) reputation as 'Austin's rudest business'. Unashamedly proud of its Texan heritage, the Lonestar BLT comes with fried green tomatoes; you'll also find the Spicy SXSW Reuben as well the Shiner Monte Cristo – an award-winning sandwich coated in beer batter and accompanied by cherry and fig jelly.

Cazamance is influenced by head chef and co-owner Ibo Thiam's West African heritage, his time spent living and working in New York and France and, of course, his mother's home cooking. It is the only food of its kind you'll encounter in the Austin street food scene. There are traditional West African dishes such as yassa chicken and mafé (peanut stew), but you'll also discover a wealth of original concoctions such as the Dakar boy's lamb burger.

Baton Creole's cooking is inspired by neighbouring Louisiana. Cajun and Creole spicy items are sometimes on the menu, but Baton Creole takes it the whole way with their traditional gumbo (cooked slowly to achieve 'ultimate badassery'), jambalaya and crayfish (crawfish) étouffée. JW

CRAYFISH ETOUFFEE
This tasty Cajun dish is made with a roux and served on rice.

SERVES 4–6
Preparation: 20 minutes
Cooking: 2 to 3 hours

115 g/4 oz butter
100 g/3½ oz plain flour
85 g/3 oz red pepper, diced
85 g/3 oz green pepper, diced
100 g/3½ oz celery, diced
1 garlic clove, finely chopped
325 g/11½ oz onion, diced
115 g/4 oz streaky bacon, chopped

15 g/½ oz fresh parsley, finely chopped
250 ml/9 fl oz beer
900 ml/1½ pints clam juice
1 bay leaf
1 tbsp Cajun seasoning
¼ tsp white pepper
¼ tsp cayenne pepper
250 ml/9 fl oz single cream
450g/1 lb cooked crayfish
Boiled rice, to serve

- In a heavy-based pan, melt the butter and add the flour to make a paste. Stir constantly over a low heat until it turns a beige colour and loses the floury taste.
- Stir in the vegetables, bacon and parsley. Add the beer, clam juice, bay leaf, seasoning and cream. Stir and cover. Simmer gently for 30 to 45 minutes.
- Near the end of the cooking time, add the cooked crayfish and heat through. Serve on a bed of boiled rice.

NEW
ORLEANS

Ever since local Indian tribes traded corn, beans, squash, shellfish, wild game and more with colonial French settlers, food has been a key part of the identity of New Orleans. The early eighteenth century saw the arrival of German immigrants who introduced sausage to the region, and the appearance of the first slaves in Louisiana brought African ingredients to the cuisine. When Louisiana changed from French to Spanish rule and then became part of the United States, other nationalities such as Italians came, bringing their own unique culinary styles. As a result this buzzing city offers a medley of French-, African- and American-influenced foods that reflect its multifaceted history and culture. Enterprising street sellers are part of the city's way of life. During the 1800s, for example, African-American women sold pralines throughout New Orleans and were the most popular street vendors.

Essentially two styles of cooking predominate here – Cajun and Creole. Cajun food originated under French influence during the seventeenth century; it is well seasoned but not necessarily spicy. Creoles were the descendants of the French and Spanish upper-class settlers who ruled the city, but also included, over time, native-born slaves of African descent and free people of colour. Creole food is a blend of the different cultures of New Orleans, including Italian, Spanish, African, German, Caribbean, Native American and Portuguese. It has more variety because Creoles used exotic ingredients from their broad mix of cultures. That is why Creole jambalaya contains tomatoes, but these are never in authentic Cajun jambalaya. Cajun cuisine is often described as 'country food' and Creole cuisine as 'city food'.

Today in New Orleans you'll find a wide choice of street foods from markets and food trucks, with an amazing variety of unique specialties, many of which have a long history. Look out for the po'boy – a substantial French bread sandwich of fried shrimp,

1 An oyster Po'boy sandwich.   2 Po'boys and jambalaya: New Orleans is famed for its Cajun and Creole cooking.   3 French colonial influence inspires the name of the city's major market.

oysters, catfish and soft-shell crab – at the French Market (see p.42). This downtown market began life as a Native American trading post in 1791. Here you'll also find other local delicacies – gumbo, a stew of West African vegetables served over rice; jambalaya, a spicy Cajun or Creole mix of seafood, meats, vegetables and rice; and beignets, square doughnuts dusted with sugar.

Uptown, near the university district, Freret Street offers further opportunities for local food across its eight blocks as well as a monthly farmers' market. St Roch Market (see p.46) on Claude Avenue is a southern food hall that reopened in 2012 after Hurricane Katrina destroyed the original building. It features food and drink vendors serving unusual Haitian-inspired dishes. The main condiment is pikliz (pronounced 'picklees'), a blend of cabbage, carrots, onions, bell peppers and fiery Scotch bonnet chillies.

You'll also come across colourful food trucks parked in locations throughout the city, serving everything from tacos to fried chicken. Several trucks can usually be found near the main university campuses on the tree-lined boulevard of St Charles Avenue, selling renowned southern-style fried chicken, fries, biscuits, waffles and sauces including creole mustard. Look out for the distinctive red and yellow hot dog-shaped carts of Lucky Dog on street corners. Their hot dogs have been a New Orleans favourite since 1948.

FRENCH MARKET
NEW ORLEANS

The French Market in New Orleans is the city's oldest street food hub, one that has survived hurricanes, civil war and encroaching property developers. It was one of the first trading posts on the Mississippi River; when New Orleans was just a village it was the only place to buy meat, seafood or dairy products. A location attracting travellers from every continent, it has spawned a fusion food culture that remains to this day and the city is now one of America's taste capitals. The atmosphere is more Mardi Gras than market; there is live music on every corner, oyster vendors holler and sing as they shuck, and traders call out to customers.

Local Cajun classics gumbo and jambalaya can be found in abundance, but there are also new delicacies to discover. Just about anything that lives in water can be a tasty snack in Louisiana – for example, gator on a stick. White alligator tail meat is seasoned, sometimes rolled in herbs or battered, then deep-fried or grilled, shish kebab style.

Look out for the local Po'boy sandwich. Bread is the key ingredient, usually baguette, the exterior crusty and the inside fluffy to absorb the sloppy filling. This is usually shredded roast beef served with a rich gravy nicknamed 'debris', or fried seafood – everything from crayfish to oysters to shrimp. The best ones include remoulade, a Cajun take on the French mayo-mustard sauce. Another local must-try is étouffée, a rich and spicy crayfish stew. Preparation uses a traditional Cajun cooking technique known as smothering, in which ingredients are cooked in a small amount of liquid to impart intense flavour to the sauce. AJ

Where: 1235 N. Peters Street, New Orleans, LA 70116
When: Daily 10 a.m. – 6 p.m.

1 In operation since 1791, the market's architecture shows clear colonial influences.   2–5 Seafood and local classics are French Market staples.   6 Stuffed full of meat, this sandwich is a winner.   7 Gator is a delicacy hard to find outside Lousiana.

CRAWFISH
ÉTOUFFÉE

VEGGIE
JAMBALAYA

BLACKENED
CATFISH
POBOY

N'awlins CAFE

Bayou Swamp
GATOR BURGER

Dressed & Pepper Jack Cheese $11.95
w/ Mango or Zulu Sauce...

MEATBALL
w/ Sautéed Creole Potatoes $13.00
& Pepper Jack Cheese

SHRIMP
SAUSAGE PO-BOY
w/ Potatoes   9.95

8 A cheese topping to a fried snack.   9 The French Market is popular well into the night.   10 Po'boys are a Louisana favourite, albeit a slightly messy meal!   11 A stylish local vendor stirs a pot of gumbo.   12 Fried plantains are one of the Creole-influenced specialties on offer.

VENDOR SPOTLIGHT

Start your quest for authentic Louisiana cuisine at the farmers' market, which can be found within the French Market. Creole favourites such as jambalaya, gumbo and étouffée (below) are made with love at **Cajun Café**. Get the original trader-style atmosphere at **J's Seafood Dock** where they shuck oysters and serve boiled crawfish. Check out the decadently sweet praline**s** made at **Aunt Sally's**.

PEPPERED SHRIMP

Louisiana locals love spice and shrimp, which are perfectly combined in this recipe by Creole food expert Janet McGowan.

SERVES 2

Preparation: 15 minutes

Cooking: 5 minutes

2 tbsp olive oil

4 garlic cloves, finely chopped

1 Scotch bonnet chilli, finely chopped

500 g/1 lb 2oz uncooked shrimp or king prawns in their shells

½ tsp sea salt

½ tsp coarsely ground black pepper

2 spring onions, finely chopped

Juice of ½ lime

Fresh parsley, chopped, to garnish

- Preheat a heavy-based saucepan on a medium heat and add the olive oil, garlic and Scotch bonnet chilli. Sauté for 1 minute then add the prawns, salt and ground black pepper.
- Stir-fry for 3 minutes, until the prawns start to change colour.
- Add the spring onions, and stir-fry for another 30 seconds, then add the lime juice and simmer for 1 minute, or until the prawns have turned pink. Garnish with parsley and serve immediately.

ST ROCH MARKET

NEW ORLEANS

New Orleans is proud of its history, but there is a new verve in the city since Hurricane Katrina as it looks optimistically to the future. Nowhere is this better celebrated than in its local food markets and festivals. A neighbourhood secret that embodies the spirit of the new soul food is St Roch Market. The historic market hall on St Claude Avenue, erected in 1875, was devastated by the hurricane in 2005. Like a phoenix rising out of the ashes, it has been rebuilt as a community space for the upcoming stars of the food scene. Dynamic food with humour is as much part of the menu as jambalaya.

Brügger's Barbecüe concoct a small menu including craft-grilled ribs, brisket and pulled-pork. Texan Damian Brügger smokes his smorgasbord of meats in a covered area onsite behind the market building. Less time spent on pretension and more time on cooking well is the ethos, with a healthy dose of creative imagination thrown in. Don't miss the barbecue 'debris' mac 'n' cheese.

There are non-meaty options at T2 Street Food, where fragrant phos, baos and noodles are complemented with US-inspired side dishes of slaws and green onions. St Roch Forage uphold the current trend, sourcing beautiful specimens of fruit and vegetables from the Gulf Coast: Louisiana, Mississippi, Alabama and Florida. Getting to grips with classic New Orleans fare is Elysian Seafood, who add fantastic twists to old favourites. Blackened catfish, a Louisiana stalwart, comes with pickled turnips and roasted garlic mayo. There's also a seafood ceviche, which is a masterful blend of seasonal fish with fresh coriander. **AJ**

Where: 2381 St Claude Avenue, New Orleans, LA 70117
When: Sunday to Thursday 7 a.m.–10 p.m.; Friday and Saturday 7 a.m.–11 p.m.

MAXWELL STREET

CHICAGO

Like Al Capone and the esteemed Art Institute, Maxwell Street Market is part of Chicago's historic legacy. Locals have a real love affair with this Sunday escape, where street food is made with passion against a backdrop of performing art and music. The market was founded in 1870 by Eastern European immigrants, and became a place to haggle for anything from sawdust to soap. Waves of newcomers from Italy, Greece, Poland and Asia joined them, selling their exotic foods.

Latin Americans influence today's market fare. The best Mexican food in town can be found here; every stall uses home-made ingredients, cooked to order. You'll soon catch the smell of roasting corn blended with spice and meat. Experimental takes on tacos, quesadillas, tortas and churros are everywhere and each stand has its own spin on the classics. Long queues gather at Rubi's for their home-made corn tortillas. A must-try are tamales (steamed banana leaf parcels of corn) at Oaxacan Tamales; look out for the chicken with salsa verde. At Taco Bernardo offal addicts can tuck into tacos made with goat's spleen, oesophagus and liver. One Latin delicacy in abundance here is huitlacoche, a black fungus that grows on corn. When prepared properly it's a salty, pungent complement to cheese and onions.

The market also has its own coveted dog of provenance, known as the Maxwell Street Polish. Spiced sausage is crammed in a bun with pickles and relish. The finest versions are at Jim's Original or The Original Maxwell Street.

Food is only the beginning of this vibrant Sunday market, which has hosted impromptu appearances from acts such as John Lee Hooker. It's probably the only street food market on the planet to earn a place in the Rock 'n' Roll Hall of Fame, for the urban blues sound it spawned, now marked by the Chicago Blues Festival. AJ

Where: 800 S. Desplaines Street, Chicago, IL 60607
When: Sunday 7 a.m.–3 p.m.

GREEN CITY MARKET

CHICAGO

Green City Market is where Chicago gourmands go to find the freshest sustainable ingredients. Everyone from Michelin-starred restaurateurs and supper-club owners to keen local cooks gather here to get the pick of the best produce sourced from local suppliers and farmers. The rule is that any street food served here must be made with ingredients found onsite.

Green City was set up as a non-profit organization long before the organic food revolution. It began in 1998 with nine farmers and now attracts 180,000 visitors a year, giving growers a platform to showcase their produce and avoid exploitation. All vendors are carefully vetted before they can set up stalls to determine whether what they sell is sustainable and organic. The result is tasty, guilt-free fast food. It's a raw food junkie's nirvana with divine salads concocted with anything from fresh mint leaves to shaved Brussels sprouts, in a compostable bowl, of course.

At Tuscan Hen you can feast on the city's best mac 'n' cheese, with pasta made fresh daily. Its lasagnes are sublime: choose from spinach, crushed meatballs or Tuscan pork ragu. Other market classics include apple cider doughnuts and marinara breads at Zullos. The market also gives cookery demonstrations and chefs such as local Rick Bayless often take part. **AJ**

Where: November–April: Peggy Notebaert Nature Museum, 2430 N Cannon Drive, Chicago, IL 60614; May–October: Lincoln Park, 1800 N Clark Street, Chicago, IL 60614

When: May–October, Wednesday and Saturday 7 a.m.–1 p.m.; November–April, Saturday 8 a.m.–1 p.m.

1 Grilled cheese as you've never seen it.   2–3 Barbecued meats are a fail-safe choice.   4–5 Vendors are vetted to ensure they deliver high-quality, sustainable street food.   6 Al fresco: dining with nature.

VENDOR SPOTLIGHT

The **Nomad Food Company** makes wood-fired pizza and sandwiches. Toasted cheese sandwiches never tasted so good as at **Gayle's Best Ever Grilled Cheese** (below), made with butter and bread produced on the same day. And if it's pure cheese you are after, **Brunknow** offers Brun-uusto, a Finnish-style baked cheese treat heated over a flame until it is crisp and buttery. Crêpes are a market specialty, being the first takeaway food originally offered by Green City founder, Abby Mandel. They come packed with farm fresh ingredients at **Gotta B**. The chicken crammed with sautéed cremini mushrooms and mozzarella is a winner. Few foods define America better than pie and the **Hoosier Mama Pie Co.** is a Chicago favourite. Their pies are hard to resist with names like Fat Elvis (chocolate, peanut butter, banana, pretzel crust). There's also gourmet quiche and savoury pies including pork, sage and apple.

CHILLI PRAWN TAGLIATELLE
A classic pasta dish of sweet prawns with tomato and a kick of chilli.

SERVES 2–3
Preparation: 20 minutes
Cooking: 30 minutes

150 ml / 5 fl oz olive oil	1 glass white wine
1 medium onion, chopped	200 ml / 7 fl oz water
4 garlic cloves, chopped	20 cherry tomatoes, halved
125 g / 4½ oz fresh parsley, chopped	250 g / 9 oz fresh tagliatelle or tagliolini
20 uncooked tiger prawns, shell on	½ tsp chilli powder
	Zest of ½ lemon
	2 spring onions, chopped

- Heat 50 ml / 2 fl oz of the olive oil in a pan and fry the onion, with three chopped garlic cloves and the parsley. Remove heads from the prawns (reserving one prawn per person for decoration) and add them to the pan, along with the wine. Cover with the water and simmer for 10 minutes.
- Process the prawn stock in a blender and then strain it through a sieve.
- Heat 50 ml / 2 fl oz of the oil in a pan and fry the remaining chopped garlic until softened. Add the prawns, tomatoes and strained stock and cook for 3 to 4 minutes.
- Cook the pasta in a large pan of boiling salted water for 2 minutes; drain and stir in the remaining oil and chilli powder. Toss the pasta into the prawn sauce and serve immediately.
- Garnish with the reserved prawns, lemon zest and spring onions.

QUINCY MARKET

BOSTON

Located in the heart of lively downtown Boston, Quincy Market is packed with an appetizing array of food merchants selling everything from New England specialties to Chinese noodles, Mexican enchiladas and Japanese sushi. The bustling indoor food hall is part of the Faneuil Hall Marketplace, a collection of four historic buildings set just back from the city's waterfront and which house a variety of indoor and outdoor stalls, shops and restaurants.

The neoclassical building, with its impressive colonnades, was built in 1826 by Mayor Josiah Quincy – in honour of whom the market has been named – to feed Boston's rapidly growing population. The current incarnation dates back to 1976, when they refurbished the building and created the Food Colonnade, an impressive linear food court that runs the full length of the ground floor. Today, you can still see signs from the original traders hung on the walls of the giant rotunda, where hungry locals and tourists now sit at communal wooden tables and benches tucking into whatever they have purchased from the market's food sellers.

There is now a choice of over thirty vendors, offering both local and international food. Most visitors head to Quincy Market to try the traditional New England dishes, such as clam chowder, lobster roll, chicken pot pie and Boston baked scrod (young cod). If you are a little overwhelmed by what's on offer – and it is easy to be with so much to choose from – ask for a free taster. Most places will be happy to oblige. If it's a nice day, the best place to eat is outside on the cobblestone plaza, where renowned street performers and musicians provide free entertainment. **NS**

Where: Faneuil Hall Market, 4 S. Market Building, Boston, MA 02109
When: Monday to Saturday 10 a.m.–9 p.m.; Sunday 12–6 p.m.

NEW ENGLAND CLAM CHOWDER

This classic New England chowder comes from Quincy Market's Walrus and the Carpenter Oyster Bar.

SERVES 6–8
Preparation: 15 minutes
Cooking: 1 hour

30 large clams	1 small onion, chopped
1.4 litres/2½ pints water	2 sticks celery, chopped
70 g/2½ oz salt pork or bacon, diced finely	60 g/2 oz plain flour
	225 g/8 oz potatoes, peeled, diced
70 g/2½ oz butter	800 ml/28 fl oz single cream
	Tabasco sauce, to taste
	Pepper, to taste
	Chopped parsley, to garnish

- Check that the clams are undamaged and tightly shut. Place them in a colander and rinse under cold running water to remove any grit. Add the clams to a pot of water, cover, bring to the boil and cook for a few minutes until they open. Discard any that remain closed.
- Strain through a fine sieve or cheesecloth and reserve the liquid.
- When cool, remove the clams from their shells and chop roughly.
- Fry the salt pork or bacon in a large pan until the fat runs out. Add the butter, onion and celery. Cook gently until softened, but not browned.
- Mix in the flour and cook for a few minutes on a low heat. Stir in the reserved liquid and simmer for 30 minutes.
- Add the diced potatoes to the pan and simmer until tender. Finally, add the clams and the cream and heat through gently.
- Add Tabasco sauce and pepper to taste and garnish with parsley.

1–2 Food trucks offer up a variety of dishes. 3–4 Classics are just as tempting as more exotic fare. 5 Clover Food Lab jazzes up a fritter. 6 Belgian waffles at Zinneken's. 7–8 Bustling throngs gather around the food trucks. 9 Famous Roxy's Grilled Cheese.

BOSTON
FOOD TRUCKS

From grilled cheese sandwiches, oozing with guacamole and bacon, to huge warm pitta breads, packed with falafel and red cabbage slaw, and authentic Belgian waffles with strawberries and bananas – Boston is brimming with choice when it comes to its food trucks. On any day, you will find trucks parked outside landmarks such as City Hall and Boston Public Library, and on college campuses including Massachusetts Institute of Technology, as well as at special events, festivals and markets. Visit the City of Boston website (www.boston.gov) for information.

One of the best places to find Boston's food trucks is SoWa Open Market (May–October) in the arty enclave south of Washington. This huge Sunday market includes a Food Truck Bazaar where ten to fifteen of Boston's most iconic food trucks line up on a parking lot at 560 Harrison Avenue. A regular at SoWa Open Market is Roxy's Grilled Cheese. After being inspired by a trip to Europe, owner James DiSabatino ditched his plans for a media career and bought a food truck instead. Roxy's menu features grilled sandwiches made with Vermont cheddar, fontina and muenster cheese on soft white, organic pain de mie bread.

Alongside Roxy's you'll often find Clover Food Lab, which offers fresh, locally sourced vegetarian food in large stuffed pitta breads. Fillings include falafel, BBQ seitan and Mayor Menino's Soy BLT (named for the late Boston mayor). Another regular at SoWa is Bon Me, who started selling their fresh, bold Asian food after winning the City of Boston's Food Truck Challenge in 2010. Bon Me are famed for their take on the Vietnamese baguette, banh mi, which they serve filled with Chinese BBQ pork or roasted soy and paprika tofu.

Redbones BBQ serves Southern comfort food – pulled-pork sandwiches, St Louis ribs and collard greens – to hungry downtown workers from a funky red truck decorated with cartoon skulls and bones. And Zinneken's proudly offer 'Belgian waffles made by actual Belgians'. Take your pick from either a Liège (soft 'n chewy) or a Brussels (light 'n crispy), which is then piled high with toppings, including fresh fruit, caramel and (naturally) Belgian chocolate. **NS**

10 With flavoursome foods and quick, easy snacks to suit every taste, no one leaves SoWa hungry.

NEW YORK

New York City's street food is a vista of world flavours from almost every culinary culture. From the oyster vendors of the eighteenth century to the present day's state-of-the-art food trucks, New Yorkers have always had a lavish choice of mouth-watering, inexpensive eats. The first cart service dates to the seventeenth century, when immigrants sold goods on the street to make a living. With the growing numbers of newcomers, especially from Europe, New York's food became more varied and constantly evolving.

If you're looking for New York's best street food, head to one of the city's many outdoor food markets. Smorgasburg (see p.66), the city's biggest and most well-known market; Red Hook Food Vendors (see p.65) on Bay Street and Queens International Night Market (see p.63), one of the city's few nocturnal markets, are all deservedly popular. Other markets include Vendy Plaza, where you'll be spoiled for choice with everything from Chicago-style Italian beef sandwiches to cupcakes. Up to twenty sellers assemble every Sunday under the Metro North railway tracks in East Harlem on Park Avenue between 115th and 116th streets. The Vendy Awards — the 'Oscars of street food' — are presented in September and celebrate the city's unique food culture. Greenmarket, the flagship farmers' market in Union Square, features 140 farmers, fishermen and bakers selling artisan foods, including home-made cheeses and heirloom tomatoes and other homegrown goods. It was founded in 1976 with the aim of promoting regional agriculture and giving small producers the opportunity to sell locally grown products direct to consumers. Stop and watch a cookery demonstration using the freshest choices of the day.

1 Coney Island institution Nathan's Famous has been serving up hot dogs since 1916. **2** Smorgasburg open-air market originated as a flea market, but is now a tourist hotspot and a definite destination for any enthusiastic foodie.

| 1 | 2 |

Chelsea Market, a short walk from the Hudson River in the Meatpacking District, is home to an array of restaurants and food stalls with more than thirty-five traders proffering every type of food. This urban food court was home to the National Biscuit Company in the nineteenth century and is one of the most written-about destinations in the city. The building's brick and timber facade adds to its unique character. LIC Flea & Food, a weekend outdoor market located at 5–25 46th Avenue in Queens, also offers a dazzling choice of artisan foods, including spicy Szechuan beef ramen and okonomiyaki (Japanese savoury pancakes).

Several years ago, a few upmarket food trucks arrived on the streets of New York, adding an exciting new dimension to street food (see p.70). Their success was quickly followed by a host of other new trucks selling foods from around the world and you'll now find them all over the city. Iconic food truck dishes include clam chowder as well as some of the world's finest bagels. Often handmade with a crunchy crust and dense, chewy interior, they're a world away from mass-produced bagels.

German butcher Charles Feltman began selling hot dogs in Coney Island in 1871. Since then, the hot dog has been a New York staple. Nathan's Famous has supplied kosher beef hot dogs for over ninety years in food trucks and diners all over the city. Complement your with thick, crinkle-cut fries – just like the locals do. Or you can take an enjoyable two-hour walking tour and discover this iconic city's street food past and present, meet some of the vendors and enjoy tastings along the way.

1 Dining in front of the Hall of Science.   2 Kebabs on the grill.   3 Bengali snack jhaal muri, served in a paper cone.   4 Korean-style taco.   5 Tofu and avocado roll.   6 Brazilian steak sandwich.   7 Mama Food's grilled squid skewer.   8 Hungarian chimney cake.   9 Entertaining the crowds.

QUEENS INTERNATIONAL NIGHT MARKET NEW YORK

A celebration of cultural and ethnic diversity is how you might describe this vibrant, sometimes frenetic open-air food market nestled in parkland in New York City's largest and easternmost borough. Although still in its infancy – the inaugural Queens International Night Market was held in April 2015 – it has already won fans for the extraordinary range of cuisines on offer and its night-picnic-meets-music-festival vibe.

Located behind the New York Hall of Science at Flushing Meadows–Corona Park, the family-friendly market has so far played host to vendors from almost sixty countries, with up to 100 featured each night. The eclectic stalls attract an equally diverse crowd, which can be partly attributed to the strict price caps aimed at making food affordable for all – at the time of writing the limit was US$6 (£5) per dish. Follow your nose and you might find okonomiyaki (Japanese pancakes), jhaal muri (puffed rice snacks) from Kolkata, sticky Thai chicken wings, hefty Brazilian steak sandwiches, Korean corn dogs, Trinidadian shark sandwiches and Chinese barbecued squid. The range is extraordinary.

Visitors bring blankets and enjoy their food sprawled on the grass or at the picnic tables and chairs provided. This is not a market for a lightning visit: guests linger over their food and drinks, watching the sun set over the park, as the New York Hall of Science lights up. Vendors themselves provide entertainment: if you're lucky, you might catch a Chinese master demonstrating the art of hand-pulled noodles. There is also music, games, dance and often fireworks. SQ

Where: Flushing Meadows–Corona Park, Queens, NY 11368
When: Saturday 6 p.m. to midnight, 23 April to 20 August and 8–29 October

VENDOR SPOTLIGHT

Travel the globe in one gustatory session at the Queens International Night Market. **Chiflez** explores Ecuadorian, Peruvian and Colombian cuisine with delicious bites, including buttered corn on the cob, kebabs and Peruvian steak sandwiches (right). Fans of Long Island's **Roosevelt Ave Fare** adore the roti tacos and Korean fried chicken cooked by the two chef owners who were both born and raised in Queens. **Catmint Wheel Cake** claims to have been the first vendor in New York City to sell the popular Taiwanese desserts, which comprise circular cakes stuffed with flavourings such as cream custard, red bean, banana chocolate, matcha chocolate, corn egg and cheese, and corn and tuna. Alternatively, you could try bubble tea or shaved ice at the **Panda Café**.

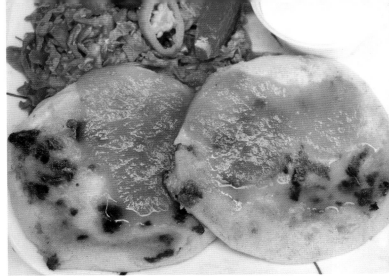

RED HOOK FOOD VENDORS

NEW YORK

Since 1974, Red Hook Food Vendors have been dishing up delicious, Latin American food. Named after its location on the edge of Red Hook Recreation Fields, Brooklyn, the market is regarded as one of the most authentic street food locations in the United States. Here you'll find honest, home-style street cooking: think huaraches (huge Mexican tortillas), tacos, quesadillas (grilled Mexican sandwiches), aguas frescas (Spanish fruit drinks), pupusas (El Salvadoran stuffed corn tortillas) and arepas (Colombian and Venezuelan stuffed corn cakes). Vendors are no culinary slouches; they've won food gongs, including four Vendy Awards – the Oscars of New York street food. It wasn't always so. More than forty years ago, it was soccer and not food that drew the crowds: players and supporters converged on the sports fields for weekend fixtures. There were few food or drink options in the vicinity, so locals responded by setting up stalls selling authentic foods from their homelands.

Decades later, the food is still extraordinary but the area's gentrification – it was once infamous for crime, drugs and prostitution – has placed a question mark over the market's status. It seems this humble market does not dovetail with everyone's vision for the future. Once upon a time, local authorities pretty much left vendors to their own devices, but over the years, layers of red tape and dwindling crowds have threatened the market with extinction. For the moment, this culinary treasure still exists – but its future hinges on continued support. SQ

Where: Red Hook Recreation Fields, 160 Bay Street, Brooklyn, NY 11232
When: Weekends 10 a.m. to sundown, April to the end of October

1–2 Pupusas being skilfully prepared at El Olomega. 3 Tacos are always a favourite. 4 Spicy condiments are a must for Latin American food. 5 Enjoying home-style cooking in the open air. 6 Shredded red cabbage adds colour to the food.

SMORGASBURG NEW YORK

Dubbed 'the Woodstock of eating,' Smorgasburg is a real-deal mecca for New York foodies, as well as gastronomic pilgrims from around the globe. Heaving with endlessly delicious food stalls, cool people and astonishing views of the Manhattan skyline, there's only one rule for visitors to this gustatory nirvana: go ravenous. Around 100 vendors set out their stalls every Saturday on an empty riverside lot at East River State Park in Williamsburg, creating a multicultural food bazaar that has visitors drooling and dazed with choice. It is little wonder that up to 20,000 people descend on the site each Saturday for a feasting session: from Mexican iced lollies and Japanese-inspired Mexican food, to kimchi burgers and stuffed patties from El Salvador, they can expect the unexpected.

This food-only 'grub hub' was launched in 2011 as a spin-off to the hugely popular Brooklyn Flea, founded by Jonathan Butler and Eric Demby in 2008. Smorgasburg – a portmanteau of smorgasbord and Williamsburg – is now deluged with applications from would-be vendors, who are interviewed and their food taste-tested before earning the right to a highly coveted stall. The result? High standards and an incredible diversity of food that has even launched worldwide food trends, such as the ramen burger. Many vendors also run acclaimed bricks-and-mortar businesses as well, so visitors can enjoy the best of NYC eating without straying from the one location. Be prepared for large crowds and long queues; however, it is generally well worth the wait.

Smorgasburg has been so successful that similar food-only markets have sprouted up in locations beyond Williamsburg. There are now fixtures in beautiful Prospect Park, Brooklyn; Seaport, Manhattan; and Los Angeles, as well as various pop-up events. SQ

Where: East River State Park, 90 Kent Avenue at N. 7 Street, NY 11211

When: Saturday 11 a.m.–6 p.m.; rain or shine

1 Outer Borough's classic braised beef sandwich.   2 Vaquero's mango on a stick.   3 Wowfulls create 1950s-style Hong Kong egg waffles.   4 Carnal's short rib beef.   5 Snacking and chatting.   6–7 Preparing and enjoying refreshing coconut water.

8–9 Grab a seat at a picnic table to stop and tuck in. 10 Salted and blistered: snack on several moreish Padrón peppers. 11 Handmade deep-fried mozzarella sticks from Big Mozz. 12 Carnal's renowned slow-cooked barbecue. 13 Eat, drink, be happy.

RED HOOK LOBSTER POUND LOBSTER ROLLS

Recreate Red Hook's signature sweet and succulent treat.

SERVES 8

Preparation: 15 minutes

Cooking: 5 minutes per batch

900 g/2 lb cooked lobster meat, as fresh as possible

75 g/2¾ oz quality mayonnaise, ideally home-made

150 g/5½ oz celery, finely chopped

2 tbsp lemon juice

½ tsp sea salt, or to taste

Pinch of ground white pepper

8 hot dog rolls, split

115 g/4 oz butter, melted

200 g/7 oz iceberg lettuce, finely shredded

3 spring onions, finely sliced

Sweet paprika, to taste

- Place the lobster meat in a mixing bowl and stir in just enough mayonnaise to bind. Add the celery and lemon juice, and season with salt and pepper. Divide the salad into eight equal portions and set aside.
- Generously brush the sides of each roll with melted butter. Grill the rolls in a hot frying pan, as you would a cheese sandwich, until golden on each side.
- Stuff some lettuce into each bun, add a portion of the lobster salad, and top with spring onions and a sprinkling of sweet paprika. Drizzle with melted butter and serve immediately.

VENDOR SPOTLIGHT

Smorgasburg is a multicultural mouth-watering mixing pot of food that is cool, interesting, unique and always changing. Deep-fried mozzarella sticks might not be considered traditional Italian fare, but fans of the **Big Mozz** claim the ones they serve up are incredible. Egg waffle ice cream cones festooned with toppings are a popular draw at the **Wowfulls** stall. **BrunchStreet** — a vendor whose head chef previously worked at acclaimed NYC eatery Eleven Madison Park — dishes up delectable skewers of crispy quails eggs (left). **Dough** sets foodie hearts aflutter with highly praised, gorgeously iced doughnuts. **East Coast Poke** is committed to fresh and authentic Hawaiian cuisine with seafood from sustainable fisheries, while **Kimchi Smoke** delivers Korean barbecue classics with a punchy serving of kimchi (fermented spicy pickled cabbage). Or how about a burrito roll stuffed with French fries at **Best Buds Burritos**? Look out for the oddball: **Raindrop Cake** sells the eponymous see-through wobbly cakes that took social media by storm.

NEW YORK
FOOD TRUCKS

The hot dog is probably New York's original staple, but as the city's immigrant population has grown over the decades the street food available has grown exponentially. Brian Goldberg, founder of **Mr Bings**, ate jianbing every day when he studied Chinese in Beijing back in 1998 and his truck is the realization of a dream to bring this northern Chinese street crêpe to wider attention. The classic vegetarian version, with scrambled egg and crispy wonton, is their take on the Beijing style that is traditionally eaten for breakfast. There's also barbecue pork, Peking duck and drunken chicken.

The Morris food truck elevates the humble cheese toastie to something nearing gastronomic heaven and should be your first stop for this snack. The Classic is made with New York State Cheddar, while the Green Machine comes with fontina, fennel butter and kale. The blue cheese Habanero Chicken is given some piquancy with pickled celery and, if you want a touch of class, the Delicate Cheese offers both truffle cheese and butter!

The Cinnamon Snail is a longstanding favourite among food truck enthusiasts. Their inventive approach to vegan sandwiches, burgers and pastries has customers consistently coming back for more. The Beastmode Burger Deluxe – an ancho chilli seitan burger grilled in maple hickory barbecue sauce with jalapeño mac 'n' cheese, rocket, smoked chilli coconut bacon and chipotle mayo on a grilled pretzel bun – is just one example of the different flavours you'll encounter on a menu that changes seasonally.

El Olomega has served the people of Red Hook, Brooklyn for over twenty years and is the only place you should go for pupusas – an El Salvadoran corn flour tortilla stuffed with chicken, pork, shrimp, sweet plantain or a specialty of El Olomega, the loroco flower. **Snowday Food Truck** gets a lot of things right. Not only does it offer a menu where the staple ingredient is maple syrup – for example, maple bacon and fried Brussels sprouts – it's run by Drive Change, a non-profit organization that supports criminal justice reform by employing formerly incarcerated youths to help keep them from reoffending. **JW**

JIANBING CHINESE CREPES
These savoury crisp fried pancakes are a much-loved Chinese street food.

SERVES 4–5 (ONE BING EACH)	16 wonton wrappers
Preparation: 20 minutes	**For the crêpes:**
Cooking: 30 minutes	5 tsp vegetable oil
For the batter:	5 eggs
85 g / 3 oz plain flour	4 spring onions, thinly sliced
85 g / 3 oz mung bean flour	5 tsp black sesame seeds
1 tsp sea salt	5 tbsp hoisin sauce
250 ml / 9 fl oz water	5 tbsp chilli paste
For the crispy wontons:	55 g / 2 oz fresh coriander leaves,
225 ml / 8 fl oz vegetable oil	finely chopped

- For the batter, sieve together the plain and mung bean flours and salt. Whisk in the water until a smooth batter forms. Set aside.
- For the crispy wontons, heat the oil in a heavy-based frying pan. Fry the wonton wrappers in four batches of four until golden brown. Remove and leave to cool on absorbent kitchen paper. When completely cool, crush the wontons into 2.5-cm / 1-in. pieces with your hands.
- For the crêpes, heat 1 teaspoon of the vegetable oil in a frying pan over a medium heat. Pour enough batter into the pan to create a thin pancake.
- Whisk one egg in a small bowl.
- Once the crêpe begins to curl at the edges, pour the beaten egg mixture on top and spread in an even layer over the entire surface. Sprinkle some of the spring onions and a teaspoon of sesame seeds over the egg and cook for one minute more until the egg begins to set.
- Carefully flip the crêpe and brush with 1 tablespoon of the hoisin sauce and 1 tablespoon of the chilli paste, then scatter over some crushed wonton pieces and coriander.
- Fold the crêpe horizontally and vertically to form a squared pancake. Cut in half and serve immediately. Repeat with the remaining ingredients.

WASHINGTON, DC
FOOD TRUCKS

When the office workers and political players of Washington, DC stride out for lunch, it is easy to imagine they're heading to smart steakhouses or fancy hotel bars. However, they are more likely to be found creasing their suits by perching on park benches or gallery steps, munching on fried chicken or slurping fragrant spoonfuls of Vietnamese pho. Since the first regulated food trucks rolled into the capital in 2009, the scene has exploded. Trucks park up at designated mobile roadway vending zones (MRVs), with the most popular hubs at Franklin Square, Farragut Square, Union Station, Metro Center, George Washington University, Chinatown and L'Enfant Plaza. The easiest way to track vendors is to follow them on Twitter or to check websites – for example, Roaming Hunger and Food Truck Fiesta. There are around 200 mobile kitchens serving up diverse cuisines, from sticky Peruvian chicken wings at **Los Wingeez** to satisfying bowls of Korean bibimbap (mixed rice and meat with tangy pickles, topped with a fried egg) at **BiBi Ja**.

With the farmlands of Virginia and Maryland as their pantry, plus quality farmers' markets in the city, local ingredients are prominent on many menus. Some trucks are owned by cooks wanting to break into the dining scene, while others are spin-offs from bricks-and-mortar locations. Launching a food truck is deemed a savvy business move for restaurateurs. **Captain Cookie and the Milkman** has a store on Pennsylvania Avenue and two vans. Locals follow their tweets to locate the huge, gooey-centred chocolate chip cookies, ice-cream sandwiches and milk from local creameries. A spin-off from Crêpe Amour, a café in Vienna, Virginia, the **Crêpe Love** truck pops up daily around the capital with savoury and sweet creations, like the banana, strawberry and hazelnut chocolate spread Carnivale. One unusual truck is **Astro Doughnuts and Fried Chicken**, often parked in Chinatown. Whimsical flavours such as peanut butter and jelly change daily; an indulgent choice is the fried chicken sandwich seasoned with Old Bay. Suited workers devour this fix sprawled on the steps of the Smithsonian's National Portrait Gallery – redefining the idea of the power lunch. **EB**

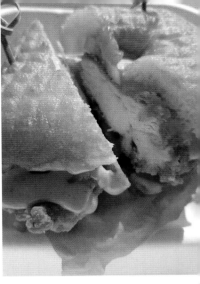

1 A vintage-style food truck proudly displays its Argentinian offerings. Renowned for steak, Argentinian cuisine offers so much more, including the national dish asado – a selection of barbecued meats cooked on a parrilla grill – and an indulgent take on grilled cheese – the provoleta.

CENTRAL AND SOUTH AMERICA

MEXICO CITY KINGSTON CUZCO SUCRE RIO DE JANEIRO BUENOS AIRES

In Central America, South America and the Caribbean, centuries of Spanish, African and European influences have combined with native flavours to offer a thrilling culinary experience. The original inhabitants of Central America were the Maya (from around 2000 BCE) who ate indigenous squash, beans, maize, chilli peppers, meat, fish, game, fruits and vegetables as staple foods. Their civilization's height was between 250 and 900 CE, until their rule in southern Mexico and northern South America declined and finally ended with the arrival of the Spanish in 1519. The Aztec Empire was located in central Mexico and ruled much of the region until the Spanish arrived, by which time turkey and duck had been domesticated. The seeds of the native cocoa tree (*Theobroma cacao*) were highly esteemed by both the Maya and Aztecs. They ground the dried fermented beans to make luxurious, highly spiced drinks.

This region's gastronomy has also been influenced by the food of Spain, Asia, France, West Africa, Portugal, India and the Caribbean. Except for Belize, all these countries were first settled by the Spanish in the early 1500s. Spanish food has had the most influence on Central American cuisine. The Spanish introduced sheep, pigs, cows, dairy products, herbs, wheat and spices. The assimilation of other cuisines including Caribbean, South American, French, West African and Portuguese resulted in a rich regional gastronomy. Belize has a large native-born population of African descent although the cuisine is a blend of Spanish and Mayan influences. Despite differences among the countries, they all have unifying features and ingredients such as corn or maize, peppers and beans.

The diverse cuisine of Jamaica has been influenced by the Spanish, British, East Indians, West Africans, Portuguese, Chinese, French and Dutch. The Spanish came with slaves who brought techniques, spices and recipes from Africa; the Spanish Jews introduced dishes such as escovitch fish; the English set up sugar plantations and immigrants from China and East India brought spicy foods. Jamaica is now renowned for its jerk-spiced dishes and curries.

From meat-loving Argentinians to the fish-loving Peruvians, South America boasts a stunning variety of street food. This is the continent that gave the world corn, tomatoes, potatoes and chillies. The first populations of South America hunted llamas, turkeys and other wild animals, and gathered wild foods such as corn, potatoes, beans and avocados. Around 8000 BCE they began to cultivate potatoes and later, corn, beans and chillies. Long before Europeans discovered South America, the indigenous peoples were cultivating plants, developing intricate irrigation systems and terracing the steep mountainsides to grow crops. When the Europeans arrived, they incorporated native dishes into their own cuisine. They took the new foods back to Europe and introduced European foods to South America such as pigs, cows, goats, chickens, citrus trees and wheat. European settlers adapted their favourite Spanish, Italian and Portuguese dishes using local ingredients. Native American ingredients and cooking methods were modified to incorporate the new European foods and a traditional regional cuisine gradually emerged.

In Colombia Spanish conquerors took their cuisine to the native Indians, the Chibchas, who grew various beans, cassava, quinoa and potatoes. The heavy Spanish influence is still apparent today in Spanish-style soups, stews and desserts, although local ingredients make them distinct. Coconut milk is used extensively – for example, in arroz con coco y pasas (rice with coconut and raisins). Fresh coriander is used a great deal, as is hot pepper sauce.

In Peru, the highly organized society of the ancient Incas had an extensive road system, linking towns and cities. As a result farmers could take their produce to markets in the nearest town. Peruvians love colourful food and the herb palillo (turmeric) is ground to a

3 A beach vendor sells traditional Brazilian snacks made from tapioca (manioc or cassava) flour in Rio de Janeiro. Cooked to order, these crêpe-like pancakes are served with a variety of sweet (*doce*) and savoury (*salgado*) fillings.

powder to colour and flavour food. The cooking is characterized by the generous use of peppers, of which there is a great variety, most of them hot. Bolivian cuisine is closest to its indigenous origins. Potatoes and corn are a main part of the diet. Like the Peruvians, they love hot, spicy food and use peppers lavishly. Quinoa was cultivated by the ancient Incas and is still grown and widely eaten.

Brazil accounts for nearly half of the land mass of South America and its ethnic groups are diverse, comprising native Indians, Portuguese, Italians, Africans, Germans and more. The arrival of the Portuguese in 1539, who planted sugarcane and brought African slaves to work in the fields saw a new type of cuisine emerging – *cozinha baiana* or Bahian cookery. The chief ingredients are palm oil, coconut, coriander, dried shrimp, peanuts, cashews and almonds and, needless to say, hot peppers. There was not a great Indian civilization in what is now Argentina. Before independence, Spanish cooking, using indigenous and introduced ingredients, produced the local cuisine, which was later modified by new arrivals – the Italians, in particular. Argentinian beef ranks with the finest in the world and there are some unusual stews with fruits such as carbonada criolla (beef stew with peaches).

Certain ingredients form the basis of South American cuisine. For example, corn is the key ingredient of arepas (cornbread) and chicha, an ancient beverage. Potatoes rival corn as the oldest and most important South American crop and are cooked in myriad ways. Every country has its own unique street food that reflects its individual climate, culture and culinary tradition. The little pastries known as empanadas are a staple street food found throughout this sprawling continent. Ceviche is also found in every market – a cold fish dish marinated in lime and chilli that 'cooks' the fish from raw – a method that predates refrigeration. Lima in Peru is thought of as the capital of ceviche.

MEXICO CITY

When the Spanish conquistadors arrived in Mexico in 1519, they were astonished to find ready-made food on sale in the Aztec markets and streets. This centuries-old tradition continues today and street food still plays an important part in Mexican daily life. With almost 21 million inhabitants, the capital of Mexico City is one of the world's most populated cities. To experience its real culture the street food is unmissable. Street food stands are everywhere – from fixed stands, market stalls, small restaurants (*fondas*) and food trucks, to vendors under umbrellas, on carts and bicycles – all offering a tantalizing, mouth-watering array of snacks, meals and beverages. Thousands of *taquerias* (taco stands) sell tacos, tamales (a traditional Mesoamerican dish made of masa or dough steamed in a corn husk or banana leaf), quesadillas, elote (roasted corn on the cob), chapulines (fried grasshoppers) and much more.

1 Located in the historic city centre, Mercado de San Juan is the place to go for exotic ingredients and gourmet products.
2 The fleshy, tender leaves of the nopal prickly pear cactus have been commonly eaten in Mexico since ancient times.

Mercado de San Juan Arcos de Bélen (see p.82) is one of the best artisanal food markets in the city. There are plenty of Oaxacan specialties to choose from such as blue corn quesadillas and tlacoyos – tortillas stuffed with mashed fava beans and grilled over charcoal, topped with nopales (prickly pear), shredded cabbage and queso fresco (mild white cheese). If you're feeling adventurous, sample roasted chapulines dusted with chilli powder or fried in garlic oil.

Mercado de Dulces Ampudia (see p. 84) is a mecca for sweet lovers. Traditional Mexican sweets abound here in a dazzling variety of colours that you won't find in supermarkets. Also available are unusual candied vegetables like calabaza (pumpkin), chilacayote (squash) and camote (sweet potato), plus local chocolate. Try tarugos (tamarind sweets with sugar or chilli) and rich creamy Glorias de cajeta (goat's milk caramel and pecan nuts) in individually wrapped balls. Look out for ollitas de barro – little clay pots filled with sweet tamarind paste mixed with sugar, salt and chilli that offers a combined taste of sweet, spicy and savoury – and sublime cocadas (toasted coconut sweets).

Central de Abasto (see p. 86) – the largest market in Latin America – is a vast hive of activity with thousands of people crowding into the marketplace daily. It's a feast for the eyes as well as the palate. Besides the enormous choice of fruits and vegetables, there are plenty of ready-to-eat treats such as esquites, a warm grilled corn salad – a popular Mexican street snack.

Bajío Street (on the corner of Bajío and Salina Cruz) is one of the most vibrant streets in Colonia Roma, a fashionable, artistic district just west of central Mexico City. As well as all the street stands, there's a market every Saturday, with a fantastic variety of food. Inside the market you're sure to hear a long, loud whistle from a camote cart selling plantains, yams and sweet potatoes cooked on a bed of charcoal inside an oven built into the cart. They are served with strawberry jam and condensed milk. The whistle comes from the steam being released from the oven through the cart's small pipe. The steam keeps the food from drying out.

Tamales are one of the best loved foods in Mexico. They were first made for warring Aztec and Mayan tribes and today are one of the most common street foods, traditionally eaten in the morning for breakfast. Made from corn masa (dough) shaped around a filling – sweet (chocolate or cream cheese with blackberry) or savoury (chicken mole or pork in green sauce) – they are wrapped (usually) in a corn husk and steamed. A massive steel bucket full of steaming tamales and pots of atole (a hot corn-based drink) are the essentials of the tamale stand.

Tortillas – thin, unleavened flatbreads made from finely ground corn – are a Mexican staple. A taco is a tortilla filled with meat, poultry or seafood, and served with salsa. Every taco stand will have at least two variations of salsa, as well as a mix of chopped onions and habañero chillies, French fries or sautéed potatoes and a large bowl of Mexican limes. Tacos al pastor ('in the style of the shepherd') – thick strips of pork shaved off a vertical rotisserie spit and served on a soft tortilla – were introduced in the 1920s with the arrival of Lebanese and Syrian immigrants to Mexico. Chilaquiles made with lightly fried quarters of corn tortilla covered with a spicy red or green salsa are another typical Mexican dish. Go to Colonia Condesa (on the corner of Alfonso Reyes and Tamaulipas, Col. Condesa, Delegación Cuauhtémoc), where there is always a queue of eager customers. Sample them inside bolillo (bread) or ask for 'la bomba' – mixed red and green chilaquiles and breaded chicken breast. Other ubiquitous street snacks include chicharrón (crisp pork crackling) and plastic cups of fruta con chile y limon – fresh fruit, such as mango, pineapple and papaya, dusted with chilli powder, salt and a spritz of fresh lime.

Mexicans also adore sweet treats and coffee and pastries can be found everywhere. It's a familiar sight to see a vendor riding a bicycle selling hot café de olla (cinnamon-flavoured coffee) from a jug and delectable pastries carefully displayed in baskets. Other sweet treats include Mexican-style egg nog (rompope), a delicious thick yellow drink made with eggs, rum, vanilla, milk, sugar and almonds. Served in small glasses, it is meant to be sipped.

MERCADO DE SAN JUAN ARCOS DE BELEN MEXICO CITY

Mercado de San Juan Arcos de Bélen (also known as San Juan Salto del Agua) is a vibrant, budget-friendly hub for locals. Less hyped in guidebooks than other Mexico City markets, it nonetheless offers visitors an incredible taste of the country's food and flavours.

Created in the 1950s after the original San Juan marketplace was split up, the market was almost destroyed by a devastating fire in 2012 that claimed around 10 per cent of the stalls. But this bustling food bazaar has clung on to its role as a source of staple food items for the city's citizens. It now comprises 125 square metres (1345 sq ft) and 400 stalls of lusciously bright fruit and vegetables, prepared foods, nuts and seeds, meat, chillies, moles (traditional sauces), juices and other Mexican favourites.

Upon entering, visitors soon become immersed in the colourful and stimulating atmosphere of this traditional Mexican food market. There are numerous options to sit and eat at Mercado de San Juan. Gloria y Familia Taco Placero boasts a selection of prepared foods to seduce the senses – grilled vegetables, rice, stewed huitlacoche (a fungus that grows naturally on ears of corn), handmade hot salsas, salads, tamales, beans and soups. Veggie friendly, it displays ceramic trays piled with delectable greenery. All the dishes on offer at Gloria's act as a vehicle for her glorious salsas and hot sauces – around ten different kinds: grilled nopal cactus, sautéed onions, yellow rice and vegetable rice, many herbs native to Mexico, as well as stuffed poblano chillies, tamales (a corn-based dough wrapped in a leaf, which is steamed or boiled) and elote (corn on the cob served with salt, chilli powder, grated cheese, lime juice and mayonnaise).

Moles Sarita is the place to go for prepared mole sauces and chillies. Stallholders are generally friendly and knowledgeable regarding the names, origins and usages of the foods. CL

Where: Arcos de Belén y Lopez Centro 06010, Mexico City
When: Daily 6.50 a.m. – 8.30 p.m.

TOMATILLO SALSA DE GLORIA

Mexico's answer to the salsa verde is a versatile partner to many foods.

SERVES 6–8 (as an accompaniment)
Preparation: 20 minutes
Cooking: 20 minutes

300 g/10½ oz tomatillos, husked and rinsed (or use unripe tomatoes with a squeeze of fresh lime juice)
1 serrano chilli, deseeded and stem removed
½ jalapeño chilli, deseeded and stem removed
3 garlic cloves, peeled
¼ onion, finely chopped
30 g/1 oz fresh coriander, chopped
Sea salt, to taste

- Preheat the oven to 200°C/400°F/gas mark 6.
- Place the whole tomatillos (or unripe tomatoes and lime juice) in a baking tray and roast for 15 to 20 minutes. Be careful not to let them burn.
- When cool, transfer to a food processor along with the remaining ingredients. Pulse briefly until everything is combined into a coarse purée – don't blitz to a sauce. Add salt to taste.

1 Sweet but strong: rolled in sugar and flavoured with liquor, borrachitos are known as 'little drunks'. 2 Mazapán de cacahuates are a peanut marizpan sweet treat, emblematic of Mexican culture. 3 Mamey fruits are native to Mexico and are used to make ice cream and milkshakes.

MERCADO DE DULCES AMPUDIA

MEXICO CITY

Mexico City's specialist sweet market sits next to its colossal, famous cousin, La Merced, on the borders of the historic city centre. The modern hangar-like complex was built in the mid-1900s, but the first market was held on this site hundreds of years ago and grew up around the remains of a sixteenth-century monastery. El Mercado Ampudia is an Aladdin's cave of shimmering colours and the intoxicating aromas of exotic fruit, flowered honey and crystallized sugar, velvety chocolate and caramelized nuts. The market prides itself on its artisanal wares and there is a distinct lack of industrially produced goods, with *casero* (home-made) concoctions prominent. *Marchantas* (sellers) at the stalls are eager to explain how they make their specialties from old family recipes.

Mexico has a long history of sweet-making dating back to the pre-Hispanic era when candies were made from indigenous fruits, grains and nuts. Cane sugar, wheat and dairy were introduced by the conquistadors, and the Spanish nuns who followed them began the venerable tradition of Mexican confectionery. This gradually absorbed European influences and today El Mercado Ampudia offers everything from amaranth-based alegrías (rice cakes) and exquisite alfeñiques (sugar paste confections) modelled from pumpkin seed marzipan to candied fruits, coconut-stuffed limes, tamarind balls, goat's milk fudge, coffee meringues and nut brittles. The choice is mesmerizing and new seasons and holidays bring a distinct change of focus: grinning sugar skulls for the Day of the Dead; beribboned baskets of candied fruit for the Christmas *posadas*; acitrón (crystallized cactus) for the Epiphany Rosca de Reyes (Three Kings' bread); and beautifully crafted eggs for Easter. IH

Where: Anillo de Circunvalación 40, Cuauhtémoc, Mexico City

When: Monday to Saturday 8 a.m.–7 p.m.

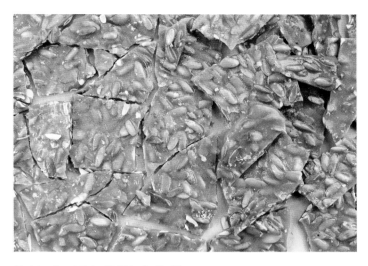

PALANQUETAS DE ALMENDRAS Y PEPITAS

Almonds partner ancient Mexican pumpkin seeds in this sweet brittle.

MAKES ABOUT 15 PIECES (depending on size)

Preparation: 30 minutes

Cooking: 20 minutes

100 g/3½ oz blanched whole almonds

100 g/3½ oz hulled pumpkin seeds

225 g/8 oz granulated sugar

100 ml/3½ fl oz water

2 tbsp unsalted butter

¼ tsp bicarbonate of soda

¼ tsp fine sea salt

- Preheat the oven to 175°C/350°F/gas mark 4. Spread the almonds on a baking tray and cook in the oven until lightly browned, about 10 minutes.
- In a large frying pan, stir the pumpkin seeds over a medium heat until aromatic and starting to pop. Mix with the almonds and set aside.
- Line a baking sheet with non-stick paper.
- Place the sugar and water in a pan and heat gently, stirring with a wooden spatula, until the mixture is transparent. Bring to the boil and leave to cook without stirring until it turns a rich golden colour. Remove from the heat and stir in the almonds, pumpkin seeds, butter, bicarbonate of soda and salt.
- Scrape the mixture onto the lined baking sheet, flatten with the wooden spatula to a thickness of 5 mm (¼ in.) and shape into a rough square or rectangle with a palette knife. Lightly oil a large knife and cut the brittle into squares or rectangles while it is still warm and slightly soft. Alternatively, break it into pieces once it is cool.

CENTRAL DE ABASTO MEXICO CITY

Imagine the biggest wholesale market in the world, a belly that feeds a capital city with twenty million citizens, bustling with activity at all hours of the day and night. This is Central de Abasto, an island of colours and scents in the centre of a metropolis, made up of produce that arrives from Mexico's thirty-one states and around the world. Since the fifteenth century, Mexico City has been the country's trading centre and its open-air markets the focus of commerce. Central de Abasto opened in 1982, on what was then farmland, with the aim of bringing together producers, wholesalers and retailers from around the country into one vast market. Now more than 2,000 businesses on a site spanning over 300 hectares (740 acres) cater to 80 per cent of the city's needs. Fruit and veg from the United States, spices and dates from Asia and olive oil from Spain are just some of the items available in what feels like a small undercover city.

Its sheer size is staggering: aisle after aisle of foods are piled sky high in colourful displays with vibrant signage. The aisles are bustling with *carretilleros*, who push trolleys towering with crates of produce and whistle to each other in their own 'language'. Vendors noisily compete to advertise their goods as the best, cheapest and freshest, calling visitors over to make jokes and entice them to buy more. The welcome is warm and it helps if you speak Spanish; vendors will suggest recipes. In an immense market filled with so many people, the availability of hot food is essential, and food stands abound; just follow the heady aromas and sizzle of cooking burners: pork tacos, smoky roasted yam, golden spit-roast chicken or barbacoa – a special dish, usually made with goat or lamb meat wrapped in maguey or agave leaves, and slowly cooked on aged oak in underground pit ovens for over sixteen hours. **MR**

Where: Av. Canal de Río Churubusco, s/n, Iztapalapa, Mexico City
When: Daily 6 a.m. – 8 p.m.

1 A carnivore's dream.   2 Roasted corn is a market staple.
3 It's not all about the meat: vegetables are ripe and ready, too.   4 Barbacoa – meat traditionally cooked over a fire dug in the ground for up to twenty-four hours.

5   Chiles en Nogada (stuffed chillies in walnut sauce with pomegranate seeds) is a traditional Mexican dish.   6   Chickens roast on a spit, with guacamole, rice and garnishes ready to serve.   7   Spices are essential in Mexican cooking; feast your eyes on their rainbow colours.

FOOD HIGHLIGHTS

From the aroma of a simmering soup and the herbal thyme scent of roasting chicken to the sweet smokiness of grilled husks of corn, Central de Abasto offers much more than tacos and quesadillas. Look out for finger-licking **pollo rostizado** (roast chicken), **empanadas de camarón** (shrimp empanadas; below) and, during August and September when they are in season, **chiles en nogada**. This Pueblan specialty is a classic dish eaten on Mexican Independence Day – the colours of the stuffed green poblano chillies coated in a creamy walnut sauce and studded with ruby pomegranate seeds echo the colours of the national flag. Seek out **esquites**, a popular Mexican street snack – toasted corn slathered in a creamy, cheesy, lime-infused, chilli-flecked sauce. Or opt for simple but much-loved **tamales** (corn-dough steamed in banana-leaf and enhanced with sweet or savoury fillings) – the ultimate Mesoamerican portable food.

CALDO DE QUESO POBLANO

A hearty cheese and potato soup from the Mexican state of Sonora.

SERVES 4

Preparation: 20 minutes

Cooking: 50 minutes

2 poblano chillies

1 tbsp extra virgin olive oil, plus extra for brushing

4 medium potatoes, cut into 1-cm (½-in.) cubes

1 onion, thinly sliced

2 garlic cloves, finely chopped

3 plum tomatoes, chopped

1 large handful of fresh coriander

Sea salt flakes

Freshly ground black pepper

1.4 litres/2½ pints chicken stock

225 ml/8 fl oz milk

350 g/12 oz Manchego cheese, cut into 1-cm (½ in.) cubes

- Roast the chillies on the flame of a gas stove, turning with tongs, until the skin is blistered and charred. Alternatively, brush with oil and roast in an oven heated to 200°C/400°F/gas mark 6 for 30 minutes. Transfer to a plastic bag, seal and set aside for 10 minutes. Peel off the skin, discard the seeds and membranes, and thinly slice.
- Heat the oil in a frying pan, add the potatoes and fry for 2 to 3 minutes. Add the onion and garlic, and fry for 2 to 3 minutes more. Add the chillies, tomatoes, coriander and salt and pepper. Cook, stirring, for 1 minute.
- Heat the stock in a pan, add the potato mixture and cover. Simmer for 15 minutes, or until tender. A few minutes before serving, stir in the milk and cheese. Add salt and pepper to taste, and ladle into bowls to serve.

1 Fried fish and dumplings – ideal for a Jamaican brunch.
2 Corn kernels bagged and ready to pop.   3 Take a taste
adventure with new fruit flavours.   4 Reggae music keeps
the market buzzing.   5 Spice it up with hot pepper sauce.

CORONATION MARKET

KINGSTON

Coronation Market in downtown Kingston, Jamaica, is known as the 'stomach' of the country. Indeed, the loud and boisterous farmers' market is where most of Kingston shops for provisions, and as the weekend approaches, the vendors, or 'higglers,' descend from their rural farms and villages to plug their wares, delivering their sales pitches in thick patois.

Here you will find all the classic staples of Jamaican cuisine at the stalls, shacks and mobile carts in and around one of the biggest markets in the Caribbean world: the legendary jerk – a fiery Scotch bonnet chilli-infused rub applied to chicken and pork, tempered down slightly for the former; delicious pastry patties filled with spicy meat or vegetables, the flaky pastry stained yellow with turmeric or egg yolk; ackee, breadfruit and saltfish. One way to enjoy the latter is in small fritters known as 'stamp-and-go,' so named because hungry customers would stamp their feet to indicate they were in a hurry.

You'll also discover a wealth of fruits on offer at Coronation Market, some you may not have heard of or seen before – but don't worry, most higglers will let you try before you buy. The market is largely under cover, but that doesn't completely protect it from the stifling tropical heat. You're going to need to cool down. What better way to do so than by sipping on fresh coconut water directly from the fruit through a straw? And all the while you'll be feeling the beat from the reggae and dancehall blaring from the local sound systems. Keep your energy levels up by chewing on fresh stalks of sugar cane. TJ

Where: Pechon Street, Kingston
When: Monday to Saturday 6 a.m. till late

FOOD HIGHLIGHTS

Find yourself a 'coconut woman' who will prepare a fresh **coconut** for you, pouring the juice into a plastic bag and shredding the succulent flesh (below). Next, find a handcart man to guide you round the market and show you all the best eating spots. **Jerk** of some kind has to be top of the list, piled high with **rice and peas**, or perhaps some **curry goat**. Sweeten up with **Johnnycakes** (fluffy fried dumplings) or **banana fritters**. And if you get peckish, beef-stuffed **patties** are a must.

JERK CHICKEN

Wear gloves when preparing the chillies for this Jamaican classic.

SERVES 6–8
Preparation: up to 24 hours
Cooking: 80 minutes

125 ml/4 fl oz malt vinegar or distilled white vinegar
2 tbsp dark rum
2 Scotch bonnet chillies, chopped
1 red onion, chopped
4 spring onion tops, finely chopped
1 tbsp dried thyme or 2 tbsp fresh thyme leaves, finely chopped
2 tbsp olive oil
2 tsp salt
2 tsp freshly ground black pepper
4 tsp ground allspice
4 tsp ground cinnamon
4 tsp ground nutmeg
4 tsp ground ginger
2 tsp molasses
2.7 kg/6 lb roasting chicken, cut in half, lengthways
125 ml/4 fl oz fresh lime juice

- Blend the vinegar, rum, chillies, red onion, spring onion tops, thyme, oil, seasoning, spices and molasses until smooth to create the wet jerk rub.
- Marinate the chicken in the jerk rub and lime juice overnight.
- When ready to cook, reserve any leftover rub. Bring this to the boil in a small pan and simmer for 10 minutes. This will be used to baste the chicken during cooking.
- Preheat the oven to 200°C/400°F/gas mark 6. Season the chicken and place it skin side down on a rack in a roasting tin. Cover and cook for 1 hour, turning and basting occasionally until the chicken is cooked through and the juices run clear. Rest the meat, loosely covered, for 15 minutes.
- Serve with boiled rice and peas and coleslaw.

SAN PEDRO MARKET CUZCO

Located around ten minutes away from Cuzco's historic centre, San Pedro market has a strong local vibe. Women wearing tall Quechua-style hats made from sheep's wool cluster around the entrance. Selling fruits, nuts and seeds, or crouched over a pan, their bright pink and blue dresses cut through the perpetual drizzle that hangs over Cuzco. The produce at the market is as colourful as their attire. Inside, women operating blenders wave their arms and call tourists over: 'Aqui! Here!'

San Pedro is famous for juices. There are over thirty juice stands, each manned by a *mami* (mother) who tries to get trade by shouting the loudest. Stalls blend strawberries and avocados (*paltas*) to make creamy and healthy drinks, while apricots and oranges spill over the side of barrels. Traders commute up to 50 km (31 miles) by local *collectivo* bus to trade here. At 3,400 metres (11,200 ft) above sea level in the Andes, Cuzco is a city at altitude. Air is thin, which makes everything smell and taste more vivid here than in Lima or Trujillo. With many varieties of quinoa, chia seeds and lucuma fruit (it looks like a mango, tastes like butter but is packed with antioxidants), Andean ingredients are among the healthiest in the world.

Browsing the market, the street food, thankfully, is not quite so healthy! Cuzco is cold, so food here is all about getting as many calories for the least cost. Peruvians enjoy fatty meat and plenty of carbs, necessary to help pull them through the bitter winters. Food can be as simple as large discs of fried batter sprinkled with sugar to trays of picarones (mini-hoops of dough drenched in sticky date syrup). The market also has savoury, carb-heavy dishes that you'll hoover up (especially if you've just hiked the Inca Trail). **ER**

Where: Calles Tupac Amaru and Cascaparo, Cuzco
When: Daily 9 a.m. – 5 p.m.

1 Fight the chill of the Andes with a carb overload.
2 A *mami* prepares huevos fritos (fried eggs).
3 Marketgoers enjoy local dishes, including saltado (steak) and lentejas (lentils). 4 A market high in the Andes.

5 Although the native crops in Cuzco are antioxidant rich and incredibly healthy, the food definitely does not lack flavour. Visitors show their appreciation, slurping up every last bite from the china dishes. San Pedro is not your typical street food market.

LOMO SALTADO

Stir-fried steak is part of Peru's Chifa (Chinese–Peruvian) heritage.

SERVES 4

Preparation: 10 minutes

Cooking: 5 minutes

3 garlic cloves, finely chopped

Salt and pepper, to taste

450 g/1 lb sirloin steak, sliced

1 tbsp vegetable oil

1 red onion, thinly sliced

1 red chilli pepper, thinly sliced

(deseeded if you prefer less heat)

3 tomatoes, thinly sliced

2 tbsp soy sauce

2 tbsp balsamic vinegar

450 ml/16 fl oz chicken
  or beef stock

To serve:

Boiled white rice

1 handful of chopped fresh coriander

- Rub the garlic, salt and pepper over the beef.
- Heat the oil in a deep pan or wok and cook the meat a few slices at a time until brown.
- On a high heat, add the chopped onion, chilli and tomatoes. Cook for 2 minutes and remove from the heat if the tomatoes become too soft.
- Add the soy sauce and vinegar, then pour the stock over the mixture and cook for 1 minute. The liquid should have reduced a little.
- Serve with rice and sprinkle with coriander.

FOOD HIGHLIGHTS

Snack on a **buttifara** (crusty French bread topped with thick slices of ham, spread with a generous portion of spicy **salsa criolla**), or pick up an **empanada** (above). These hand-sized pastries are often crammed with minced beef and cumin, or, for a vegetarian option, pick up a carb-on-carb tender potato empanada. **Lomo saltado** (stir-fried steak) is one of Peru's most loved dishes – the salty, sticky, tender meat is served with rice. The animal market is a visceral display of flesh. The donkey heads on display are not for the faint-hearted. Street food hawkers pop over to the produce stalls to pick up a lime or two, or a bag of diced chicken for a stir-fry. This is a bustling market filled with the sweet smell of toasted corn over charcoal, tangy orange juices and roasted skewered meats. It's an homage to the variety of Andean cuisine, from the plain unusual (snout stew) to the downright delicious (corn heads sizzling in butter).

MERCADO CENTRAL SUCRE

The constitutional capital of Bolivia is rich with history – but it's even fuller of top-quality, budget-priced food, nearly all of which is on sale at street stalls in and around the city's main farmers' market. The Mercado Central in Sucre occupies a large three-storey building in the heart of the city. On the top floor a vast self-service cafeteria, which runs the whole length of the building, more than makes up in quality and variety of food what it lacks in comfort: dedicated to traditional Bolivian cuisine, this is the place for anyone who likes street food but doesn't want to eat it on the hoof.

The middle floor offers cheese in every conceivable shape and size, from wheels as big as traffic circles to minuscule tasting slivers, and an even more extensive range of herbs and spices, some of which taste rocket powered. The ground floor is a cornucopia of meat and chicken, vegetables, and dried food. But all of this produce put together pales into insignificance beside the fruit on offer here, which ranges from the familiar – orange,

banana, pineapple, papaya, peach and strawberry – to the exotic chiramoya, an Andean specialty that tastes like a combination of all of them. These are all sold either whole or as amazingly cheap made-to-order drinks for consumption on the spot. Don't miss the truly delicious jugo de tumbo (unripe passionfruit juice).

Another delicacy that all visitors should sample is Bolivian chocolate, which is quite unlike the packaged, branded confections that are ubiquitous throughout the northern hemisphere, but a tangy, bitter product that is much closer in every way to its Mesoamerican roots. **JP**

Where: Calle Ravelo, Sucre
When: Daily 8 a.m. – 7 p.m., but the stalls that orbit the main concourse stay open later, normally until 11 p.m. or midnight

1 Juice combinations are endless.   2 Papas rellenas – hard-boiled egg coated in mashed potato and then deep-fried.
3 Salteñas – baked empanadas filled with meat and spicy sauce.   4 Cooking in a typical Bolivian market kitchen.

SILPANCHO

This hearty beef dish can be pepped up with llajwa, a spicy salsa.

SERVES 4
Preparation: 20 minutes
Cooking: 30 minutes
250 g / 9 oz white rice
3 potatoes, peeled and sliced
450 g / 1 lb minced beef
Salt and pepper
175 g / 6 oz breadcrumbs
4 eggs
1 tomato, diced

½ small red onion, diced
1 small green pepper, diced
2 tsp malt vinegar
2 tsp olive oil, plus more for frying
For the llajwa:
2 large green jalapeño peppers, deseeded
1 large red tomato
A handful of fresh coriander leaves
Salt

- Boil the rice and sliced potatoes separately in water for 10 minutes. Drain and leave to cool.
- Season the beef with salt and pepper and divide into four equal balls (one per portion). Roll the balls in the breadcrumbs until lightly coated, then flatten each ball with a rolling pin. Fry each, flipping regularly, until brown, then set aside.
- Fry the eggs individually and brown the potato rounds. Put to one side.
- Line the bottom of each serving dish with the rice and potatoes and place the meat patty and egg on top. Surround with a salad of tomato, red onion and green pepper dressed with the vinegar and olive oil. Repeat for the remaining portions.
- For the llajwa: finely chop the ingredients or blend in a food processor. Serve on the side.

FOOD HIGHLIGHTS

There are plenty of traditional Bolivian snacks and dishes to enjoy in and around Mercado Central. Made from mashed yucca and cheese, **zonzo** is wrapped on sticks and grilled over charcoal (below). **Ch'arki** is the South American version of jerky – strips of dried meat, sometimes beef but traditionally llama. You'll have plenty of opportunities to eat **choripan** – a chorizo sandwich with bread baked at the market. **Salteñas** are the Bolivian version of empanadas – savoury pastries filled with meat, spices, egg, potatoes, olives and a distinctive sauce. If you're in need of heartier sustenance, look out for the typical Bolivian dishes **pique macho** (beef stew with sausage, potato, onion, capiscum, boiled egg, mustard and ketchup) and **silpancho** (rice and potato topped with meat, chopped tomato, onion and fried egg). You can wash it all down with **yungueño** – a potent drink made from local brandy and orange juice.

Street food has been an integral part of life in Rio de Janeiro since the beginning of the nineteenth century and is characterized by the wide variety of food sold by the *camelôs* (street vendors) and at *feiras* (markets). This fascinating city has a rich heritage of African, Amerindian and European cooking traditions that are packed with intense flavours, spices and diversity – a perfect illustration of Rio's colourful history. Local dishes were primarily influenced by the Portuguese colonizers and African slaves who arrived in the city from the late seventeenth century. The best way to experience this vibrant cuisine is in the parks, on the beaches, at the many street markets and from food trucks throughout the city. Street food carts are everywhere in Rio, but are especially clustered downtown around Carioca metro station. Rio's food truck scene is relatively young, but has been gaining momentum since the 2016 Olympics when mobile eateries helped feed hungry

spectators at the Olympic Park. There are now around 150 trucks in Rio including Tapi who have given traditional tapioca pancakes a gourmet twist with more exotic fillings such as smoked salmon.

The biggest and most impressive market is CADEG (Centro de Abastecimento do Estado de Guanabara, pronounced 'kah-day-gee') in the northern neighbourhood of Benfica (see p.105). Here, stalls selling flowers and fruit trees stand alongside food vendors offering local favourites such as bacalhau (salted cod), roasted meats, plump barbecued sardines, sanduiche de pernil (a substantial sandwich of slow-roasted pork in a crusty white bread roll with lime wedges on the side) and traditional pastries. Bolinhos de bacalhau (salt cod fish cakes) are a famous specialty and the best are said to be found at Cantinho das Concertinas (Accordion Corner, named after a musical instrument similar to an accordion used in the Minho region of Portugal), where

1 Eat like a local and have pastéis (thin crust pies) fresh from the fryer for breakfast.   **2** A mobile food truck parks up on Itacoatiara Beach – a popular surf spot – to wait for customers hungry after hitting the waves.

2

1

Rio's Portuguese community gather on Saturdays to enjoy classic Portuguese dishes and live music. There are plenty of eateries dotted about that use the best and freshest ingredients from the market; most of them use the covered walkways to create pop-up dining areas with plastic tables and chairs.

Held every Sunday next to the Glória metro station, Feira da Glória is a dazzling tumult of colour and noise. The Avenida Augusto Severo is closed to traffic and dozens of stalls are set up, packed with exotic fruits, vegetables, cheeses and food to go. Copy the locals and enjoy a breakfast of pastels – piping hot, crisp, fried pastry parcels filled with meat, cheese or palmito (heart of palm). Sweet versions usually contain tropical fruits, chocolate or caramel. Wash it down with a refreshing drink of pure caldo de cana (sugarcane juice).

The first Saturday of the month is when you'll find the lively Mercado Mistureba on Avenue Mem de Sá, selling clothes, trinkets and mouth-watering food. Feijoada, a main staple of the Brazilian diet, is a spicy dish of black beans in pork or beef gravy, served with crisp yellow potatoes, crunchy pork crackling, shredded kale, fluffy farofa (toasted cassava flour) and orange slices. This is a favourite Saturday lunch for locals. Caldinho de feijão is a lighter version, more of a thick bean soup although still with meat.

Elsewhere, on the second Sunday of every month, Rio's black community come together and set up their stalls at Feira das Yabás at Praça Paulo da Portela, which focuses on traditional Brazilian food and music. You can feast on dishes including galinha com quiabo (chicken with okra) and rabada com angu (oxtail with polenta).

Carts selling sweet snacks are on practically every street corner in Rio. Cakes, pastries and desserts are a national passion. The sweet-toothed Brazilians enjoy masses of sweet treats, particularly brigadieros (Portuguese for brigadier). These chocolate truffles are made with condensed milk and cocoa powder. They are Brazil's most iconic sweet and are delectably moreish. Gourmet versions add various fruits, nuts and even whisky to the mix.

CADEG MARKET

RIO DE JANEIRO

CADEG may represent a rather cumbersome name – Centro de Abastecimento do Estado da Guanabara (or Supply Centre of Guanabara State) – but this market in Benfica, Rio de Janeiro, is a large and colourful hub that serves many of the restaurants and hotels within the region. With upwards of 92,903,00 square metres (1 million sq ft) of food and supplies within its locale, the four-storey CADEG building is peppered with eateries offering diverse Brazilian cuisine. With myriad influences from its rich history, Brazilian food offers African- and Portuguese-inspired snacks, as well as a number of characteristic meats, fish and seafood. Although the 350-plus vendors here are largely wholesale, the main attraction for visitors is to come and eat. There are dozens of food stalls scattered around the market, usually offering casual, makeshift dining areas consisting of plastic tables and chairs. By contrast, however, look out for Brasas Show (store 110) where a quirky interior has been constructed out of market pallets, wine boxes and barrels with a vintage yellow VW van as its centrepiece. They produce *petiscos* (small plates) drawing on pork, beef and seafood, including their signature dish of crispy golden galeto (roast chicken). Illustrating some of the chaos that is associated with Rio, the market, while riven with hungry tourists, will not stop and pose for photos. While there is on-site parking and an elevator to make getting around easier, bear in mind that there is no air conditioning and it can get hot wandering around. Serving up to 10,000 people a day, CADEG is not the most attractive market, but it has a vibrancy that speaks of native Brazil, and some of the best street food on offer. LB

Where: R. Cap. Félix 110, Benfica, Rio de Janeiro, RJ, 20920-310
When: Daily 8 a.m. – 7 p.m., but the stalls that orbit the main concourse stay open later, normally until 11 p.m. or midnight

ACARAJE WITH VATAPA

The perfect Brazilian snack – crispy bean fritters stuffed with a mix of shrimp, crab and nuts.

MAKES 15
Preparation: 20 minutes
Cooking: 25 minutes
For the fritters:
650 g/1 lb 7 oz tinned black-eyed
  beans
3 garlic cloves, crushed
1 small onion, finely diced
1 small chilli, finely chopped
1–2 tbsp flour
1 tsp ground coriander
Salt and pepper to taste
Small handful of fresh coriander,
  roughly chopped

Oil for frying
For the vatapá (filling):
2 tbsp palm oil
1 medium white onion
1 red chilli, finely chopped
2.5 cm/1 in. piece root ginger,
  finely chopped
300 g/10½ oz small shrimps
150 g/5½ oz white crab meat
250 g/9oz stale breadcrumbs
100 g/3½ oz plain cashew nuts
Salt and pepper to taste
Hot sauce or mayonnaise,
  to serve

- For the fritters, blitz all the ingredients in a blender until smooth.
- Shape into quenelles (ovals) using two spoons.
- Heat the oil in a frying pan and cook over a low heat until golden on the outside and cooked through. Set aside to cool.
- For the vatapá, heat the oil in a frying pan and gently fry the onions, chilli and ginger over a low heat for about 10 minutes, until transparent and soft.
- Blitz the shrimps, crab, breadcrumbs and cashews in a blender and add to the softened mixture. Cook through for 2 to 3 minutes over a low heat.
- Cut a small slit in the side of each fritter, fill with a small amount of the filling and serve with either hot sauce or mayonnaise.

VENDOR SPOTLIGHT

Wandering around the wholesale market at CADEG, you will encounter food stalls selling everything from grilled meats to barbecued sardines and more traditional Brazilian street fare such as acarajé (deep-fried black-eyed bean fritters) and bolinhos de bacalhau (fried codfish balls) cooked fresh from many nameless stalls. As CADEG is the major supplier in the area, you can be assured that all the ingredients have been sourced from the market itself and brought to you fresh on the day. Look for the ladies wearing headdresses, called *baianas*, who serve various variations on the acarajé recipe (left). There are many outstanding eateries around the market. With a predominant Portuguese influence, Saturdays see canteen **Cantinho das Concertinas** transform into a street party with salted cod bites and grilled sardines served accompanied by live music. Small shop and trendy burger joint **Ex Touro** cook up artisan hamburgers and steaks – they really know how to handle meat and bring out the best flavours. **Adega Cesari** serve satisfying sanduiche de pernil – slow-roasted pork shoulder in crusty bread (below). There are also plenty of Portuguese wines on offer, such as refreshing white vinho verde.

1 A late-night *carrito*.   2 Choripán with chimichurri sauce.
3 With views of a nature reserve, Costanera Sur is a relaxed and
beautiful setting.   4 Make your order your own with a plethora
of toppings.   5 Fuelling a day out with a quick snack stop.

COSTANERA SUR BUENOS AIRES

Running the length of an attractive walkway bordering an
ecological reserve in the east of Buenos Aires, Costanera Sur is
probably one of the most relaxed and unfussy street markets
you're likely to come across. Street food culture is not yet as
prevalent in Buenos Aires as it is in other major cities, as
Argentinians tend to prefer long and relaxed dining, so a visit
to Costanera Sur will feel more akin to a late-night stop at the
burger van on the way back from the pub or a bar. Rest assured,
however, that you'll encounter a substantially better and tastier
selection of meat on offer. Seeing as this is Argentina, don't
expect to find many (if any) vegetarian or vegan options. You're
sure to find empanadas and facturas (sweet and savoury filled
pastries) in locations around the city, but more substantial snacks
are to be found at mobile grills, known as *carritos*.

These vendors deal in Argentine sandwich staples. Here you
might find bondiola al limón, a piece of pork shoulder dowsed in
a mix of lemon juice, water and garlic while it grills, or lomito, a
prime piece of Argentinian steak with tomato, lettuce, fried egg,
ham and melted cheese. Then, possibly most loved of all, there is
choripán. Known to locals as 'chori', this beef and pork chorizo
sausage is commonly served with a healthy dose of chimichurri
and tucked inside a crisp white baguette or roll that has itself been
allowed to soak, just briefly, in the meat's juices.

When you finally have your hot sandwich in hand, you can get
creative with the condiments. Chimichurri is ubiquitous: the
combination of finely chopped parsley, oregano, minced garlic
and white wine vinegar lends itself perfectly to any of the meats
on offer from the *parrillas* (grills) and is as deeply ingrained in
national culture as football or the Argentine beef on which it is
served. Or there's salsa criolla made from red onion, chillies, lime
juice and fresh coriander leaves. You can, though, find all sorts of
combinations of fresh vegetables, sautéed onions and spices. JW

Where: Avenida Tristán Achaval Rodríguez 1550, Buenos Aires
When: Times vary for each stall, but many are open 24 hours a day

CHORIPAN
BIFE de CHORIZO
BONDIOLA
HAMBURGUESA
CHURRASQUITO
LOMITO
GASEOSAS
PARRILLA
EL
CHIRIBIN

CHORIPAN

This chorizo sandwich gets its name from the two key ingredients used.

SERVES 2–4

Preparation: 20 minutes

Cooking: 15 minutes

For the chimichurri:

½ bunch of parsley, finely chopped

2 tbsp finely chopped fresh oregano

4 garlic cloves, crushed

1 large red onion, finely chopped

1 small red chilli pepper, finely chopped

2 tbsp red wine vinegar

1 tbsp fresh lemon juice

100 ml/3½ fl oz olive oil

Salt and pepper, to taste

For the sandwich:

1–2 quality chorizo or beef
  sausages per person

Baguette or crusty rolls

Grated cheese, to serve (optional)

- Combine all the ingredients for the chimichurri and allow to stand for as long as possible; generally it lasts well for up to two days.
- Cook the sausages either whole or butterflied in a frying pan until cooked through. Set aside and place the sliced baguette on the meat juices.
- Put the sausages into the baguette and serve with chimichurri to taste. Sprinkle with grated cheese, if liked.

VENDOR SPOTLIGHT

Although you won't find a great deal of variation from stall to stall, there's plenty of opportunity to make your way from either end of the street to try a little of everything. The best bet if you want to make just one stop would be at **El Parrillón**, generally considered to be *the* place for choripán in the city, thanks to the quality of its sausage and bread as well as the variety of home-made salsas on offer. Try the green onion mayo for an excellent alternative to chimichurri. Also, it's fittingly located next to a gold statue of one of Argentina's most famous sporting icons – footballer Lionel Messi. For the best bondiola al limón, head to **Parrilla Mi Sueño** where the white wine mixture that keeps the meat tender is generously laced with ají molido (red chilli flakes) for a little extra kick. Don't miss **Parrilla El Torito** (below), they serve up music with their bondiolas. One of Costanera's oldest vendors is the **Parrilla Los Hermanitos** which, alongside the usual options, offers the specialty vacío – a whole cut of beef flank cooked slowly, sliced and served to order. A further wander into the neighbouring ecological reserve provides the ideal way to work off any overeating from this Argentinian take on street food.

EUROPE

HELSINKI STOCKHOLM COPENHAGEN
EDINBURGH BRISTOL LONDON PARIS
MADRID BARCELONA LISBON ROTTERDAM
BERLIN MUNICH VIENNA ROME NAPLES
PALERMO KRAKOW BUDAPEST

The cuisines of Europe represent a medley of history, culture and ingredients that has slowly evolved over hundreds of years and reflects the rich mosaic of its different peoples. Colonialism and trade also introduced new foods from outside Europe. Street food is nothing new – it has been a widespread global trend throughout history; evidence of street food sellers was discovered in the 2,000-year-old ruins of Pompeii in southern Italy. As street food evolved throughout the European continent, thanks to both native and immigrant vendors cooking their own national cuisines, it has become part of contemporary life. In Europe the diversity of street food on offer not only embodies the traditional cuisine of particular countries, but also the ethnic foods of its immigrant populations. People today are deeply interested in different ingredients and cuisines, and are eager to experience the myriad ways in which food can be prepared. Street food is affordable and has the advantage, with today's busy lifestyles, that it can be eaten quickly and on the go. People have changed the way they think about eating out and want the option of a more informal and relaxed way of dining.

Many different cultures have left their mark on the cooking and ingredients of Austria and Hungary, once part of the Hapsburg Empire. The borders with Germany and Italy have strongly influenced the food and bear many similarities. For example, the world-famous Austrian dish Wiener schnitzel originally came from Milan and was introduced to Viennese cuisine in the sixteenth century. Cakes and pastries are also much loved with some gaining international renown, such as the Austrian Linzertorte. Meat is also at the forefront, especially pork, beef and chicken, although Wiener schnitzel is usually made with veal. Potatoes and dumplings (nockerln in Austria, gnocchi in Italy and knödel in Germany) are staples in these countries.

Austria and France had a considerable influence on cooking techniques and cuisine in Italy; for example, noodles in the far north of Italy are very similar to those of Austria. The varied landscape, climate and culture of Italy encompass many culinary traditions, from the hearty fare of the south to the more refined dishes of the north. Cheese is an indispensable ingredient and, of course, the ice cream is of unrivalled quality.

Germany's hearty cuisine also shares many dishes with Austria and the Nordic countries, including herring, pork, a huge variety of potato dishes, dumplings and kuchen (cakes and pastries) and over a thousand different sausages.

Throughout history, the food of the Netherlands has reflected the tastes of a maritime trading nation with a strong preference for fish, vegetables – particularly potatoes – dairy products and sweet, spicy dishes. Diverse influences include Arab flavours of the early Middle Ages, fifteenth-century French cookery, the Indonesian colonial period of the nineteenth century and the country's own religious traditions. Combined these influences have resulted in a plethora of popular street food dishes from heart-warming stews, sweet and savoury pancakes (pannenkoeken) to rijsttafel (a Dutch word that translates to 'rice table') – an Indonesian meal consisting of many small side dishes accompanied by rice prepared in several different ways.

Nordic cuisine is rooted in seafaring Viking traditions. Surviving the long, cold dark winters required relying on foods that had been preserved during the growing seasons. The Vikings mastered the art of preserving meats and fish by smoking, drying and salting and these types of foods remain popular in Scandinavian street markets today.

Food in Denmark, Sweden and Finland shares many similarities, with fish, and herring in particular, being highly popular. It is eaten

fresh, smoked and pickled, but varieties of pickled herring are less sharp than elsewhere in Europe, as the brine is sweeter. Cured and smoked salmon is also much loved, the most famous being gravadlax (salmon cured in dill, sugar and salt). Pork is an important meat while further north and in Finland, reindeer and elk are enjoyed. *Smörgåsbord* literally means 'buttered table', and in Sweden a selection of small dishes, both warm and cold are displayed, usually starting with fish, then on to cold meats, followed by warm dishes. In Denmark (where it's called *det kolde bord*, or 'the cold table'), a combination of hot and cold dishes are sent to the table during the meal. Nordic pastries favour cinnamon and cardamom, with Danish pastries at the forefront. Kanelbullar (cinnamon buns) are a favourite in Sweden (sometimes with a hint of cardamom). Other sweet favourites in all Nordic countries include anything crammed with seasonal fruit and berries.

Polish cuisine shares some similarities with other Central and East European cuisines, as evidenced by pickled vegetables, thick soups, game and heavy breads. Buckwheat is an important cereal, and curd cheese and smetana (sour cream) is used in many recipes.

British cuisine has absorbed the cultural influence of the many settlers and invaders that settled on its shores. Romans, Vikings, Normans, British colonies and countries of the British Empire, especially India, have all left a significant mark on British food, frequently producing hybrid dishes such as the Anglo-Indian chicken tikka masala. Much has changed in British eating since Victorian street vendors served pies and jellied eels, and today's street food culture offers innovative and exciting flavours. Scotland's game, fish and cheeses are staples of its cooking. It has its own distinctive recipes, but shares a great deal with wider European cuisine thanks to foreign and local influences. French food changed the cuisine in 1561, when Mary Queen of Scots brought her French cooks back with her. In the nineteenth and twentieth centuries, there was an influx of Italian immigration that dramatically affected Scottish cooking.

Spain's food is similar to that of other Mediterranean countries, with olive oil and rice much in use. Over the centuries, explorers and conquerors introduced new cooking techniques and products that left their mark on Spanish cuisine. After the expulsion of the Muslim Moors in the fifteenth century, there was an emphasis on the meat of the pig and pork predominated. However, many Moorish influences have endured, particularly in the south of Spain, with the use of spices, saffron and almonds still prevalent.

French food is regarded as the epitome of world gastronomy, due to its tradition of great chefs and the opening of the world's first restaurant there. Chefs are revered and they constantly explore new tastes and techniques, transforming food and introducing new trends. Before the French Revolution, distinct regional cuisines dominated and these are now a source of pride and can be found across the country. For example, cassoulet – the bean and meat casserole from Gascony – is now found everywhere. Bread has a special status in France and bread riots played a significant role leading up to and during the Revolution. Today, the baguette, a long loaf with a golden crust, is regarded by everyone as a symbol of France – often called simply 'French bread'.

Street food is so popular across Europe that it has entered the mainstream, with high-end chefs opening stalls and vans, and publishing cookbooks with street food recipes. Street food is a key part of savouring the authentic gastronomic experience and traditions of a country. Whether traditional age-old delicacies or innovative modern dishes from a stall or kiosk, it's at street markets, with the flavours, excitement and buzz of street food that you get the real sense of a place.

KAUPPATORI

HELSINKI

This lovely scenic marketplace borders the Baltic Sea and is Helsinki's most international and famous market, dating back to 1818. The Old Market Hall next to the Market Square also has plenty of food stalls and has been a favourite meeting place and popular tourist attraction since it first opened in 1889.

Both the indoor and outdoor markets are a hive of activity, with vendors hawking a range of delectable Finnish and world foods including Belgian waffles, reindeer meatballs, berries, vegetables and fresh fish. As well as traditional treats, you can also find Japanese sushi and delicacies from Lapland. Mushrooms are in abundance in the autumn and every type is on sale, including the pricey pakurikääpä (a parasitic fungi that grows on birch trees). A firm Finnish favourite is salmiakki (black salty liquorice).

Other tasty local treats that are a must include munkki (cardamom-flavoured doughnuts); leipäjuusto (a mild cheese that is fried or baked and served in wedges with cloudberry jam); and grillimakkara (big fat grilled sausages), served by themselves or in a bun with mustard and washed down with a cold beer.

There are lots of outdoor cafés to sit and enjoy a leisurely lunch or a snack. Don't miss the renowned and incredibly delicious meat pastries lihapiirakka – a traditional meat pasty made with bread dough, filled with mince, onion and rice and then deep-fried. The orange-roofed Toripojat eatery claims to sell the 'best meat pies in Finland' and has been patronized by distinguished customers including the Finnish prime minister and George Bush. Every October Helsinki's oldest annual event, the Silakkamarkkinat – herring fair – takes place and has been popular since the mid-eighteenth century. In winter, head to the heated café tent where you can happily sip a welcoming cup of piping hot coffee on the coldest days. **CW**

Where: Eteläsatama, 00170 Helsinki

When: Monday to Friday 6.30 a.m. – 6 p.m.; Saturday 6.30 a.m. – 4 p.m.; during summer, Sunday 10 a.m. – 5 p.m.

1 Hot roast beef sandwich with red cabbage slaw.   2 Fried muikku, calamari and salmon roll.   3 Stuffed cabbage rolls.
4 Fresh and tasty seafood delicacies from Kalaliike Marja Nätti.   5–6 The harbourside market at the heart of Helsinki.

OSTERMALMS SALUHALL

STOCKHOLM

Since 1888, both locals and tourists alike have been inspired by the splendid foods at this lovely old brick market hall with medieval-style spires. It's chock-full of celebrated family businesses, restaurants and stalls selling the finest ingredients along with traditional Swedish delicacies and sparklingly fresh seafood.

At Melanders, for example, there's an amazing choice of fresh fish, shellfish, ready-cooked dishes, fresh salads and delicacies, plus game, meats and cured meats. Every Friday the chefs there prepare 'Friday food bags' containing a superb three-course dinner for two, usually with seafood as the main ingredient. B. Andersson Fågel & Vilt sell traditional Swedish favourites such as deer and elk alongside game and their own duck sausages, smoked reindeer heart, barrel-aged balsamic vinegar and white truffles, all well worth trying. At Seger's you'll find meats and cured meats you can't find anywhere else. They make their

popular sausages in their own small sausage factory, cure their meats and joints and hang their meat. Try their fine old classics including minced beef wrapped in cabbage and paltbröd (blood bread). Don't be put off by the name – this is a type of black pudding made with rye flour, pigs' blood, onion, herbs and spices. The cheese counter, with a wide range of Swedish and foreign cheeses, is just as inviting, plus there is a tempting selection of accompaniments – sauces, jellies and a whole lot more. **CW**

Where: Östermalmstorg, 114 42 Stockholm
When: Monday to Friday 9.30 a.m. – 7 p.m.; Saturday 9.30 a.m. – 6 p.m.

1 The striking red-brick Ostermalms Saluhall – Stockholm's premier food institution.   2 Smoked herring mousse.
3 Saluhall's grilled chicken stall.   4 Fresh fish of every variety takes pride of place at this classy Swedish food hall.

5 Delectable baked goods, including chocolate-dipped kokoskakor (Swedish coconut cakes). 6 Sweet and succulent freshly cooked crayfish. 7 Inside the gourmet food hall there is plenty of space to sit and eat comfortably while admiring the stylish market interior.

LUSSEBULLAR

These saffron-flavoured buns are eaten on St Lucia's Day in December.

MAKES 12
Preparation: 2 hours 45 minutes
Cooking: 30 minutes

1 tsp saffron threads
250 ml/9 fl oz warm milk
500 g/1 lb 2 oz strong white
   bread flour

10 g/¼ oz easy-blend yeast
1 tsp salt
55 g/2 oz caster sugar
55 g/2 oz unsalted butter, melted
100 g/3 ½ oz soft cream cheese
1 egg yolk, beaten
24 raisins

- Soak the saffron in the milk for 10 minutes.
- Mix together the flour, yeast, salt and sugar in a mixing bowl and make a well in the centre. Stir the melted butter into the milk and saffron mixture and pour into the well. Add the cream cheese and mix to a dough. Knead on a floured surface until smooth, then place in a greased bowl, cover with oiled cling film and leave in a warm place for 1 to 2 hours until well risen.
- Heat the oven to 220°C/425°F/gas mark 7. Grease a large baking sheet.
- Knead the dough lightly on a floured surface and divide into twelve pieces. Roll each piece into a rectangle about 20 cm (8 in.) long. Twist each rectangle into an 'S' shape and place on the baking sheet. Cover loosely and leave for 30 to 45 minutes until well risen.
- Brush the rolls with egg yolk, then place one raisin in the centre of each circle (two raisins per roll). Bake for about 15 minutes, until golden brown on top.

FOOD HIGHLIGHTS

Herring has long been a staple of Swedish cuisine. The fish has two names in Swedish — sill for the slightly larger fish found off the west coast, and strömming for the herring sourced from the Baltic. Strömming is often enjoyed breaded and fried as the street snack **stekt strömming** (below), whereas sill is usually pickled. Try S.O.S — **Smör Ost och Sill** (butter, cheese and herring) — a classic, lipsmacking appetizer usually accompanied by schnapps. Delicious spiced cinnamon buns — **kanelbullar** — can be found just about everywhere. They are often also flavoured with cardamom and saffron — favourite spices in Sweden. Enjoy them served for a fika — the daily practice of sitting down with a cup of coffee and a cake or sandwiches. The distinctive and most famous cake in Sweden is **Prinsesstårta** — a domed sponge cake layered with crème patissière, whipped cream and jam and covered in green marzipan and sold by the slice. The shade of the cake varies distinctly from one baker to another — some are bright vivid green, while others are paler.

COPENHAGEN

The cuisine of this elegant city dates back to the Vikings and displays an enduring preference for pork, fish and preserved meats such as salami (spegepølse) and sausages. Food was preserved by salting, pickling or smoking so that it could be stored for considerable periods and eaten during the long harsh winters. Modern Danish cooking reflects this history and these types of foods are still prevalent. During the Middle Ages trade with other countries instigated the use of imported spices, particularly cinnamon, cardamom and pepper, which are still very popular today and feature in most sweet pastries.

Sausages are a Danish passion; by the end of the eighteenth century, there were several different kinds available. The most famous is the bright red sausage (røde pølser); this sausage was originally dipped in red dye to disguise whether it was less than fresh, but the tradition of colouring them continues and over one hundred million are eaten in Denmark every year. The first pølsevogn (sausage wagon) was established in Copenhagen in 1921 and there were over 400 of them in the city by the 1950s. They have remained a cultural institution and street food tradition ever since and it is still possible to grab a hot dog on almost every corner across the city. There are two different hot dogs that are most popular: the riset is a long, thin sausage served inside a bread roll and topped with pickled cucumber, crisp onions, mustard, ketchup and sweet mayonnaise. The fransk dog is a hollowed-out baguette filled with a frankfurter sausage and topped with a squirt of piquant mayonnaise. The best ones can be found near the tower in the city centre. Look out, too, for open barbecues serving burgers as well as hot dogs.

1   2
3

1 A typical Danish *pølsevogn* (hot dog stand) on Strøget, one of
Copenhagen's longest pedestrian streets.   2 A classic røde pølser
hot dog – Danes eat over a hundred million of them every year.
3 Copenhagen's Street Food Warehouse on Papirøen (Paper Island).

It's easy to eat well in this city. Torvehallerne (see p. 126) is a Danish institution and a mecca for food lovers. The eye-catching open sandwiches known as smørrebrød are practically a national dish and you'll find them everywhere, but they're especially good at this market. They come with a variety of toppings, including veggie, fish or meat. Copenhagen Street Food takes place daily from midday in an old warehouse on Papirøen. It is home to some excellent international food stalls and trucks. There's plenty of seating both indoors and outdoors, but at weekends it gets crowded, so go early. This is the place to come for wonderful sushi, innovative smørrebrød or Korean burgers. Other highlights include double-fried duck fat fries with home-made spicy ketchup and gourmet pulled-pork sandwiches – tender seasoned pork in a

brioche bun with sides of creamy coleslaw, pickles and smoky barbecue sauce. Denmark is renowned for its pastries, so don't miss sampling flødeboller (chocolate-coated cream buns sprinkled with coconut) here, along with a wide selection of cakes and desserts that change according to season.

The Meatpacking District holds a weekly food market, Kødbyens Mad & Marked, where vendors change regularly to promote diversity. You can enjoy a satisfying lunch at the communal tables here; try frikadeller – fried meatballs made from fish, pork or a mix of pork and beef, with a side of potatoes and parsley sauce. Fish frikadeller are eaten cold with remoulade and fried onions. Food trucks also feature at this market, offering a tempting choice of authentic imported charcuterie and cheeses as well as traditional Danish fare.

TORVEHALLERNE COPENHAGEN

Saunter through the light, spacious and airy Torvehallerne on the cobbled square and marvel at how immaculate and orderly it is as you inhale the tempting aromas of cooking meat, sausages and pasta, mingled with freshly brewed coffee. Designed by architect Hans Hagens, the market opened in September 2011 and now has about eighty stalls, housed in two glass and steel market halls on opposite sides of the square. You'll find traditional Danish delicacies such as hams and seafood, plus ready meals and more unusual items such as rhubarb juice and ox-meat sausages.

Traditional gems include hot dogs packed with flavour from one of the many street-side stands; smørrebrød, attractive open sandwiches on dark rye bread; and, of course, the myriad sweet Danish pastries, a firm favourite of locals. Interestingly in Denmark, these world-famous delights are called wienerbrød (Vienna bread), as they were first made in Denmark in 1840 by Viennese chefs. At the Fiskerikajen (fish market), sellers will happily fry torske (cod) for a meal of fish and chips. Wash it down with a pilsner from the Gourmet Bryggeriet (microbrewery). Gourmet shops have stalls including fashionable Italian bakery Il Fornaio and Summerbird Chocolaterie, which produces handmade chocolates of every description. The shop is named after their butterfly-shaped marzipan covered in dark chocolate (the Danish word for 'butterfly', *sommerfugl*, translates as 'summerbird'). Sip a cup of hot chocolate while you decide what to buy. Try rich, fluffy flødebolle – a marzipan base, topped with soft meringue foam, smothered in dark chocolate. The chocolate-covered almonds dusted with cocoa, lemon, raspberry or liquorice powder are addictive. **CW**

Where: Israels Plads, Frederiksborggade 21, 1360 Copenhagen
When: Monday to Thursday 10 a.m.–7 p.m.; Friday to 8 p.m.; Saturday to 6 p.m.; Sunday 11 a.m.–5 p.m.

1 At Torvehallerne, over sixty stands sell everything from sushi and tapas to Nordic cuisine. 2 Many stalls sell local organic produce. 3 The classic Danish open sandwich. 4 Garlic butter shrimp. 5 Herring salad smørrebrød.

6 Roast pork and rare roast beef smørrebrød.   **7** Thin crispy pizza with smoked horsemeat, broccoli and rocket from Gorm's – named after the Dane who brought authentic pizza to Copenhagen.   **8** Torvehallerne may be in the busy city centre, but the dining style is casual and relaxed.

SMORREBROD FISK
A popular Danish open sandwich of fried fish fillets on rye bread.

SERVES 4

Preparation: 25 minutes

Cooking: 20 minutes

4 tbsp rye flour

4 sole or plaice fillets

1 egg, beaten

Butter, for frying

For the sauce:

3 egg yolks

1 tbsp water

115 g / 4 oz butter, softened

Pinch each of salt and cayenne pepper

1 tsp lemon juice

1 tbsp light cream

To serve:

4 slices Danish rye bread, buttered

To garnish:

1 tbsp capers

Lemon wedges

Fresh dill sprigs

- Put the rye flour in a bowl and season with salt and pepper. Dip the fish fillets in the egg and coat in rye flour. Heat the butter in a pan and fry the fish over a medium-high heat until golden (3 to 4 minutes per side). Remove from the pan and cool on absorbent kitchen paper.

- For the sauce: beat the egg yolks and water together in the top of a double boiler set over simmering water, until the mixture is pale. Gradually add the butter, a few pieces at a time, and continue beating until the mixture thickens. Add the salt, cayenne pepper, and lemon juice. Stir in the cream. Remove from the heat.

- Top each slice of the buttered rye bread with a warm fish fillet and a spoonful of sauce. Serve garnished with capers, lemon wedges and dill.

FOOD HIGHLIGHTS

Danish **smørrebrød** (left) – slices of buttered dark rye bread beautifully stacked with a choice of mouth-watering fillings – are like works of art. Some of the finest open-faced sandwiches in Torvehallerne market can be found at Hallernes Smørrebrød. Ingredients are all local and change daily: try juicy roast beef topped with pickles and crispy fried onions; chicken liver pâté with pickled cucumber salad and beets; or citrus-marinated salmon with fennel cream, lemon and dill. Don't miss **kanelsnegle** (sweet cinnamon rolls) from Laura's Bakery. Excellent smoked salmon, herring, langoustines and scallops are available at HAV fish market. Or enjoy the Danish national dish **stegt flæsk med persillesovs** (crispy fried pork belly with creamy parsley sauce) – an old country recipe that originated in the sixteenth century.

1 Edinburgh Castle provides a stunning backdrop to the farmers' market.
2 A perfect locally produced Scotch pie – a traditional double-crust pie filled with mutton.   3 Food-to-go at the market includes bhaji, split pea dal and naan bread.

EDINBURGH FARMERS' MARKET EDINBURGH

Scotland's capital is a city that oozes history, and many of the streets speak of its food heritage – Fleshmarket Close, Old Fishmarket Close and Cowgate all point back to a time when food and livestock were traded on its cobbled streets. The modern market in the city centre sits directly below the imposing castle rock, which forms the majestic backdrop to a weekly farmers' market of fresh produce and street food vendors alike. It focuses on Scottish produce with a mix of heritage and cosmopolitan flavours, reflecting the modern cuisine that makes up contemporary Scottish cooking.

Scotch eggs have taken on a contemporary feel at Aye Love Real Food, with haggis, venison and chickpea varieties available alongside the traditional pork. Washed down with a small-batch soda, mixing local and exotic ingredients such as rhubarb with Thai basil, the fare on offer is eclectic. Flat Out Food clearly have their tongues firmly in cheeks as their Citroën H van, affectionately known as Belle, has a top speed of 72 km/h (45 mph), but their flatbreads and meatballs, featuring everything local and seasonal, are quirky and ever changing.

The Scots have a love affair with pastry and will put it on or around just about anything. At the market you can find it in many guises, from Annanwater's mutton pies to Ridley's game parcels filled with venison, duck and pigeon. Hammond Charcuterie offer reestit mutton, an ancient Shetland delicacy of smoked mutton, while for dessert Blacksmith's Butter will toss you a stack of pancakes with a knob of their hand-churned butter melting on top. With artisan soups, buffalo burgers, pizza and Scottish tablet also available, there is something for everyone and the market is reflective of the vibrant food scene across Scotland. **GT**

Where: Castle Terrace, Edinburgh EH1 2EN
When: Saturday 9 a.m. – 2 p.m.

HAGGIS SCOTCH EGG
Aye Love Real Food's classic Scotch egg pairs pork and haggis.

MAKES 1
Preparation: 15 minutes plus
   30 minutes chilling
Cooking: 7 minutes
70 g / 2½ oz pork sausage meat
30 g / 1 oz haggis, coarsely chopped

1 soft-boiled egg,
   chilled in its shell
Vegetable oil for deep frying
Plain flour for coating
1 egg, beaten
85 g / 3 oz wholemeal breadcrumbs

- Combine the sausage meat and haggis until homogenous. Flatten into a patty large enough to completely cover the boiled egg.
- Peel the egg and place it in the middle of the patty. Gently wrap the patty around it, cover it in cling film and chill in the refrigerator for 30 minutes.
- Heat the oil to 175°C/350°F in a pan, making sure it is deep enough to completely cover the egg. Remove the cling film from the covered egg, then roll the egg in the flour. Coat with beaten egg, roll in the breadcrumbs, shake off the excess crumbs, then repeat.
- Lower into the hot oil and cook for 7 minutes, remove from the oil and drain on absorbent kitchen paper.

ST NICHOLAS MARKET BRISTOL

At Bristol's bustling heart, in Corn Street, lies the historic, covered St Nicholas Market. Founded in the late eighteenth century, St Nicks remains a time capsule. The prevailing vibe transports visitors back to the late 1970s and 1980s, where food counters mingle with rugged knitwear boutiques, diverse accessories and 'healing' crystal vendors.

Happy hippies flock to stalwarts Royce Rolls for soul-satisfying soup, earth-mother pies, sweet and savoury oat slices or the more decadent siren call of a deep, dark espresso tart. Communal tables are happily shared with eternally popular, neighbouring, traditional curry house Spice Up Your Life, where Indian food devotees are spoilt for choice.

Bristolians seeking a wholesome buzz head for Juice Therapy to down a speedy herbal shot or a sustaining mega-blend. Creative types home in on Brozen, where twins Ben and Joe don protective goggles to invent liquid nitrogen ices, frozen to order. Be prepared to expect good-humoured but lengthy lunchtime queues, especially at Middle Eastern Matina, Eat a Pitta, Grillstock, Pieminster or one of the myriad, mouth-watering cake stalls.

It is particularly worth visiting on Wednesdays (until 2.30 p.m.) and Fridays (until 4 p.m.) when the market spills outside onto Wine Street. Wednesday showcases a farmers' market – perfect for stocking up on abundant, locally sourced seasonal produce.

Friday has a more international feel, with the opportunity to travel the culinary world from France and Italy to Brazil, via Nepal and Japan. Tantalizing street food highlights include multi-textured octopus dumpling balls (takoyaki) at She Sells Sushi and indulgently warming, sell-out tartiflette at Raclette Raclette. **AK**

Where: The Exchange, Corn Street, Bristol BS1 1JQ
When: Monday to Saturday 9.30 a.m.–5 p.m.

RACLETTE RACLETTE'S TARTIFLETTE
This cheesy potato gratin hails from the Savoy area of the French Alps.

MAKES 4–6
Preparation: 35 minutes
Cooking: 30 minutes

1.2 kg/2 lb 10 oz waxy potatoes, diced
200 g/7 oz smoked streaky bacon, diced
2 white onions, thinly sliced
2 garlic cloves, finely chopped

150 ml/5 fl oz white wine
300 ml/10 fl oz double cream
220 g/8 oz Reblochon cheese, roughly chopped
200 g/7 oz raclette cheese, roughly chopped
Salt and freshly ground black pepper

- Boil the potatoes in a pan of salted water, until just cooked through.
- Fry the bacon lightly; add the onion, cook until soft, stirring occasionally.
- Add the garlic, cook until golden; pour in the wine and cook for 2 minutes, until the liquid has almost disappeared.
- Add the boiled potatoes to the onion and bacon mixture, stirring constantly.
- Reduce the heat, add the cream and the cheeses; stir well until the cheese has melted. Meanwhile, preheat the oven to 190°C/375°F/gas mark 5.
- Season with salt and pepper. Finish in the oven for 10 minutes until golden and crisp on top.

LONDON

Londoners have long been lovers of street food. Archaeological digs in the city regularly unearth oyster shells discarded by Roman Londinium residents, who would buy fresh oysters from roadside stalls. In Victorian times, the streets were filled with vendors, who sold such culinary delights as pickled whelks and eel-filled 'penny pies'. Today, the city's street food reflects its multicultural diversity. Successive waves of immigration throughout the second half of the twentieth century each brought with them different culinary cultures, opening up the conservative British palate to new and exciting flavours. Traditional staples – fish and chips, sausage rolls and Scotch eggs – can still be found, but you are just as likely – if not more – to come across all kinds of curries from the Indian subcontinent, jerk chicken from Jamaica or noodle dishes from China.

There are good street food markets in just about every area of London. Some have been there for centuries; others have sprung up in the last decade or so. A visit to any one of them is the best way of experiencing the vibrancy of the city and the staggering variety of food on offer. From Brixton to Brick Lane, you'll be overwhelmed by the range of delicious food to suit every taste.

Located next to London Bridge, iconic Borough Market (see p.137), which has existed for over 1,000 years, is the best known of the capital's markets and is considered by many to be the birthplace of the modern British street food movement. It houses more than 100 stalls, selling both fresh produce and ready-to-eat dishes. From hearty hog roast sandwiches to delicately spiced samosas, the choice is endless.

Ropewalk Maltby Street (see p.141) is a more intimate version of its close neighbour, Borough Market. Each weekend, the railway arches along the narrow street are populated by food vendors, selling everything from tartiflette to peri peri chicken buns. Pop-up bars serve craft beers and innovative cocktails.

Brixton Village and its sister arcade, Market Row, (see p.145) were saved from demolition in 2009 and transformed into a bustling foodie market, filled with informal restaurants and cafés offering the very best street food from around the world. Europe, Asia, Africa, South America and the Caribbean are all represented.

East London, in keeping with its reputation as the city's most fashionable area, is another popular hub for street food. Brick Lane, the street renowned for its Indian and Bangladeshi restaurants, comes alive at weekends with several markets in and around the Old Truman Brewery, including the Boiler House Food Hall, the Sunday UpMarket and Ely's Yard. Broadway Market, in nearby Hackney, is another wonderful place to while away a Saturday: the street is crammed with stalls, serving everything from crispy French crêpes to fragrant Malaysian laksa (noodle soup).

North London has also earned a name for itself as a foodie destination. In 2011, street food collective KERB set up a market just behind King's Cross railway station with a handful of the city's most popular food trucks. The success of this first venture led to the opening of KERB Camden in Camden Market's West Yard, where its canalside terraces are lined with stalls offering an array of British and global specialties.

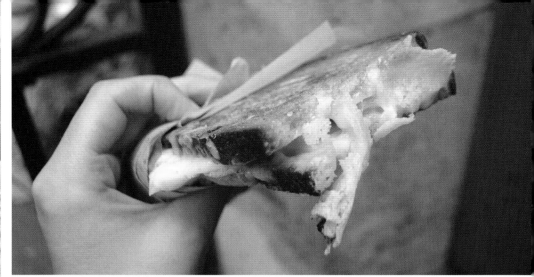

BOROUGH MARKET LONDON

This 1,000-year-old market, home to 113 food traders – from sweet makers to bakers, butchers, cheesemongers, flower sellers and street food traders – is Britain's most renowned food and drink market. It has had a chequered history, having adapted and survived through two world wars and the mass arrival of supermarkets. Now running six days a week, with a reduced market from Monday to Thursday, it attracts sixteen million visitors annually for its immense range of British and world food, and specialty produce.

The market in its earliest form is thought to have first started in 1014, when it then adjoined the southern end of London Bridge, for centuries the only route across the River Thames into the capital. It subsequently moved south to its current location, and in the nineteenth century became one of London's most important food markets due to its proximity to the riverside wharves. The present buildings were designed in 1851, with the beautiful Art Deco-style entrance added on Southwark Street in 1932.

The market went into brief decline, due in part to the dawn of supermarkets, but received a much-needed boost in 1998 when a three-day specialist food fair was held here as part of Southwark Festival. Early artisan producers such as Neal's Yard Dairy and Spanish food specialist Brindisa soon started trading and were endorsed by top London chefs; the market has grown and thrived ever since, in size as well as stature.

Today the market is recognized by the Slow Food movement for its commitment to traditional food, as well as its waste culture: much of the food waste is distributed to local charities or turned into fertilizer. **VS**

Where: 8 Southwark Street, London SE1 1TL
When: Monday to Saturday 10 a.m. – 5 p.m.

1 Doughnuts from Bread Ahead.   2 Toasted cheddar sandwich.   3 The atmospheric interior.   4 Stoney Street entrance.   5 Raclette from Kappacasein.   6 Goat kofta.   7 Wheatberry salad.   8 Artisan cakes, breads and pastries.

GOURMET GOAT'S KID GOAT LOIN WITH SPINACH AND WHEY CHEESE SALAD

A satisfying salad filled with the flavours of the east Mediterranean.

SERVES 2

For the goat:

1 tbsp olive oil

Grated zest of ½ lemon

1 tbsp fresh marjoram, chopped

1 kid goat tenderloin

Sea salt

For the salad:

140 g / 5 oz anari or ricotta cheese

½ tsp ground cinnamon

125 g / 4½ oz fresh spinach, chopped

4 oven- or sun-dried tomatoes

10 black olives, pitted

2 seeded crisp breads, broken in pieces

- Preheat the oven to 150°C/300°F/gas mark 2. For the goat, mix the olive oil, lemon zest and marjoram in a shallow bowl large enough to fit the loin. Add the goat, turning to coat, then cover with cling film and leave for 30 minutes.
- For the salad, crumble the cheese into an ovenproof dish and mix in the cinnamon. Warm in the oven for 10 minutes.
- Place the spinach, tomatoes, olives and crisp breads in a salad bowl.
- When the cheese is ready, add to the salad and drizzle with olive oil.
- Turn up the oven to 200°C/400°F/gas mark 6 and heat a griddle pan. Place the tenderloin on the hot griddle for 2 minutes each side. Finish in the oven for 6 minutes for medium cooked. Season with salt and allow to rest.
- Carve the meat in thick slices and serve on top of the salad.

VENDOR SPOTLIGHT

Given the high standard of produce at Borough Market, it is no surprise that its street food provides rich pickings. No visit is complete without a visit to **Kappacasein**, where cheesemaker Bill Oglethorpe has been selling his raclette and toasted cheese sandwiches since 2003. Oglethorpe makes his own cheese, Ogleshield, which he combines with Montgomery Cheddar and Comté cheeses, onions, leeks and garlic on sourdough bread. **Brindisa**, the Spanish food specialist that arrived in 2004, does a roaring trade at its stall serving grilled chorizo and rocket rolls. Visitors at **La Tua Pasta** shop can buy hot ravioli, gnocchi and papardelle – the pumpkin tortellini is unrivalled. **Bread Ahead** specializes in sourdough bread, but is famed for its fresh doughnuts filled with fruit curds and creams (below). Other street food gems include **Gujarati Rasoi**, where Urvesh Parvais and his mother Lalita concoct spiced vegetarian dishes; **Gourmet Goat** where Nadia and Nick Stokes make Cypriot-inspired kid goat wraps; and **Northfields Farm** stall for Aberdeen Angus salt beef sandwiches on rye bread with gherkins and mustard.

ROPEWALK MALTBY STREET LONDON

Often seen as an offshoot of nearby Borough Market, Ropewalk at Maltby Street has been its own hive of market activity since 2010. Started by Anita Leroy of Monmouth Coffee and later curated by food writer Rachel McCormack, the market began operating out of arches beneath a railway viaduct. (Ropewalk's name refers to the narrow street's historic use for laying out materials used in rope-making.) Today the market runs along the newly developed Ropewalk, a lane between Maltby Street and Millstream Road.

Comprising stalls, shops, pop-up bars and eateries, Ropewalk is a buzzing, thriving foodie destination. Twenty-five traders operate and one hundred more are on the waiting list, such is the market's gastronomic cachet. Top spots are Waffle On, whose signature dishes include brunch specialties such as Southern fried buttermilk chicken with maple syrup butter. The Cheese Truck serves its grilled Cheddar and Ogleshield cheese toasties, made with bread from Lambeth's Bread Bread Bakery. Comptoir Gourmand has earned a loyal following for its tartiflette, a rich and bubbling cheese and potato dish served from giant pans.

Visitors flock to St John Maltby, owned by chef Fergus Henderson, the market outlet for the firm's baked goods, including rhubarb, custard and lemon curd doughnuts. It has now expanded into an eatery serving British small plates. There's also sherry and tapas at Tozino and peri peri chicken buns at African Volcano. Ropewalk is popular for grocery shopping between bites to eat. Offerings include Greek oils and honeys from Maltby and Greek, oysters from Market Gourmet and gin libations at the pop-up Sparrow Bar. **VS**

Where: Ropewalk, London SE1 3PA

When: Saturday, 9 a.m.–4 p.m.; Sundays 11 a.m.–4 p.m.

1 Burmese fermented tea leaf salad from Lahpet.   2 Dirty Little Secret Burger at African Volcano.   3 LASSCO's architectural salvage shop.   4 Doughnuts from St John's.   5 Peri peri prawns.   6 Tending the tartiflette.   7 Totally tasty: Waffle On.

8

8 Maltby Street Market on Ropewalk offers the finest gourmet street food in a characterful London setting.

BRIXTON VILLAGE AND MARKET ROW LONDON

This vibrant, covered market, located in the arches beneath Brixton railway station, started life in the early 1900s as a series of arcades. Threatened by potential closure in recent years, Granville Arcade (now Brixton Village) and Market Row were thankfully saved by local petitions. Now, it's a bustling culinary and cultural hub, comprising restaurants, cafés and shops as diverse as the population of Brixton itself. Home to over 120 businesses — including shops offering everything from African fabrics to fresh fish, specialist wines and cuisines from around the world — it's a market steeped in cultural variety, making the food options innovative, exciting and diverse. For London, it's remarkably cheap; the settings are small and cosy, and most of the time you'll see the food or drinks being made directly in front of you, or you'll be sitting under the cover of the arcade, soaking up the atmosphere.

Your biggest challenge will be deciding where to eat, but given that premises are reasonable and informal, you could try a course at each. From Pakistani to Jamaican, and Chinese to Mexican, you'll find food from all over the world. Many of today's traders will become the stars of tomorrow: look at sourdough pizza specialists, Franco Manca, who now have more than 20 restaurants in London, but still have people queuing at their original Brixton joint for a taste of their infamous twenty-hour, slow-rising sourdough. **KR**
Where: Brixton Village, 10–11, 8LB, Coldharbour Lane, London SW9
When: Monday 8 a.m. – 5 p.m.; Tuesday to Sunday, 8 a.m. – 11.30 p.m.

1 A burger with rosemary-salted fries from Honest Burgers.
2 Spreading the sauce on pizza dough.   3 The street market — known for its African and Caribbean produce.   4 The arcade is home to cafés and takeaways serving a variety of cuisines.

5   5 Brixton's Village Market has become a cosmopolitan culinary food
hub. 6 Breakfast at Burnt Toast Cafe: sourdough toast with poached
eggs, smothered in hollandaise sauce and chilli jam. 7 Rustic tables
add to the trendy atmosphere of this affordable destination.

DEEP-FRIED VEGETABLE BALLS

This delicious recipe is from Beijing street food specialist, Mama Lan.

MAKES 8
Preparation: 20 minutes
  Cooking: 5 minutes
100 g / 3½ oz carrots, grated
2–3 spring onions, finely chopped
20 g / ¾ oz fresh ginger,
  finely grated

10 g / ¼ oz fresh coriander, chopped
½ tsp salt
¼ tsp Chinese five-spice
100 g / 3½ oz plain flour
60 ml / 2 fl oz water
Vegetable oil for frying
Sweet chilli sauce to serve

- Mix together all the ingredients except the oil until well combined. Shape into small balls.
- Fill no more than half of a deep, heavy-based pan with oil and heat to 175°C / 350°F. Fry a few balls at a time until they float to the top.
- Drain on absorbent kitchen paper and serve with a sweet chilli sauce.

VENDOR SPOTLIGHT

For brunch with a twist, head to the intimate setting of **Okan** for okonomiyaki, a Japanese pancake straight from the streets of Osaka topped with brown sauce, Japanese mayonnaise, green seaweed flakes and bonito fish flakes (below). Or perhaps a big serving of yaki soba (buckwheat noodles) or yaki udon (thick white noodles) will take your fancy. **Mama Lan** also serves up steaming bowls of noodles, as well as handmade Chinese dumplings from a forty-year-old recipe. Try king prawn and Chinese water chestnuts; pork and Chinese leaf; and wood-ear mushroom, spinach and vermicelli. If meaty fare is your thing, **Honest Burgers** are renowned for their juicy patties. Order rosemary-salted fries on the side. Pulled-pork lovers should visit **The Joint**, who have sixteen-hour pulled-pork burgers and hushpuppies (fried cornmeal batter rolls) on the menu.

LONDON
FOOD TRUCKS

London's street food scene is thriving and there is no shortage of exciting new meals on wheels popping up around the British capital. The best areas to go in search of food trucks are King's Cross, Shoreditch, Dalston, Soho, Canada Water and the South Bank, but hidden gems can also be found further out, in places such as Peckham and Brockley. Read up on the latest street food festivals on the *Time Out* or *Evening Standard* websites and use the Twitter and Facebook pages of individual trucks to track their current location.

Look out for the colourful, garland-bedecked van of **Everybody Love Love Jhal Muri Express**, which sells Bengali street food. Their jhal muri cones – filled with puffed rice, roasted dhal, noodles, vegetables and a tamarind sauce – are unmissable. **Bleecker** was established by native New Yorker Zan Kaufman with the aim of serving the best burger in London. Try the classic cheeseburger – the secret burger sauce is the transformative ingredient. **Luardos** offers the best Mexican food in town. The original turquoise van, Jesus H, has been joined by a hot-pink sister, Mary, and they do a roaring trade in burritos and tacos in locations around Camden and King's Cross. Everything is home made, including the hot sauces. Also causing a stir are the team at **Mother Clucker**, with their tea-brined, buttermilk-soaked, southern fried chicken. Order with a side of Cajun fries and mac 'n' cheese for the full experience.

To top things off, you'll be pleased to hear there's plenty of options for dessert on the go. **Blu Top Ice Cream** scoop up delicious ice-cream sandwiches – made with their own handmade filling – from the back of their Piaggio van. Just pick from a choice of two cookies, including red velvet, lemon cornmeal and pistachio, then choose an ice cream flavour and some toppings.

It wouldn't be London if tea wasn't available on every corner and **Good & Proper Tea** pour plenty of cups of tea and crumpets from their 1974 Citroën-H van at events and pop-ups around the capital. A cup of Darjeeling 2nd flush – known as the 'champagne' of teas – goes perfectly with a Marmite melt crumpet. **KR**

PARIS

Parisian street sellers crying their wares of pastries, pies and drinks were a common sight during the Middle Ages, their shouts echoing through the city's streets and passageways. As Paris grew and the population increased, so too did the number of street vendors, who sold an ever-expanding range of ready-to-eat food. A nineteenth-century favourite was fried strips of potato – the forerunner of modern French fries. This beautiful city is rightly famed for its cuisine and the growing trend for gourmet street food only adds to its distinguished reputation.

In the French capital there is a wonderful choice of markets and food trucks offering top-quality artisan food from around the globe. The city's oldest market, Marché des Enfants Rouges (see p.153) and the boutique Marché Raspail (see p.157) are deservedly popular with locals and tourists alike, but it is well worth making time to try the other culinary choices around the city. You can eat very well at wallet-friendly prices.

The fabulous food market at 24–34 Boulevard de Belleville is packed with fresh and ready-made food. You can eat outdoors at the market, sitting at a table or standing at the stalls, which offer everything from authentically French to Moroccan, Mexican and vegan dishes. The small open-air market in the leafy square of Place Monge opened in 1921 and sells a range of ready-to-go foods, including West Indian and Lebanese, alongside typical French fare.

The picturesque Marché Saxe-Breteuil in the 7th arrondissement starts at Place de Breteuil and extends to Avenue de Ségur. Choose from a wide range of delicious ready-cooked foods such as beef

MARCHE DES ENFANTS ROUGES PARIS

Created in 1615 and named after the red-coloured jackets worn by children of the nearby orphanage, the Marché des Enfants Rouges is the oldest surviving market in Paris. Four hundred years on, it is a thoroughly modern experience, perhaps not surprising given its prime position in the dynamic and progressive Marais district of the French capital.

Like much of the area, the market was initially fashionable among the city's wealthiest residents, before experiencing a decline as the rich moved south and west. At one point it was threatened with demolition, but its future was secured following a major clean-up of the Marais in the 1960s, when a new affluent professional class moved in. Renovated over several years at the end of the 1990s, the market quickly re-established itself as an attraction for local residents as well as large numbers of foodies from across the city.

The market's glass, wood and iron structure shelters barely twenty stands, making it an intimate and welcoming experience. There are fruit and vegetables available, and a fishmonger, but the Marché des Enfants Rouges is more about consuming onsite than the weekly shop these days, with most stands providing stools and tables. The vibe is international. Although you can purchase typically French crêpes, galettes, toasted sandwiches, freshly prepared quiches, salads and organic soups, most vendors offer more exotic fare. Take your pick from Lebanese meze, Italian pasta, Japanese bentos, Moroccan couscous and a lively corner unit from the French Antilles serving rum cocktails to accompany plates of fish and accra fritters. **AR**

Where: 39 Rue de Bretagne, 75003 Paris
When: Tuesday to Saturday 8 a.m.–8.30 p.m.; Sunday 8.30 a.m.–5 p.m.

6 The Moroccan food at Marché des Enfants Rouges is especially delicious and colourful – from fragrant couscous and succulent grilled meat skewers to stuffed vegetables and hearty lamb tagines.

GALETTE DE SARRASIN COMPLETE

These savoury Breton-style pancakes are made with buckwheat flour.

MAKES 4

Preparation: 20 minutes
 plus 2 hours resting

Cooking: 6–8 minutes

325 g/11½ oz buckwheat flour

A generous pinch of sea salt

75 ml/2½ fl oz water

1 egg

Salted butter or lard, for frying

For the filling:

Slices of ham and grated Emmental

4 eggs

- Place the flour and salt in a large bowl and make a well in the centre. Add the water little by little, mixing briskly to incorporate some air. Add the egg and mix well. Cover with cling film or a clean cloth and leave to rest for at least two hours in the fridge.
- Melt a knob of butter or lard in a heavy frying pan and pour in a ladleful of batter. Quickly swirl to coat the base. Cook the pancake for 1 to 2 minutes, then carefully loosen the edges with a spatula and flip.
- Place the ham and cheese (as much as desired) in the centre and crack an egg on top. Fold in the edges to form a square, and cook until the egg is done. Repeat with the remaining batter and filling. Serve immediately.

VENDOR SPOTLIGHT

This atmospheric market offers visitors the chance to munch their way through food from around the globe. Enjoy plates of oysters, breaded pigs' trotters and Sunday brunch in the charming **Estaminet des Enfants Rouges** eatery or feast on traditional Italian fare at **Mangiamo Italiano** (above). The **Taeko** stand offers reasonably priced bento boxes brimming with grilled sardines, ginger-infused tuna, miso soups or crispy chicken. If you still have room, top things off with a bowl of white sesame ice cream. Housed in a two-sided unit on the market's edge, **Versant Vins** offers natural wines, plates of cheese and charcuterie. On certain days, you can even enjoy eating fish and chips on large barrels placed outside the shop.

Chèvre aux
herbes
4,60 €

galette
de Pommes de
Terre
2,50€

1 A traditional open-air market.   2 Artisan cheeses.   3 Vegetarian paella to go.   4 A side of rustic roast potatoes.   5 Don't miss galette de pomme de terre (potato pancake) from Les Gallatins.   6 The best poulet rôti (spit-roast chicken) in Paris from Romain & Ses Poulettes.

MARCHE RASPAIL PARIS

When the Marché Raspail was first created in the 1920s, the Left Bank of Paris was teeming with students, writers and artists who were more often than not 'belly-empty, hollow-hungry', as Ernest Hemingway once wrote. Times have changed, and although the area remains intellectual in spirit, it is now also wealthy in pocket, making it the ideal location, since 1989, for the French capital's first fully organic market.

Raspail is very much the archetypal open-air Parisian market, with its striped awnings snaking down a Haussmannian boulevard. On Tuesday and Friday mornings it is home to more traditional vendors, but it is the organic market, organized each Sunday, that has really given Raspail its particular identity. This incarnation may be known as 'le plus chic et le plus cher' (the most exclusive and expensive) and a place where celebrities fill their fridges, but it also has a surprisingly laid-back atmosphere. Many vendors have been here since the market's beginnings; as well as being passionate about their produce, they are also happy to provide samples and explanations. With shoppers coming from across the world, most vendors are also at ease conversing in English.

The market's natural produce remit includes clothing, carved wood implements, soaps and perfumes, the inevitable esoteric books and potions, and even flowers. However, the food and drink is the biggest draw. The choice on the fifty or so stands is vast, spanning fruit and vegetables, meat, bread, jam and honey, wine, dairy products and seafood. Prices may be geared towards Left-Bank budgets, but the quality is high. Local producers display bunches of carrots still wearing the mud they grew in, pleasingly misshapen tomatoes, and dew-sprinkled apples and pears. Satisfying the appetites of regular clients and visiting tourists, many stands also offer ready-to-eat food, including rotisserie chicken from Poulet Roti or potato galettes from Les Gallatins. AR

Where: Boulevard Raspail, 75006 Paris
When: Tuesday and Friday 7. a.m. – 2.30 p.m.; Sunday 9. a.m. – 3 p.m.

TARTE AU CHEVRE ET TOMATE
Creamy goat's cheese and sweet tomato in a classic tart.

SERVES 8
Preparation: 20 minutes
Cooking: 1 hour
300 g / 10½ oz sheet puff pastry
Dijon mustard
4–6 medium ripe tomatoes, sliced

180 g / 6 oz goat's cheese log, sliced
1 tbsp fresh thyme leaves,
   finely chopped
Sea salt
Freshly ground black pepper
2 eggs, beaten

- Preheat the oven to 190°C / 375°F / gas mark 5 and place a baking sheet inside. Line a 28-cm (11-in.) diameter tart tin with the pastry, trim the edges and prick all over with a fork. Line the tin with baking parchment and fill with ceramic baking beans or rice. Bake for 10 minutes, then remove the beans/rice and set aside to cool.
- Generously spread the mustard over the base of the cooled pastry case. Top with the tomato and goat's cheese slices, sprinkle with thyme and season with salt and pepper. Pour over the beaten eggs.
- Slide the tin onto the pre-heated baking sheet and bake for 40 minutes, or until the top has browned and the pastry is crisp and golden. Serve warm or at room temperature.

1 The Vietnamese Triple B from Le Camion BOL.   2 French burger outfit Le Réfectoire.   3 Nathalie Nguyen of Le Camion BOL.   4 Cantine California burger.   5–6 Le Camion qui Fume cooks gourmet burgers to order.   7 Delicatessen food truck Bügelski.

PARIS
FOOD TRUCKS

The food truck phenomenon took its time to arrive in Paris. Today, however, there are dozens of *restaurants ambulants* on the city's boulevards and streets. Most are truly nomadic, appearing at a different spot daily and releasing the details of their location via Twitter or Facebook. Hotspots include Place de la Madeleine, La Défense, the MK2 Bibliothèque cinema and the Point Ephémère.

The first truck to appear on the scene was **Le Camion qui Fume** (literally 'The Smoking Truck'), which arrived in November 2011, and many would maintain that it still offers Paris's best burger. Its bestseller is the Barbecue burger, topped with onion rings, Cheddar and the signature barbecue sauce. There are three trucks, one of which is permanently parked next to the MK2 Bibliothèque cinema.

Cantine California offers Californian-inspired dishes, which include spicy pork tacos and burgers topped with blackened red peppers and avocado, all made from organic meat and produce. If you don't want to join the long queue at lunchtime, try to get there early for the excellent brunch dishes. The van is normally located at either Marché Saint-Honoré or Marché Raspail.

If you're in search of street food with more of a French touch, try **Le Réfectoire**. Young chef Valentine Davase has given a Gallic spin to American classics, with options such as hot boeuf – a hot dog filled with slow-cooked beef bourguignon – and the Larry – a burger topped with honey-roasted goat's cheese. The secret is in the ingredients: Charolais beef, artisan bread and hand-cut fries.

Le Camion BOL offers revisited versions of classic Vietnamese dishes. Try the burger-style banh mi – mini sandwiches with a pork, prawn and shiitake mushroom filling – or the Triple B (bò bún), which is made up of finely sliced fillet beef, covered in a peanut and sesame crumble and accompanied by crispy mini nems (sausages).

Bügelski Deli, which is usually found just north of the périphérique in Saint-Denis, specializes in bagels; classic pastrami, smoked turkey and roast chicken are served with cream cheese, cornichons and salad. The bagels are made fresh daily by a bakery in Rue des Rosiers, the heart of Paris's Jewish quarter in the Marais. JL

1 The cafeteria at the centre of the market is a congenial place to stop for refreshment. 2 Scallops, mussels, prawns and razor clams. 3 Pinchos. 4 Stuffed sea urchin stars on a seafood platter. 5 Paper cones filled with freshly fried squid and calamari.

MERCADO DE SAN MIGUEL

MADRID

In Madrid, you can eat Spain. The city has always been a magnet for the best ingredients and cooking traditions from every part of this vast country. It became the capital in the sixteenth century, largely because it was right in the centre of the peninsula. Like spokes on a wheel, all the long, straight roads from the Spanish regions converge on the Puerta del Sol — the raucous meeting place where a plaque officially marks Kilometre Zero, the spot from which all distances are measured. It is at the very heart of Spain, and the beautifully renovated, *fin-de-siècle* Mercado de San Miguel, just off the Plaza Mayor, makes the most of its enviable position at the national gastronomic crossroads.

Inside the early twentieth-century, wrought-iron and glass walls, there are tables, counter bars and stalls selling beautifully displayed fresh produce and a bewildering array of endless temptations: oysters, sea urchins, chocolate, cheese, caviar, ice cream and hand-carved, acorn-fed cured ham. Tapas cover the range from prawns with garlic to olives stuffed with sun-dried tomatoes to duck salad; pinchos of monkfish liver or spicy octopus are unmissable. One could easily spend an entire day browsing, grazing, nibbling and sampling paper cones stuffed with deep-fried squid, Malaga anchovies, slices of chorizo or pork scratchings as well as portions of paella, gazpacho with shrimp or grilled Padrón peppers. All night as well: the market is open until very late to match the nocturnal eating habits of Madrileños. San Miguel is less an everyday market than an elegant, gourmet food court with a vibrant atmosphere and superb quality of food and drink. It might not be the cheapest market in the city and the crowds can be crazy, but churros and hot chocolate will restore your faith in the old saying, 'After Madrid, heaven.' But, finish your churros first. CH

Where: Plaza de San Miguel, s/n, 28005 Madrid

When: Sunday to Wednesday 10 a.m.–midnight; Thursday to Saturday 10 a.m.–2 a.m.

6 The lively lunchtime crowd at Mercado de San Miguel enjoys cold beers with their food. 7 For a taste explosion, share several plates of pinchos – bar snacks spiked on wooden sticks. 8 Tasty tapas consisting of mussels and garlic pan-fried prawns.

POLLO CON AJO Y LIMON

A delicious tapas dish of tender fried chicken with garlic and lemon.

SERVES 4

Preparation: 10 minutes

Cooking: 15 minutes

4 tbsp olive oil

8 fat garlic cloves, peeled and flattened with the flat of a knife

500 g/1 lb 2 oz boneless, skinless chicken cut into strips or small pieces

Sea salt

Juice of 2 lemons

3–4 tbsp chopped flat-leaf parsley

- Heat the oil in a large pan over a medium-high heat. Fry the whole garlic cloves until they start to turn golden brown. Remove with a slotted spoon before they burn.
- In the same oil, add the chicken and stir-fry for about 10 minutes until cooked. Add sea salt to taste, the lemon juice and parsley, and combine.
- Serve immediately, sprinkled with lemon zest.

VENDOR SPOTLIGHT

Lhardy have been renowned for classic excellence for over 170 years in Madrid and the elegant, gourmet tapas fit the updated context perfectly with a choice that ranges from breadcrumbed scallops in the shell to exquisitely light croquetas (above). The fish delicacies of north-west Spain can be enjoyed at **La Casa del Bacalao**: Santoña anchovies, Galician-style octopus, cod foie gras and ajoarriero (cod stew with red peppers) as well as salt cod pinchos (bar snacks) to sample and take away. Fish is also the big attraction at **El Señor Martín** where the choice ranges from goose barnacles to razor clams, langoustines and seafood cocktails plus the irresistible attractions of fresh squid and anchovies fried Andalucian style at El Señor Martín's Fish Cart. Paella is now synonymous with Spain and there are daily specials of rice and paella dishes to explore at **Paella y Olé**. Don't leave without a bag of wonderful Calasparra rice.

Frozen yoghurt may be a fairly recent arrival in Spain, but it would be hard to better that from **La Yogurería**. Made daily with fresh milk and skimmed natural yoghurt, fresh fruit and crunchy toppings, the colourful selection available is practically psychedelic. The choice of liquid refreshment is equally wide: try **La Hora del Vermut** for a draft vermouth aperitif, a caña (small beer) from the **Beer House** or taste sherries paired with tapas at **The Sherry Corner**.

BARCELONA

Street food has been part of Barcelona's culture for centuries. Based on centuries of culinary history, its cooking style reflects its Provençal heritage (Provence was once part of Spanish Catalonia). Barcelona's traditional dishes are typical of classic Catalan cuisine, ranging from brilliantly simple tapas to sumptuous fish stews. Seafood plays a significant role in the time-honoured foods of Barcelona, so it is no surprise that a Catalan favourite is suquet de peix, a flavoursome potato-based seafood stew, made with a variety of fish cooked with garlic and tomatoes. Unmissable specialties found everywhere include escalivada, a dish of smoky chargrilled vegetables made with aubergines, potatoes, onions and peppers. Anyone with a sweet tooth will love panellets; these small round confections are incredibly moreish. Made with almonds, sugar and eggs, they're traditionally rolled in a coating of pine nuts. All these delights can be found in the city's markets.

Barcelona's markets are lively affairs and part of the city's rich history. One of the most renowned and perhaps one of the oldest is located on the Ramblas – La Boqueria (see p.166). A market on this site is thought to date back to 1217, when tables were first set up near the old door of the city to sell meat. The market as we see it today was built in 1840, with the iron roof added in 1914, since when it has offered a diverse range of fresh produce. The city's

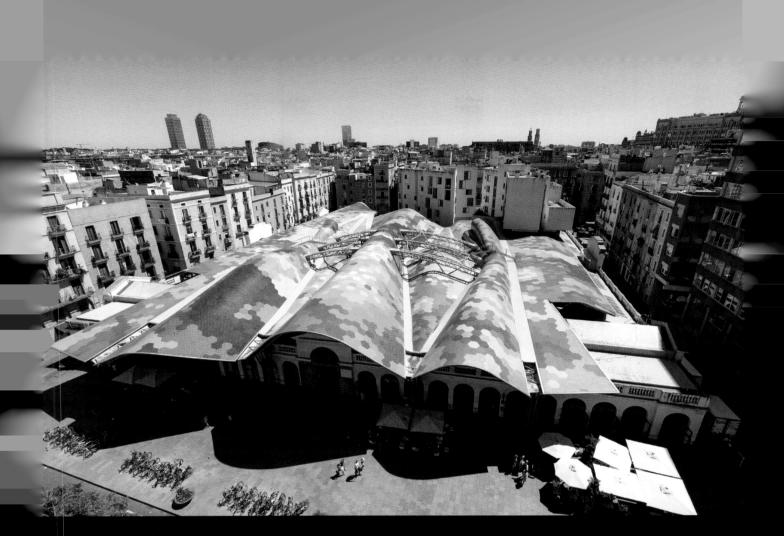

restaurateurs, as well as the locals, come here to shop in search of Catalonian specialties ranging from bacallà salat (dried salted cod) to percebes (gooseneck barnacles).

There are other great Barcelona markets, such as Fira Artesana (also known as the honey market) in Plaça del Pi, on the first Friday and Saturday of every month, where local producers gather to sell great food. It is famous for its delectable home-made cakes. Mercat de Sants on Carrer de Sant Jordi, in a large and airy brick building, sells fresh produce along with stands where you can purchase ready-made meals, snacks and salads. For a tasty lunch sample the wonderful charcuterie and cheese. You can take a seat at a counter to enjoy a freshly made sandwich with mouth-watering fillings, including Iberian ham, pork or cheese.

The Mercat de Santa Caterina, a covered market in Avenue de Francesco Cambo, is worth seeing for its eye-catching curved roof alone – a vast Gaudí-like mosaic of coloured ceramic pieces. You can also sample excellent tapas from the bar located by the main entrance. The small and charming Sant Andreu Market stands in the centre of a beautiful porticoed square, the Plaça del Mercadal in the Sant Andreu district. It dates back to the nineteenth century and a time when selling goods in Barcelona was regulated with the building of covered markets. One of the highlights here are the high-quality chocolates and ice creams.

The steel-and-glass Mercat del Ninot on Carrer de Mallorca is modern and bright, and it is a pleasure to stroll around its wide aisles. Particularly recommended here are the delicious charcuterie, tapas and croquetas de jamón (ham croquettes). The Rooftop Smokehouse at Carrer del Consell de Cent offers creative street food with a distinctive smoky taste. It began smoking food in an old wine barrel on a rooftop in 2014. Today it produces a sublime range of smoked food, including pastrami, duck, octopus and more, all served with a selection of home-made pickles.

LA BOQUERIA BARCELONA

This huge covered market, situated in the Old City (Ciutat Vella) district is regarded by many as the best in Spain, if not the world. It dates back to the Middle Ages and was built over a long period, from 1840 to 1914, on the site of the former St Joseph's monastery. Walk into the market and you'll be awed by its colour, buzz and sheer energy, as well as its huge range of artisan foods. It's packed with locals, tourists, top chefs and restaurateurs, who buy their produce here, a tribute to the renowned culinary traditions of the Catalan region. Notably, the market also houses the Boqueria Food School, which offers cookery courses taught by professional chefs.

At the heart of the market every type of seafood is on sale: live in tanks, glisteningly fresh, salted and dried, cooked and canned fish, plus a variety of shellfish. The fishmongers shout out their bargains and are happy to advise you on preparation, cooking and serving. If you're lucky, you'll find callos de bacalao (salt cod tripe), which is very rare. Around 500 stalls offer an infinite variety of foods, including meats, charcuterie, cheeses, fruit, vegetables,

edible flowers, breads, pastries, sweets, wines, freshly squeezed juices and ready-to-eat snacks. A popular Spanish treat is cecina de caballo (cured horsemeat).

You can take a guided tour of the market that lasts for about three to four hours, and there are plenty of places to eat dotted around the market if you fancy lunch or a light snack. The best tapas are at the popular El Quim de la Boqueria stand located in the centre, which specializes in tellines — tiny sweet delicate clams steamed in wine, baby squid (chipirones) sautéed with garlic and olive oil with fried eggs, and much more besides. The market does get very crowded, so it's best to go early in the day. **CW**

Where: La Rambla, 91, 08001 Barcelona

When: Monday to Saturday 8 a.m. to 8.30 p.m.

1 This beautiful medieval covered market is located on the former site of a monastery.   2 Seasoned artichokes.   3 Barcelona's take on the Mexican burrito – tortilla with fried seafood or chorizo and egg.   4 Crisp, deep-fried anchovies.

BURRITOS 4'50 €

5 Feast on the finest and freshest marisco (seafood) inside Barcelona's bustling La Boqueria market – washed down with a cold glass of beer.

PAELLA

This vibrant dish is named for the flat round pan in which it is cooked.

SERVES 4

Preparation: 15 minutes

Cooking: 30 minutes

16 mussels, beards removed and scrubbed

50 ml/2 fl oz olive oil

300 g/10 oz chorizo, diced

1 onion, finely chopped

1 bell pepper, roughly chopped

2 garlic cloves, finely chopped

½ tsp dried chilli flakes

½ tsp smoked hot paprika

500 g/1 lb 2 oz Calasparra or paella rice

1 large glass of white wine

1.2 litres/2 pints fish or vegetable stock

4 tomatoes, chopped, plus any other items: spring onions, peas or baby corn

Salt and pepper

12 uncooked prawns in their shells

- Place the mussels in a colander and rinse under cold running water. Discard any mussels that do not close when tapped firmly.
- Heat the olive oil in a large wok-type pan. When the oil is hot, add the diced chorizo and cook for a few minutes.
- Add the chopped onion and pepper and gently stir for a few minutes. Next add the garlic, chilli flakes and paprika. Stir together for another minute.
- Add the rice and stir for a further 2 minutes until well mixed.
- Pour in the wine and keep stirring. When most of the liquid has been absorbed, add the stock and tomatoes and simmer on a reduced heat for up to 15 minutes, until the rice is soft and all the stock has been absorbed.
- Add the prawns and mussels. You can also add chopped spring onions, peas and baby corn. Season and add a little more stock if the mixture is too dry.
- Cover and cook over a medium heat for 5 minutes until the seafood is cooked. The mussel shells should have opened (discard any that remain tightly closed) and the prawns should have turned pink. Serve with lemon wedges.

FOOD HIGHLIGHTS

Barcelona's iconic La Boqueria is a true gastronomic experience. Enjoy sublime **paella** from the Paella Bar, situated just outside the market entrance. All ingredients are sourced from La Boqueria. Another celebrated Spanish delicacy is **jamón ibérico** (Iberian ham), the rich, smooth, cured ham from pastured pigs that have been fed on a combination of acorns and grain. The finest – **jamón ibérico de bellota** – is from free-range pigs that roam oak forests along the border between Spain and Portugal, and eat only acorns in the final period before slaughter. The ham is cured for thirty-six months. This rich, savoury ham can be enjoyed served in a paper cone (above) or as an accompaniment to the rustic Catalan tapas snack **pa amb tomàquet** (grilled bread with tomato, olive oil, salt and garlic). For seafood lovers, **percebes** (gooseneck barnacles) are a rare delicacy served with garlic and parsley sauce. To finish **xuixo** – a flaky, deep-fried pastry that is filled with crema catalana – will satisfy any sweet craving.

MERCADO DA RIBEIRA LISBON

Lisbon's Mercado da Ribeira sees more than two million visitors pass through its doors each year, making it one of the country's most popular tourist attractions. Renovated in 2014 when part of it became Time Out Market Lisboa, it was once a building that had seen better days. Today this canteen-style food hall is a street food mecca, housing some of the city's best eats all under one roof. With each offering chosen by *Time Out* magazine's editorial team, this street food market is a unique concept (and unsurprisingly one that is to be replicated in London). The market's convenient location is also a big draw for visitors, being only a short walk from Cais do Sodré train station (with links to Belém, Cascais and beyond) as well as the bustling Chiado and Bairro Alto districts.

Proving that there is more to Portuguese cuisine than piri piri chicken (delicious as it is), Lisbon's *Time Out* market is home to stalls from some of the country's finest chefs and restaurants – three of the original establishments behind the market's pop-up eateries have Michelin stars. However, it's not only gourmet food

that you can savour at a fraction of the price; you'll also find Portugal's most revered snacks in abundance here, from bacalhau (salted cod) to pasteis de nata (custard tarts). The building's original food and vegetable market, which dates from 1892, is still next door – be sure to browse the wide selection of local produce.

With over thirty eateries to choose from, communal benches big enough for 500 hungry visitors (plus an extra 250 seats outside for sun worshippers) and late-night opening hours, this market is the perfect destination whatever your hunger levels. Just don't be surprised if you end up here for breakfast, lunch and dinner. KR

Where: Avenida 24 de Julho, 1200 Lisbon
When: Sunday to Wednesday 10 a.m.–midnight; Thursday to Saturday 10 a.m. to 2 a.m.

1 The vast canteen-style food court showcases the best street food. 2 The bright white entranceway features a distinctive clock. 3 Serving up fine local cuisine. 4 The Manteigaria Silva deli specializes in Portuguese hams.

PEIXINHOS DA HORTA E DO MAR

These deep-fried green beans and fish tempura are a variation of a traditional dish that has been a hit at chef Marlene Vieira's restaurant.

SERVES 4

Preparation: 20 minutes

Cooking: 15 minutes

8 large uncooked peeled prawns

Salt and pepper

1 litre/1¾ pint cooking oil

100 g/3½ oz green beans, ends trimmed and cut into strips

150 g/5½ oz cod loin, cut into strips

Microgreens, to garnish

For the tempura batter:

150 g/5½ oz flour

150 g/5½ oz cornflour

1 tsp baking powder

1 egg

½ tsp fine salt

250 ml/9 fl oz very cold sparkling water

- Season the prawns with salt and pepper.
- For the tempura batter, whisk together all the ingredients except the water in a bowl.
- Whisk in the sparkling water.
- Heat the oil in a deep heavy-based pan to 175°C/350°F.
- Dip each of the pieces of bean, prawn and cod individually in the tempura batter.
- Fry in batches in the oil until golden and crisp. Drain on absorbent kitchen paper. Garnish with microgreens, if liked, and serve immediately.

VENDOR SPOTLIGHT

Take a gastronomic tour of Portugal in a single sitting and at a fraction of the speed and price of traditional eateries. **Honorato** have been causing a real stir across the city with their unbelievable double-decker artisan burgers (above) and now you can have a taste of them on the go here. You'll also want to take advantage of Lisbon's abundance of fresh fish – **Confraria** serves up mouth-watering nigiri. Devour barriga de porco com puré de ervilhas (pork belly with mashed peas) from **Alexandre Silva** and if you're just passing through, **Pizza a Pezzi** is ideal for a quick slice. For the ultimate sandwich look no further than **Miguel Castro e Silva,** whose francesinha (sandwich from Porto) is guaranteed to fill you up for hours. If you're a fan of all things sweet, Porto-based **Arcádia** serve delectable chocolates. Perhaps looking to wash it all down with something? **Garrafeira Nacional** stocks excellent regional wine from throughout Portugal.

MEERZADEN PAVÉ
Bruinvierkant broodje van 'zampremy' tarwe, zonnebloempitten, sesamzaadjes, geel en bruin lijnzaad, micut en roggebloem. Bereid volgens de 'pousse lent' methode.

MULTIPLE SEEDS PAVÉ
Squared bun of brown bread prepared from 'zampremy' wheat, sunflower seeds, sesame seeds, yellow and brown linseeds, malt and rye flour. Prepared according to the 'pousse lent' method.

2,25

MARKTHAL

ROTTERDAM

Opened in October 2014 by Queen Máxima of the Netherlands, the impressive Markthal, located next to Rotterdam Blaak station, is vast with around one hundred fresh food stands, fifteen food shops and several restaurants, all offering a diverse variety of delicious food and drink. It presents a feast for the eyes as well as the taste buds, with eye-catching architecture and amazing foods and produce from around the globe. Uniquely, the building – designed by architects MVRDV – houses apartments, the food market, a supermarket and underground parking. A horseshoe-shaped arch of 228 residential apartments forms the roof of the building, which has a glass window facade. The interior is adorned with the biggest artwork in the Netherlands – the stunning, three-dimensional *Horn of Plenty* by Arno Coenen and Iris Roskam. Inspired by the classical cornucopia, it takes in fruit, fish, bread, flowers and the tower of the adjacent Laurenskerk church.

And the Markthal certainly delivers an abundance. More than one hundred market stands offer a fantastic variety of foods on the ground floor, while the first floor houses shops and a great choice of restaurants. De Wereld van Smaak (The World of Taste) is a focal point of the Markthal, where you can enjoy dishes made with fresh seasonal products, sourced directly from the farmers; a bonus is the wonderful view from the sixty-nine seats on the roof.

Enjoy a meal or a snack at any of the numerous food stands. Try sharing platters and cocktails at Obba Foodbar in the centre of the market. Munch on a delicious Dutch cheese sandwich from Henri Willig's Cheese & More on the first floor, while you browse the marvellous artisanal cheeses. Be sure to sample the Polderkaas and Hooidammer cheeses; the baby cheeses in several flavours (including coconut) make great gifts to take home. **CW**

Where: Dominee Jan Scharpstraat 298, 3011 GZ Rotterdam
When: Monday to Saturday 10 a.m.–8 p.m.; Sunday 12–6 p.m. (though bars and restaurants stay open till midnight)

1 Cromwijk Kaasdok – purveyors of the finest Dutch cheeses
2 Artisan pavé breads.   3 Fresh crab and shrimp rolls.
4 Crispy calamari.   5 Diners can admire the mural inspired by the cornucopia – a symbol of nourishment and abundance.

SMOKED MACKEREL SALAD

The Dutch love smoked mackerel – the perfect dish for a summer's day.

SERVES 4

Preparation: 15 minutes

Peppery salad leaves	75 ml / 2½ fl oz extra virgin olive oil
1 red bell pepper, cut into long strips	3 tbsp white wine vinegar
200 g / 7 oz canned sweetcorn, drained	Salt and pepper
10 cherry tomatoes, chopped	400 g / 14 oz smoked peppered mackerel, roughly flaked

- Place the salad leaves in a bowl, then add the red pepper, sweetcorn and tomatoes and toss together.
- Whisk together the oil and vinegar, seasoning with salt and pepper. Add the flaked mackerel to the salad ingredients and toss with the dressing.

FOOD HIGHLIGHTS

This Rotterdam food mecca will not disappoint. Enjoy the ubiquitous Dutch **friets** – thick, crispy fries served in a paper cone with a liberal dollop of creamy mayonnaise. **Patatje oorlog** (meaning war chips) is a tasty combo of friets with mayo, raw onions and Indonesian peanut satay sauce (above). There's an amazing variety of cheese in the market – **jonge kaas** is very soft and mild, but once the cheese ages it becomes **jonge belegen** with a more pronounced flavour. **Extra belegen** or **oude kaas** is matured for longer and develops a subtle sweetness and slight crunchiness from the crystals that form in older cheeses. The Dutch enjoy **overjarige kaas**, a flavoursome, crumbly cheese served with sweet apple syrup. Seafood at the Markthal is plentiful, especially **smoked mackerel** and rich **smoked eel**, **fried cod** and sharp **soused herring** – perfect with an ice-cold beer. If you want to take fish away, it can be vacuum packed for you. For those with a sweet tooth, seek out delectable **stroopwafels** (caramel sandwiched in two thin wafers). Enjoy them like the Dutch: warm a stroopwafel on top of a steaming hot cup of coffee or tea for about a minute, when it will transform into a warm, melted-caramel treat.

MARKTHALLE NEUN BERLIN

The historic Markthalle Neun draws food lovers from across the city to the West Berlin area of Kreuzberg every Thursday for a taste of the best street food the city has to offer. Every week, Berliners from all walks of life flock to this century-old market hall, just a stone's throw from the Spree River that intersects the German capital. Markthalle Neun was one of fourteen stunning market halls designed by Hermann Blankenstein towards the end of the 1800s. This charming nineteenth-century building is one of only three to survive World War II. Once the trading centre of Kreuzberg, the market hall now plays host to delicacies from around the globe.

Culinary masterminds from all sides of the city descend on Markthalle Neun every Thursday to feed hungry Berliners with classic street food from across the world and fill the hall with exciting aromas, from freshly steamed Korean buns and decadent Moroccan tagines to spicy South African bunny chow and Italian arancini (rice balls). Tourists can enjoy a more authentic central European experience by dining on traditional German bouletten (meatballs), kässpätzle (cheesy noodles) and fresh Belgian waffles.

Staying true to its roots as Kreuzberg's main hub for fresh produce, hungry visitors are also treated to expert butchers, great selections of cheese and vast collections of wine, all under one roof. Markthalle Neun is a perfect marriage of Berlin's cultural movements old and new, allowing visitors to sample Turkish meze next to vegan burgers and craft beer – or, in the winter months, a steaming hot mug of glühwein (German mulled red wine). RB

Where: Eisenbahnstrasse 42–43, 10997 Berlin
When: Thursday 5–10 p.m. (some vendors are permanent and so are accessible whenever Markthalle is open, most days 12–10 p.m.)

1 Sesame-crusted fried fish with vegetable chips and a caviar remoulade. 2 Steak marinaded in cider. 3 Mexican pork tacos. 4 Street Food Thursday attracts a diverse crowd to the hip district of Kreuzberg.

VENDOR HIGHLIGHT

Since Markthalle Neun was revamped in 2011, it has become an essential destination for foodies and tourists. Flagship events such as Street Food Thursday and weekend favourite Breakfast and Vinyl Market draw in locally famous names such as **Brammibal's Donuts**, beloved for their inventive vegan pastries, **Cheezus**, well known across the city for their gooey raclette cheese, and Mexican food truck legends **Eddielicious**. Regular vendors at Kreuzberg's historic market hall include **Big Stuff BBQ**, a pilgrimage site for meat lovers searching for gargantuan ribs and juicy pulled-pork, and Italian bakery **Sironi,** which offers up delectable focaccia loaded with toppings. Butchers **Kumpel & Keule** serve up fresh burgers made from only the finest meat, **Kame Japanese Bakery** provide everything from stuffed buns to matcha green tea cheesecake, and the folks at **Mani in Pasta** (above) are often rolling dough by hand for spectators while selling their freshly made wares by the bagful. Whether you're looking for something special to cook at home or you want to sample some of Europe's finest flavours, this market has what you need. And if you're thirsty, resident brewers **Heidenpeters** are on hand to serve their renowned craft beer.

HEISSER HOBEL'S KASSPATZLE

This food truck's award-winning recipe uses specially made cheeses, but Emmental works as well for this decadently cheesy dish.

SERVES 2
Preparation: 10 minutes
Cooking: 3 minutes
1 small onion, finely sliced into rings
325 g/11½ oz plain flour, plus extra for dusting
1–2 tsp paprika
30 g/1 oz butter

2 eggs
100 ml/3½ fl oz cold water
1 tsp salt
100 g/3½ oz grated Emmental cheese

To garnish:
2 tsp fresh chives, chopped
Freshly ground black pepper

- Dust the onion rings with enough flour and paprika to coat.
- Melt the butter in a pan over a high heat and fry the onions until crisp and browned. Set aside to drain on absorbent kitchen paper.
- Boil a large pan of salted water. Mix together the flour, eggs, water and salt in a bowl until a dough is formed. It should be loose enough to start slowly moving if the bowl is tipped upside down.
- Hold a colander with large holes (at least 5 mm/¼ in.) over the boiling water and scoop the dough into the colander. Use the back of a spoon or ladle to push the dough through the holes in the colander and into the water.
- Wait until the noodles start to float, then remove them from the water after 1 minute and place in a bowl with the grated cheese. Stir until the cheese is completely melted, then serve garnished with the fried onion rings, chives and black pepper.

BERLIN
FOOD TRUCKS

Street food in Berlin has long been dominated by greasy kebabs and currywurst (sausages with spicy ketchup), but the food truck scene is now bringing healthier and more varied options for city dwellers to grab eats on the go. Nothing draws a crowd of hip foodies in the German capital quite like a gathering of mobile kitchens offering affordable and tasty alfresco food. The Street Food auf Achse event in Prenzlauer Berg is a pilgrimage for many hungry locals every Sunday, offering up burritos, burgers, porchetta and other exciting food in the beautiful Kulturbrauerei courtyard. **Bite Club** prides itself on being a revolutionary force in the local food scene by mixing Berlin's love of partying with its affinity for open-air dining. Trucks from all over Europe regularly descend on a nightclub in Kreuzberg for Burgers & Hip Hop, a locally beloved combination of meaty mouthfuls and old school rap music. Yet it's not only meat and burgers in the German capital's street food scene – the Green Market has been hosting events since 2014, featuring some of the city's most inventive vegan food trucks.

The most popular food trucks can also be found parked at a number of weekly markets across the city, at hotspots such as Südstern, Winterfeldtplatz, Hermannplatz and Maybachufer. Housed in a converted horse transporter, **Le Pique-Nique** serves up entirely vegetarian fare; the fried pitta pockets filled with autumn vegetables are a highlight. Brazilian-run Tapiocaria sells delicate, crispy-edged pancakes made from cassava flour – try the 'Coalho', made with Brazilian cheese and coconut flakes. The award-winning **Heisser Hobel** specializes in German comfort food, offering hearty dishes such as cheese spätzle (home-made noodles). **La Criolla** makes the best empanadas, whereas **Fish 2 Go** is the place to get fish and chips with a contemporary twist.

Hungry visitors and locals alike in Berlin need only search for the nearest flea market, food festival or market hall to find diverse street food – from vegan burgers served from the back of an old Ford Transit van, grilled cheese sandwiches from a renovated Cold War-era US Army truck and tacos from a vintage milk truck to home-made cakes dished up on an old double-decker bus. RB

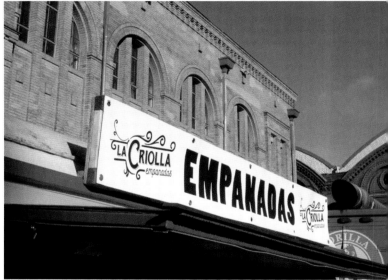

VIKTUALIENMARKT MUNICH

Strolling through the Viktualienmarkt is a treat for all the senses. Every type of food is here from time-honoured Bavarian specialties to sushi. It's a great place to enjoy an inexpensive lunch or snack. Created in 1807, over the years the market has progressed from a farmers' market to a popular destination for fresh food and deli goods. Now around 140 stalls and shops offer an amazing variety of foods, plus freshly squeezed fruit juices and outstanding Bavarian beers. Located in the pedestrian zone in the heart of the city's *Altstadt* (old town), it is the oldest farmers' market in Munich. Its name is derived from the Latin word *victualia*, which means 'provisions'.

Browse the butchers' stalls for an amazing variety of sausages such as steamed weisswurst (white sausage, traditionally eaten before noon), grilled bratwurst, substantial bauernwurst, slim polnischers and spicy paprika debreziners. Try some authentically Bavarian Leberkas (or Leberkäse) – a baked meatloaf of ground beef and pork, generally served with mustard in a bread roll.

Buy a picnic lunch in the market and enjoy a mug of beer in the beer garden in the centre of the Viktualienmarkt under the century-old chestnut trees, while you listen to the buskers. (There is a law that people can bring any food they choose to any beer garden in Bavaria.) Only fresh beer straight from the barrel is served and the type of beer changes daily. Check the sign above the beer counter for the brewery of the day. With seats for over 600 people, it includes some of the finest Munich beers and is the perfect place to sit and relax after a morning's shopping. The beer garden is also open during the winter months, selling hot Glühwein in addition to beer. **CW**

Where: Viktualienmarkt 3, 80331, Munich

When: Monday to Friday 10 a.m. – 6 p.m.; Saturday 10 a.m. – 3 p.m.

1 Visitors enjoying the beer garden.   2 Vendor selling giant pretzels and other specialty breads.   3 A wild mushroom stall.   4 An aerial shot of the sprawling, 200-year-old Viktualienmarkt, with its beer garden in the centre.

FOOD HIGHLIGHTS

Munich's gourmet food market offers visitors a unique opportunity to sample the delights of Bavarian cuisine. **Weisswurst** is a favourite Bavarian breakfast sausage that combines veal, bacon, onion, lemon zest, herbs and spices. Never eaten with a knife and fork, the correct way to eat this treat (as the locals do) is to cut it in half, pick it up in your fingers, dip it into the mustard and suck it from its skin. This staple is always eaten with bread rolls or pretzels and sweet mild mustard. **Pretzels** are another staple – distinctively shaped, their dark brown, crisp, salty crust conceals a soft interior. You can find them topped with coarse salt crystals, sesame seeds, sunflower seeds or poppy seeds. Look out for **obatzda** (below) – a Bavarian delicacy made with a pungent blend of aged white soft cheeses, paprika and onions. With your coffee, try **ausgezogene**, a type of rich sweet doughnut or **strietzel**, a braided yeast pastry, often filled with poppy seeds. Don't miss **schmalznudel** – a Munich institution. Served warm and generously sprinkled with sugar at **Café Frischhut**, these rings of rich, deep-fried dough surrounding a thin, almost transparent centre resemble a large, flat doughnut.

SCHWEINEBRATEN

This Bavarian pork roast is served with bread dumplings or potatoes.

SERVES 4
Preparation: 25 minutes (plus marinating time)
Cooking: 3 hours
2 kg/4 lb 8 oz pork shoulder
2 tbsp caraway seeds

1 tbsp salt
2 tsp black pepper
2 tbsp vegetable oil
2 onions, roughly chopped
225 ml/8 fl oz beer
Rosemary sprigs to garnish

- Rub the pork all over with the caraway seeds, salt, pepper and oil and marinate for at least 1 hour, preferably overnight. Remove the meat from the refrigerator for up to 1 hour before roasting to bring it to room temperature.
- Preheat the oven to 175°C/350°F/gas mark 4. Place the onions in a roasting tin big enough to comfortably fit the pork shoulder. Pour the beer into the tin.
- Place the pork, fat side down, in the roasting tin on top of the onions. Cover the tin with foil, place in the oven and roast for 1 hour.
- Remove the foil and turn the meat fat side up. Cut crosshatches in the fat in a diamond pattern, but try to avoid cutting into the meat itself. Place the roast, uncovered, back in the oven. Roast for another 1½ to 3 hours, until the roasted meat is tender and well browned on the outside.
- Garnish with rosemary sprigs. Serve with dumplings, vegetables and gravy.

GEFÜLLT MIT
FRISCHKÄSE
100 g € 2,40

DATTELN
GEFÜLLT MIT
SCHAFSKÄSE
100 g € 2,40

ZUCCHINI GEF
MIT SCHAFKÄSE
PINIENKERNE
100 g € 2,40

PEPERONCINI
GEFÜLLT MIT
SCHAFSKÄSE - MILD
100 g € 2,40

GEMÜSE
KRÄUTER

NASCHMARKT VIENNA

Vienna's best-known market has around 120 market stands and restaurants offering a sensational selection of Viennese specialties as well as international foods and produce. *Naschen* is the German verb meaning 'to nibble' and as you'd expect, the market is a fantastic place to find all kinds of food. It has become a trendy destination, particularly at the weekends after shoppers have left and a young crowd gather in the wine bars and eateries to listen to live music until late.

Originally a dairy market in the sixteenth century, Austrians have been enjoying culinary delights from all over the Austrian Empire at the Naschmarkt for centuries. The market has been increasingly renovated over the years, but many of the original stalls from the early twentieth century have been kept.

Do try the sauerkraut sold straight out of wooden barrels, along with breads, cheeses, wine and the myriad variety of sweet treats – desserts, pastries and cakes – for which Vienna is deservedly renowned. The most famous specialty is Sachertorte – a rich, dark chocolate cake glazed with apricot jam and coated in bittersweet chocolate icing. Grab a bite to eat at a market café or bar – it's a more relaxing experience than the formality of most traditional Austrian coffeehouses – and enjoy a glass of sturm, the Austrian fermented wine. There are plenty of ethnic eateries to choose from, too. Tewa offers organic cuisine; Neni serves Israeli-Oriental specialties such as shakshuka (eggs poached in a cumin-spiced tomato sauce); Orient & Occident provide good Turkish home cooking. Great fish restaurants include Fischviertel, Nautilus, La Marée and Umar (regarded by many as the best fish restaurant in Vienna.) Restaurants and cafés stay open until late. **CW**

Where: Wienzeile, Kettenbruecke, 1060 Vienna
When: Monday to Friday 6 a.m.–7.30 p.m.; Saturday 6 a.m.–5 p.m.

1 Fresh falafel wrap.   2 A colourful display of deli goods, including stuffed peperoncini and ricotta wrapped in parma ham.   3 A florist sells fresh herbs to grow.   4 Schaumrollen (cream pastry puffs).   5 The market is popular at night.

6 Firing up the rotisserie grill at a doner kebab stall. **7** With fresh fruit, vegetables and herbs this market is also perfect for a weekly grocery shop. **8** Kaiserschmarrn (shredded pancake) with sweet apple sauce.

WIENER SCHNITZEL

One of the celebrated dishes of Viennese cuisine – these tender, crispy breaded escalopes are most authentically prepared from veal.

SERVES 4
Preparation: 15 minutes
Cooking: 15 minutes
4 fresh veal slices or cutlets, 115 g/4 oz each
Salt

Freshly ground black pepper
100 g/3½ oz plain flour
100 g/3½ oz breadcrumbs
2 eggs, beaten
2 tbsp butter or vegetable oil
Lemon slices to garnish

• Lay out the veal slices between two sheets of cling film and pound gently with a meat mallet or rolling pin until they are thin escalopes. Season well on both sides with salt and pepper.
• Place the flour and breadcrumbs on separate flat plates. Put the beaten eggs on another plate.
• Coat each escalope on both sides in flour, then draw through the beaten eggs, ensuring that they are completely coated. Coat in the breadcrumbs, carefully pressing the crumbs into the escalopes.
• Heat the butter in a large frying pan. Place the escalopes in the pan and cook for 2 to 4 minutes (depending on the thickness) on each side until golden brown.
• Drain on absorbent kitchen paper and serve garnished with lemon slices.

FOOD HIGHLIGHTS

At the Naschmarkt the most-loved Austrian specialties include, not surprisingly, **Wiener schnitzel**, as well as **Wiener schnitzel vom schwein**, which is made with pork instead of the customary veal. Like their German neighbours, the Viennese love their meat. Look out for **Tafelspitz**, beef boiled in broth and served with minced apples and horseradish; **Beuschel**, a ragout containing veal lungs and heart; and **Selchfleisch**, a salty, smoked ham served with sauerkraut and dumplings. **Kaiserschmarrn** is a sweet, shredded pancake made with raisins, dusted with icing sugar and served with stewed plums or apples. **Palatschinken** are delectable thin crêpes, often filled with apricot jam (above).

MERCATO DI TESTACCIO ROME

What is described as Nuovo Mercato di Testaccio is in fact the original Testaccio market, which is now located in a contemporary covered building in one of Rome's central neighbourhoods. Opened in 2012, the market is considered *nuovo* thanks to Testaccio's long history with food, which stretches back nearly 2,000 years. One street down from the market on Via Galvani is Monte dei Cocci, a high hill made entirely of broken terracotta amphorae shards over which olive oil from Africa (used then for lighting lamps as well as for culinary purposes) was transported in ancient times. Directly across the road from the market entrance is the *ex-mattatoio*, a decommissioned slaughterhouse that is now home to a modern art museum.

Beyond this long history the market's newness is relative, as many of the same vendors that have been a fixture for decades – when it was located outdoors at Piazza Testaccio – are still operating. The move to the new complex has been welcome. Now equipped with running water, vendors with ready-to-eat offerings have expanded, seamlessly integrating into the classic market setting alongside fruit and vegetable sellers and butcher shops. Chef Marco Morello is a recent arrival with his gourmet Italian and international food to go – Foodbox.

The market is undeniably one of the best places in Rome for street food. Between attractive piles of courgette flowers and ripe figs, small but efficient stalls specialize in snack-sized classics such as supplì (fried balls of rice stuffed with cheese), cannoli (tube-shaped pastries filled with sweet ricotta), piadina (Roman flatbread sandwiches) or polpette agli agrumi (meatballs with citrus zest). Serious shoppers arrive early for their pick of produce, but the market is busiest at lunchtime. Venture past the food stalls and you'll find shoe shops and even a hairdresser, but the market's edible offerings remain the real draw. NA

Where: Via Galvani & Via Alessandro Volta, 00153 Rome

When: Monday to Saturday 9 a.m. – 3 p.m. (open later on Fridays)

LINGUE DI SUOCERA

These crunchy, thin flatbreads are known as mother-in-law's tongues.

SERVES 4

Preparation: 25 minutes, plus 3 hours standing

Cooking: 20 minutes

For the starter:

5 g/⅛ oz fresh yeast dissolved in 30 ml/1 fl oz of water

30 g/1 oz strong white bread flour

For the dough:

250 g/9 oz strong white bread flour

125 ml/4 fl oz water

2 tbsp olive oil

1 tsp salt

20 pitted green olives for topping

- Add the flour to the yeast mixture to create the starter. Knead into a ball, cover and leave to stand for 1 hour.
- For the dough, mix the flour and water, and then stir in the oil and salt. Add the starter and knead well until a smooth ball forms. Cover and leave to stand for at least 2 hours and up to 12 hours.
- Preheat the oven to 200°C/400°F/gas mark 6.
- Divide the dough into five pieces and roll out into narrow strips. Top with pitted olives, drizzle with olive oil and sprinkle with salt.
- Place on a baking tray and bake for 20 minutes, or until the top is very lightly browned. Cool on a wire rack and serve the same day.

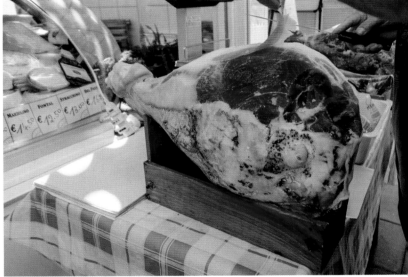

LA PIGNASECCA NAPLES

In general, Naples is a cacophony. At the market, the noise level and the action skyrocket. La Pignasecca is the oldest outdoor food market in Naples, snaking its way through narrow streets in the Quartieri Spagnoli of the city centre. Primarily located on Via Pignasecca, the market is a daily fixture near the Montesanto station. It features fruit and vegetable vendors, fish sellers and *tripperie* (tripe shops), as well as a series of small bakeries and specialty shops selling dried goods, cheese and salami.

La Pignasecca is a typical Neapolitan street market with few frills and no apparent attempt at formal organization. From one to the next, the stands alternate from buckets of octopus to boxes of onions, interspersed with the occasional rack of undershirts, then circle back around to glass cases displaying slices of thickly cut pizza to take away. However, what La Pignasecca lacks in order it richly compensates for in character. Wander through the various outdoor stalls as locals haggle for vegetables, and snack on the best fritti (fried appetizers) in Naples. While women harass you

to buy bunches of garlic, you can eat piping hot arancini (fried risotto balls in crispy breadcrumbs) or indulge in a calorific slice of parigina – a layer of pizza dough, melted provolone cheese, ham and tomato sauce topped with a layer of flaky pastry. Don't miss snacking on the bready snacks (tarrali) from Panificio Vincenzo Coppola as you wander the noisy market streets. Venturing behind the umbrellas of daytime vendors, you can also find affordable *trattorie* (restaurants) for simple sit-down lunches, as chairs and shade are otherwise difficult to find. From there you can engage in the fascinating activity of watching the lively Neapolitan natives as they go about their daily lives. NA

Where: Via Pignasecca, 14–28, 80134 Naples
When: Monday to Saturday 8 a.m.–1 p.m.

1 A typical fresh fruit stall at La Pignasecca.   2 Frittatine – fried pasta balls with pork, béchamel sauce and cheese.
3 Arancini – great to eat on the go.   4 The Neapolitan streets provide a charming setting.   5 Alici fritti (fried anchovies).

melanzane - provola
prosciutto cotto
€. 1.50

6 6 A slice of parigina – a rustic pizza covered in crisp pastry.   7 Thick pizza slices topped with aubergine, prosciutto ham and provolone cheese.   8 A fresh vegetable stall with an abundance of aubergines, courgettes, peppers and green beans.

VENDOR SPOTLIGHT

While produce and fish vendors set up shop along the sunny walkways, Via Pignasecca is also lined with storefronts that require you to step inside and jostle for room at counters selling bread, salami and cheese. Stop by **Antica Panetteria** (Via Pignasecca 20) for a fresh loaf, to be combined with pecorino cheese and cured meats from **Alimentari Russo Gabriele** (Piazza Pignasecca 1). As the market turns onto Via Portamedina, visit **Pescheria Azzurra** (number 4) for fresh seafood salads to take away (below). Alternatively, opt for a *coppo*, a cone of simple brown paper brimming with fried sardines and calamari. The finest selection of fried foods can be found at **Fiorenzano dal 1897** (Via Pignasecca 48), a short walk from Via Toledo. Ogle the delights behind the glass, and be sure to try the frittatine – deep-fried pasta balls stuffed with minced pork, béchamel sauce and peas.

FRITTATINE DI PASTA
These fried pasta balls are a staple of Neapolitan street food.

MAKES 8
Preparation: 30 minutes,
  plus 2 hours chilling
Cooking: 15 minutes
For the filling:
250 g/9 oz bucatini (or maccheroni)
  pasta, broken
200 g/7 oz fresh peas
200 g/7 oz diced prosciutto cotto
  (cooked ham)

200 g/7 oz provolone cheese,
  cubed
300 ml/10 fl oz béchamel sauce
4 tbsp Parmigiano Reggiano
  (Parmesan cheese), grated
For the batter:
300 g/10½ oz flour
Pinch of salt
500 ml/18 fl oz cold water
Olive oil for frying

- For the filling, break the dried bucatini in quarters and cook the pasta in a large pan of salted boiling water, draining a few minutes earlier than recommended on the packet to ensure that it is very al dente.
- Lightly cook the peas, and combine in a bowl with the ham and provolone cheese. Add the drained pasta, and stir in the béchamel sauce.
- Top with the grated Parmesan cheese and mix well. Set aside in the refrigerator for at least 2 hours.
- For the batter, whisk the flour and salt in the cold water.
- Using a small glass, divide the pasta mixture into rounds. Dip the rounds in batter and fry lightly in very hot olive oil, turning until the flattened balls take on a golden colour.
- Drain on absorbent kitchen paper and serve immediately.

BALLARO MARKET PALERMO

Step into Palermo's Ballarò market on a bright, sunny morning and you'll be greeted by a din of voices. The vendors cry out, proudly vaunting the merits of their produce, while housewives haggle to get the best prices. Bikes and scooters weave their way through the crowds. The market, which is in the heart of the city's historic centre, extends along the Via Ballarò towards Piazza Carmine. The narrow, cobbled streets hum with activity from early morning to late evening.

The outdoor market tradition in Sicily dates back to the ninth century, when the island was under the rule of the Saracens, which explains the striking similarity of Sicilian *mercati* to Arab souks. Ballarò – Palermo's oldest street market – preserves a strong sense of the city's Arab traditions: according to some, even its name is derived from the Arabic *Souk el Ballarak*, meaning 'market of mirrors'. A new wave of North African newcomers has been making Palermo their home, establishing businesses in the Palermitan souks.

Expect to encounter exotic finds such as the frittula, the raw ingredients of which include the pieces of meat from a calf that would have been deemed as waste. It is somewhat like a meaty version of kebab, but in Sicilian style. Another well-famed street snack is pane ca meusa, veal spleen cooked in lard and served in a soft bun. As the street market is within half a kilometre from the sea, you can also find the freshest cuttlefish, anchovies, swordfish, octopus, sardines and other creatures of the sea. *Friggitorie* (fried-food stalls) sell them battered and fried – the fritto misto di mare (fried mixed seafood) is unmissable. TL

Where: Via Ballarò, 90134 Palermo
When: Monday, Tuesday, Thursday to Saturday, 7 a.m. – 8 p.m.; Wednesday and Sunday 7 a.m. – 1 p.m.

1 The atmospheric open-air market pulses with activity.
2 A vendor making Palermitan sandwiches filled with panelle and crocchè.   3 Sicilian sfincione – a thick-crust pizza using focaccia bread.   4 Grilled stigghiole (offal) – a local delicacy.

5 Locals meander past a seafood and fish stall at this famous market.   6 A frittola sandwich, ready to eat on the spot. Frittola may sound grisly (fried calf fat, leftover meat and cartilage) but it is a must-try.   7 Vendors making panelle (chickpea fritters).

FOOD HIGHLIGHTS

One of the best-known street foods to try at Ballarò market is the North African-inspired Palermitan sandwich with **panelle** (chickpea fritters) and **crocchè** (potato croquettes). The best panellari can be found heading south-west to Palermo's Quattro Canti crossroads. Be sure to ask the vendor to put some **melanzane a fette** (thinly sliced eggplant) in your sandwich for that extra layer of tastiness. Look out for the barbecues grilling **stigghiole** (below, lamb or calf's intestines). Sellers, known as *stigghiolaru*, start to set up their stalls towards 5 p.m. In order to alert potential customers to their presence, they drop lard on the hot coals to send up a cloud of smoke – so just follow the smoke to find them!

PANE CON PANELLE E CROCCHE

This hearty Palermitan sandwich, combining chickpea fritters and potato croquettes, is often eaten for breakfast.

MAKES 4
Preparation: 40 minutes, plus chilling
Cooking: 35 minutes
For the panelle:
250 g / 9 oz chickpea (gram) flour
450 ml / 16 fl oz water
For the crocchè:
500 g / 1 lb 2 oz potatoes, peeled

1 tsp cornflour
A handful of fresh parsley, chopped
Salt and pepper for seasoning
Vegetable or olive oil for frying
To serve:
2 sesame seed white bread rolls, cut lengthways
Lemon wedges

- Grease a baking tray.
- For the panelle, mix the chickpea flour and the water in a saucepan, bring to a boil and stir until the mixture thickens to a paste. Season.
- Scoop the mixture onto the greased baking tray and spread in an even layer, about 5 mm / ¼ in. thick.
- When the panelle mixture has completely cooled down, slice it into pieces and refrigerate for at least 30 minutes (or up to 24 hours).
- Cook the panelle in a deep fryer, rotating them until golden brown.
- For the crocchè, dice the potatoes and boil in a pan of boiling salted water until they have softened.
- Mash the potatoes with the cornflour and parsley; season with salt and pepper.
- Take palm-sized amounts of the mixture and shape these into croquettes. Fry them in a deep fryer or heavy-based saucepan.
- Cut the bread rolls and fill with a few slices of panelle and two or three crocchè. Serve with lemon wedges.

Sekret Smaku
PIEROGI RUSKIE
DUMPLINGS WITH COTTAGE
CHEESE AND POTATOES
31.50 /KG

1 One of the three main aisles of the covered market. 2 Spindle-shaped oszczypek – a smoked sheep's cheese from the Tatra Mountains. 3 Hearty Polish dumplings filled with cheese and potato. 4 Doughnuts and pastries to satisfy the sweet tooth. 5 Sausage and fried onions.

STARY KLEPARZ MARKET KRAKOW

Situated north of Kraków's Barbican stands 600-year-old Stary Kleparz. Every day 200 traders flock to this market, many of whom are the fourth generation to work there. In medieval times, the market was larger, filling Matejko Square as well, but even at this scale it provides a quintessentially Polish experience. Stalls vary in size, from home-made tables to glass affairs with orderly displays. The market's three aisles are mostly covered, making it a welcome refuge during harsh weather. Despite the arrival of big supermarkets, Stary Kleparz still attracts a loyal clientele, the old arriving as the market opens, the young filing in when their lectures finish.

Smoked sausage, freshly baked bread and a hint of dill pickles waft through the air year-round. A third of the market is dedicated to fresh fruit and vegetables: polished bell peppers, colossal cabbages and pumpkins in varying sizes and shades of green and amber – all perfect for stuffing. In autumn, stalls are filled with freshly picked wild mushrooms: chanterelles, boletus and saffron milk caps. The rest of the year they're available either dried or pickled. In summer, such earthy aromas are replaced with the sweet scent of berries and stone fruit.

Cheese is another staple. Although smoked bundz – a sheep's milk cheese – has become popular, the unsmoked is considered the original, authentic version. However, you will find it flavoured with herbs and spices such as fenugreek, nettle and nigella seeds. Vendors are happy to slice off a slither, so you can compare each one. Those with a sweet tooth are also well provided for. Dried fruits, Polish sweets and traditional cakes including sharlotka (apple cake), serniki (cheesecake), pączki (doughnuts) and makowiec (poppy seed cake) are sold in abundance. CJ

Where: Rynek Kleparski, 30-962 Kraków

When: Monday to Friday, 6 a.m. – 6 p.m.; Saturday 6 a.m. – 4 p.m.; Sunday 8 a.m. – 3 p.m.

RUSKIE PIEROGI

These delicious filled dumplings are a national food in Poland.

SERVES 4
Preparation: 35 minutes
Cooking: 30 minutes

500 g/1 lb 2 oz Maris Piper potatoes, peeled and diced	500 g/1 lb 2 oz plain flour
50 g/1¾ oz ricotta cheese	250 ml/9 fl oz water
75 g/2¾ oz grated Cheddar cheese	1 medium egg
Salt	1 onion, sliced and fried until crisp
Pepper	100 g/3½ oz bacon lardons, fried
	Sour cream, to serve
	Small handful of fresh dill, to garnish

- Boil the potatoes until soft. Drain, mash and cool slightly.
- Mix in the ricotta and Cheddar cheeses. Season well and set aside.
- Mix the flour, water and egg until a dough forms.
- Knead the dough on a floured surface. Roll the dough until 3 mm (⅛ in.) thick. Cut into rounds using an 8-cm (3¼-in.) pastry cutter.
- Roll the potato and cheese mixture into balls 1 cm (½ in.) in diameter.
- Place one ball of mixture in the centre of each dough round. Fold over and pinch the edges together to make the pierogi.
- Place the pierogi in a large pan of salted, boiling water. When they rise to the surface, remove them from the pan and drain well.
- Sprinkle the pierogi with crisp fried onions and bacon lardons. Serve with sour cream and garnished with sprigs of fresh dill.

1 Warming, rustic Hungarian food for a winter's day. 2 Chimney cakes. 3 The impressive market hall is striking when illuminated at night. 4–5 Lángos is the national street food – topped with sour cream and cheese or with smoky roasted red pepper.

GRAND MARKET HALL BUDAPEST

Known as the pearl of the Danube, Budapest is one of the most enchanting cities in Europe. In reality it comprises two separate cities divided by the river. Buda is sprawled across the hills that form the base of the Transdanubian Mountains on the right bank, and on the left bank is the more compact Pest. The historic Grand Market Hall is located right at the Pest end of Liberty Bridge, which connects the two cities. The construction of Budapest's Grand Market Hall started in 1894. Two years later, a few days before the opening, a fire destroyed the roof. Repairs ensued and the splendid neo-Gothic hall finally opened in March 1897.

Designed by architect Samu Pecz, the spacious interior hosts a festival of vivid colours. Fresh products are attractively displayed in stalls with strings of red paprika and garlic, Hungarian salamis and meats festooned above. Browse for fresh pastries, dairy products, kitchen utensils, Hungarian wines and pálinka (traditional fruit brandy), honey, tea and herb mixes. The fine selection of mustards and goulash sauces packed in tubes make great souvenirs and will add a dash of flavour to many dishes. Be sure to stock up on them as well as the excellent, reasonably priced saffron.

The second floor of the market houses several outlets for Hungarian embroidery and a few places to sit. So grab a plate of hot food from one of the stands – töltött káposzta (stuffed cabbage rolls), beef goulash or palacsinta (stuffed crêpes with fillings varying from walnut and chocolate to meat) – and head upstairs to observe the action on the second floor. OR

Where: Vámház krt. 1-3, district IX, Pest end of Liberty Bridge

When: Tuesday to Friday 6 a.m.–6 p.m.; Saturday 6 a.m–3 p.m.

6 Lángos with deep-fried goose crackling. 7 The ornate market is the largest in Budapest; its architecture has been described as a 'symphony in iron'. 8 Cutting into a tray of traditional cheesy pizza. 9 A fruit-filled Hungarian pastry.

FOOD HIGHLIGHTS

The upper level of Grand Market Hall draws tourists for its embroidery, chessboards and other crafts, but it is also the place to go for a cheap, tasty bite to eat. Here you'll find a great selection of Hungarian specialties: **töltött káposzta** (stuffed cabbage rolls with minced pork), steaming bowls of beef **goulash**, **lángos** – the national street food – (fried flatbreads topped with garlic, sour cream, cheese or ham), **roasted goose thigh** and **chicken paprikash** (roast chicken in a red pepper and paprika sauce with home-made noodles). **Paprika** is a national treasure of Hungary. Made from New World capsicum peppers that were brought back to Europe, the plant used to make the Hungarian version of the spice (which is more robust in flavour than the Spanish kind) was grown in 1529 by the Turks at Buda (now part of Budapest). There are eight grades, ranging in colour and intensity from delicate and mild to strong and hot. Here you can buy all varieties and the small ceramic pots with wooden spoons make great gifts to take home (below).

PALACSINTA

These thin Hungarian pancakes have a sweet ricotta cheese filling.

SERVES 3–4
Preparation: 20 minutes, plus chilling
Cooking: 15 minutes
For the batter:
3 eggs
1 tsp caster sugar
Pinch of salt
225 ml/8 fl oz milk
140 g/5 oz plain flour
225 ml/8 fl oz carbonated water

Vegetable oil for frying
For the filling:
1 egg yolk
1 tbsp caster sugar
A few drops of vanilla extract
150 g/5½ oz ricotta or cottage
    cheese
Grated zest of ½ lemon
Fruit jam (optional)
Icing sugar, to serve

- For the batter, combine the eggs, sugar, salt and milk. Stir in the flour to form a smooth batter. Refrigerate for at least 2 hours or overnight.
- For the filling, beat the egg yolk with sugar and vanilla extract until creamy.
- In a separate bowl soften the ricotta cheese with a wooden spoon or a fork, then beat in the egg mixture and add the lemon zest. Stir in the carbonated water just before cooking.
- Coat a frying pan lightly with oil and put over a medium heat. When hot, pour some of the batter into the pan. Tilt the pan so that the batter coats the surface evenly. When golden, flip the pancake to cook the other side.
- Spread each pancake with the ricotta mix and fruit jam, if desired, and roll up. Sprinkle with icing sugar and serve immediately.

AFRICA

MARRAKECH CAIRO DAKAR ACCRA CAPE TOWN

2 Tasty seafood tacos from Tacos Locos — just one of the diverse international street foods on offer in South Africa at Cape Town's cool foodie spot, Bluebird Garage.

Street food has a long history throughout Africa. The souk at Khan el-Khalili (see p.221) in Cairo, for example, dates back to 1382 and Africans have created a profusion of inspired street foods over many generations. Selling food on the streets is an established way of life across this immense continent, dating back hundreds of years. When the first Europeans arrived in the fifteenth century, they found a flourishing street food scene and many local souks and bazaars. Today sellers can be found near offices, factories, schools, markets, construction sites, beaches, lorry and bus stations and along almost every street and alleyway. By providing convenient, inexpensive dishes and snacks, vendors meet the needs of millions of workers, a large and fluctuating population who, away from their families and home, move in and out of main rural and urban centres for work and who largely depend on street foods for their daily nourishment.

Most street vendors are women and it is customary in many African countries for street food operations to be inherited by the female members of a family. Street foods show great variation from region to region in ingredients and how they are prepared, based on local knowledge and tradition. Yet they can also have similar associations across wide areas; for example, spices are common ingredients, with each country using them in its own unique way. Africa's range of climates and growing conditions has resulted in cuisines that vary greatly throughout the continent. Colonial rule by European powers in the late nineteenth century also had a significant influence on African food and cooking.

North Africa's gastronomy has been heavily influenced over the centuries by ingredients introduced by traders, invaders and immigrants. The Arabs introduced spices such as saffron, ginger, nutmeg, cinnamon and cloves. The Ottoman Turks brought sweet pastries and other baked foods. Wheat and its by-product, semolina,

were introduced early on. The nomadic Berbers adapted semolina into couscous, which remains one of the main staples of the region. Other key foods here include seafood, goat, lamb, beef, dates, olives, almonds, vegetables and fruit. Moroccan sweets are world famous and are usually eaten with sweet mint tea. Chebakia is a traditional Moroccan pastry that is shaped into a rose, fried and coated in rosewater, runny honey and sesame seeds. Bessara is a traditional Moroccan breakfast food — broad beans are cooked in chicken stock, onions, garlic, paprika and cumin, then puréed to a silky smoothness.

Central Africa's location in the core region of the continent meant that many food trends did not infiltrate that far inland. Indigenous cooking has therefore continued to rely on local ingredients such as cassava, plantain, beef, chicken and crocodile. Stews with spinach and peanut are also very popular.

East Africa has long been a cattle-rearing area, but cattle, sheep and goats were used as currency, rather than as a food source. This tradition lingers today and some people do not eat meat, but consume the milk and blood of cattle. In other areas farmers grow grains and vegetables, with starches making up a majority of dishes. Maize is a staple and appears in traditional dishes such as fufu, a mash of yams or other starches served with meat or vegetable stews. In Uganda, a green banana called matoke provides the starch for most meals. Doro wat (spicy Ethiopian chicken stew) is served with rice and vegetables. Rolex (a Swahili chapati stuffed with scrambled eggs, shredded cabbage, tomatoes and onions) is a favourite fast breakfast food among Ugandans. The name is derived from the Lugandan pronunciation of 'roll of eggs'. Coffee lovers must try the wonderfully fragrant coffee in Ethiopia, for it is where the coffee bean first originated. Freshly roasted ground beans are gently brewed in a ceramic pot

called a *jebena*, then strained through a fine sieve and served in small cups, traditionally with plenty of sugar. Over the years, many immigrants and colonists brought their foods to East Africa including the Arabs, British, Indians and Portuguese. The Arabs brought rice and spices; the British and Indians lentil soup and vegetable curries; the Portuguese chillies and pineapples.

West Africa's cuisine tends to rely on heavy, starchy foods. Local staples include rice, black-eyed beans, brown beans and root vegetables such as yams. Typically, West Africans flavour these with hot spices and chillies or sauces such as peanut. Fufu (mashed yam, cassava or plantain) is served in West Africa as an accompaniment to meat or vegetable stews. Grains of paradise (the seeds of Guinea pepper) come from a West African plant and are used as a spice. The meat of choice in Western Africa is goat, but you can also find chicken and beef kebabs at roadside stands. Do try kelewele, a Ghanaian snack made of fried plantain seasoned with cayenne pepper, salt and ginger. The plantain is crunchy and golden on the outside and soft and juicy inside.

Early South Africans were mostly hunter-gatherers who depended on local foods to survive. The indigenous tribes of Southern Africa were divided into several groups, each of which had its own culture and style of cooking. The largest of these groups were the Bantu who grew grain and raised cattle, sheep and goats. They also grew and continue to grow pumpkins, beans and leafy green vegetables. Dutch colonists (Boers) built the first European settlement at the Cape of Good Hope in 1652. They planted pumpkins, watermelons, cucumbers, pineapples and potatoes. The Dutch East India Company increased trade between South Africa, Europe and India, bringing new cuisines to South Africa. Slaves, mostly from Malaysia, brought with them spices that added flavour to bland Dutch and English stews and dishes.

Early settlers simmered potjiekos (stew) in a three-legged iron pot over an open fire. Ingredients were added to the pot as they became available, such as meat from animals caught by hunters and vegetables and plants harvested from fields. For the early pioneers, preserving food was important. Biltong (dried, salted, spiced meat) and beskuits (dried, sweetened biscuits or rusks) were popular foods and both are still enjoyed today.

South Africa's modern cuisine has evolved out of a mixture of influences from ethnic tribes, British and Dutch colonists and settlers from the Dutch East Indies, other parts of Europe and India. The French established vineyards; the Germans introduced baked goods and pastries; the British brought meat pies; Malays and Indians introduced curries and spices. Foods from India, China and Indonesia also infiltrated the South African diet, with spices being added to popular European dishes such as meat pies. Bobotie – minced beef cooked with dried fruit and spices including curry powder, then covered with an egg-custard topping and cooked until golden – is thought to have been introduced by Indonesian slaves of the Dutch Empire during the seventeenth century. It is now considered South Africa's national dish.

Other South African specialties include sausages (made of beef or pork), sosaties (seasoned lamb or mutton on a skewer, often served at a barbecue, or *braai*), frikkadels ('little hamburgers' usually seasoned with nutmeg and sometimes served wrapped in cabbage leaves), bredies (slow-cooked meat and vegetable stews) and the popular dessert of melktert (milk custard tart).

With shifting contemporary lifestyles and very driven economies, street food vending has become a very popular business as well as an enduring feature of African culture. Food stalls, kiosks and carts can be found not only at markets, but on practically every street corner and at stations and beaches.

MARRAKECH

Markets or souks have played an important role in Moroccan life for centuries — ever since caravans loaded with goods passed through selling their wares. The expansion of the city saw markets grow in number and size, but these were — and still are — more than simply markets. They have become social and cultural events that remain a significant part of the culture here, with families travelling into the city from remote regions and villages to buy goods. Although until 1867 Europeans were forbidden from entering the city unless they were granted permission by the sultan, the French later colonized Morocco.

The exotic street food of Marrakech is a genuine feast for the senses. Morocco is a renowned spice trading centre and the amazing aromas and colours of the myriad spices are delightful. Food is rich, vibrant and unmistakably Moroccan. Bargaining is very much part of the culture here and it is traditional and customary to haggle over prices.

The hectic main square of Djemaa el-Fna (see p.216) is possibly Morocco's biggest tourist attraction. There is, in fact, no central market area in Marrakech, but a staggering number of stalls and kiosks are dotted in and around its labyrinthine streets and alleys. Smiling traders beckon you to their stalls while carts pulled by donkeys and people on motorbikes weave expertly through the throngs of people. At night the square springs to life with a host of food stalls serving classic Moroccan dishes from makeshift dining tables. A particular favourite are snails. The tender brown snails are served in a spicy thin soup, seasoned with citrus peel, aniseed, mint and other herbs. Another popular soup is harira made with chickpeas, spices, lentils, tomatoes and lamb.

B'stilla (or pastilla in Spanish) is one of the most elaborate and fascinating dishes in Moroccan cuisine and it has an Andalusian influence. Layers of ouarka (paper-thin pastry), squab pigeon, almonds, eggs, and fresh herbs and spices are baked in a dish, then dusted with icing sugar after baking. Today you can also find this unique pie stuffed with shredded chicken or fish. M'semen are buttery, flaky square pancakes that are appreciated by both tourists and locals. You'll see women making these by hand over big flat iron stoves. Be sure to eat them fresh and hot. For a cheap filling snack try ma'qooda, little deep-fried potato balls, often served with spicy harissa sauce or a fried egg, stuffed into bread and squashed together.

Morocco's oranges are world famous and you mustn't miss a glass of the fresh sweet juice obtained from the myriad orange trees in the city. It's easy to spot stallholders juicing fresh oranges; some also squeeze blood orange juice, though this is more expensive. Locals sit at tables sipping small glasses of hot, sweet tea made with fresh mint. Tea is much more than a drink here – it has deep cultural significance and is a symbol of friendship, tradition and hospitality. Wherever there's juice and mint tea you'll find pastries. Moroccans love sweet things and there is a variety of sweet treats in Marrakech. The best known are kaab el ghzal (gazelle's horns) – orange blossom-scented almond paste flavoured with cinnamon and wrapped in delicate pastry is moulded into a crescent shape and baked until beautifully golden. Chebakia are delectable sesame cookies, folded into the shape of a flower, then fried and coated in honey or syrup.

1 As darkness falls, the snake charmers and water sellers give way to many pop-up food stalls with dining tables.   2 Sheep heads and meat are slow cooked in clay vessels called tangia jars.   3 Lamb and apricot tagine.   4 Tangia jars on sale.

DJEMAA EL-FNA SQUARE
MARRAKECH

More than just a food market, the Djemaa el-Fna (and don't let one of its possible translations – 'assembly of death' – put you off) is not only at the cultural heart of Marrakech, but also the world. The famous *halqa* (street theatre) has performed on the site since the year 1050 (when the square was also the location for public executions) and the presence of this vital and idiosyncratic part of Moroccan history inspired UNESCO to proclaim the area one of the Masterpieces of the Oral and Intangible Heritage of Humanity, the first such site to be accredited in this way in 2001.

Although during the day the market bustles with storytellers, musicians, healers, snake charmers, magicians, peddlers, *chleu* (dancing boys) and sellers of traditional medicine, it is at night that the spectacle of the food is bought to the forefront. There are few more evocative sights than that of the rising smoke as grills fire into action, most commonly accompanied by the smell of lamb fat dripping onto coal or blood-red merguez sausage, and huge vats of stewed snails are set to simmer. From harira soup to b'stilla, the aromas, tastes and sensations evoked by the market's multifarious food stalls are only some of the elements that, combined with the rich history of the site, make Djemaa el-Fna one of the most unique places on earth to eat. JW

Where: Place Djemaa el-Fna, 40000 Marrakech
When: Daily 8 a.m. – midnight, dinner tables ready from 6 p.m.

5 The Marrakech air is filled with the smoke, aroma and drama of cooking.   6 Visitors enjoy their food sitting around a popular grilled meat sandwich stall in the square.   7 White snails are a staple snack – cooked in a peppery, spice-laden broth and served in a teacup.

FOOD HIGHLIGHTS

If you're feeling adventurous, there is every opportunity to try more unusual offerings such as **camel spleen** and any number of different offals. Simpler and maybe more palatable, options include traditional **couscous**, **b'stilla** and **harira soup** of lamb, chickpeas and lentils. However, it's imperative that the **freshly squeezed orange juice** is tried at any one of the many stalls, as it is said to be the most naturally delicious to be found (below). There is also a row of vendors that sell a hot, spicy galangal drink called **khoudenjal**, thought to be an aphrodisiac, which is usually eaten with a portion of nutty cake. If you want a soft drink or mineral water with your meal, the stallholders will send a boy to get it for you.

The best way of getting stuck into the food at Djemaa el-Fna is to simply take a seat on one of the benches, ask the price of a plate of food and order. It is probably worth avoiding places that try to hustle you, and it is always wise to check the price of a dish before you order. Keep an eye out for stalls with mainly Moroccan customers, as they are invariably better than those whose customers are tourists.

HARIRA SOUP

This thick, spicy lamb soup is eaten to break the fast during Ramadan.

SERVES 6–8
Preparation: 20 minutes
Cooking time: 2 hours

1 tbsp vegetable oil
450 g/1 lb lamb, cut into 1-cm/ ½-in. cubes
1 large onion, finely chopped
1 tsp turmeric
½ tsp ground cinnamon
½ tsp ground ginger
½ tsp paprika
1 saffron thread
2 tbsp chopped fresh coriander

4 large ripe tomatoes, skinned, seeded and chopped
1.4 litres/2½ pints water, more if needed
100 g/3½ oz Puy lentils
100 g/3½ oz dried chickpeas, soaked overnight and drained
115 g/4 oz vermicelli pasta
4 tbsp fresh flat-leaf parsley, chopped
Lemon wedges, to serve

- Heat the vegetable oil in a deep pan or casserole and add the lamb. Cook for 10 minutes or until softened and lightly coloured. Add the onion, turmeric, cinnamon, ginger, paprika, saffron and coriander and cook for another 2 minutes. Add the tomatoes.
- Pour in the water and add the lentils and chickpeas. Bring to a boil, then reduce to a gentle simmer, covered with the lid ajar.
- Let the soup simmer for 60 to 90 minutes, checking on the consistency of the soup regularly. It may be necessary to add more liquid.
- Add the vermicelli and stir constantly for about 5 to 10 minutes. Add the parsley before serving with the lemon wedges.

KHAN EL-KHALILI MARKET

CAIRO

No trip to Cairo is complete without a visit, day or night, to this busy and colourful open-air marketplace filled with stalls, coffee houses, restaurants and authentic Egyptian street food. The term 'meals on wheels' perfectly encapsulates this unique market with many quintessentially Egyptian dishes being cooked on brightly decorated food carts, or via holes-in-the-walls on its bustling and narrow streets. Nor is this mobile way of cooking and eating a new trend, as it currently is in many other parts of the world – Egyptians have been creating this moveable banquet here since the fourteenth century.

This historic market is undoubtedly a feast for the senses – expect to come across copious amounts of mint tea, alongside specialties including shawarma, shisha, fatayer (vegetarian parcels), mixed grills and kofta. Khoshary is one of the country's most traditional street foods; typically comprising rice, pasta, lentils and tomato sauce, it's a carb-fest that will fill you up for just pennies. You'll also want to track down a stall offering the traditional combination of tamiya (Egyptian falafel cooked with fava or broad beans) and ful mudammas (cooked fava beans with oil, garlic and lemon). Keep your eyes peeled as well for stalls serving fiteer, an Egyptian-style pizza. You'll see this exotic pancake being made at all times of the day, with lots of theatrical tossing involved. You may want to wash it all down with a refreshing mint tea from one of the many coffee stalls, but you could also try hot salep, a delicious drink made of milk, flour and orchid flowers. KR

Where: El-Gamaleya, Qism el-Gamaleya, Cairo
When: Open daily from early morning to sundown (except Friday morning and Sunday)

FUL MUDAMMAS
An Egyptian staple dish of broad beans, tahini, garlic, cumin and lemon.

SERVES 4
Preparation: 10 minutes
Cooking time: 5 minutes

400g/14oz tin of broad beans
2 tbsp tahini
1 garlic clove, crushed
Juice of ½ lemon
½ tsp cumin

2 tbsp olive oil
1 small tomato, diced
Salt and black pepper
Handful of chopped
   fresh parsley
4 slices of lemon,
   for garnishing
Pitta bread, to serve

- Simmer the broad beans in a medium pan of boiling water for approximately 10 minutes.
- Drain well and rinse with cold water. Add the beans to the pan again and gently press them with a spoon or fork to mash together.
- Stir in the tahini, garlic, lemon juice, cumin, olive oil and chopped tomato.
- Season with salt and black pepper, garnish with parsley, drizzle with olive oil and serve with warm pitta bread and a slice of lemon.

1 A woman makes traditional fish and rice. **2** Puffy fried beignets (dough balls) are a popular Dakar street snack. **3** A colourfully attired vendor tends her cooking pot. **4** Thieboudienne – a bold one-pot dish of fish, rice and vegetables simmered in tomato sauce.

MARCHE SANDAGA DAKAR

Food here is enriched by a myriad of European, African and Middle Eastern influences and your first task should be to track down some dibi, a grilled meat (usually mutton or lamb) dish of Arabic origin but with a French touch. The diced meat is tossed in spices before being cooked and served with onions, mustard and baguette, usually on brown paper to catch the drippings. It is Senegal's most popular street food.

You can taste the sea in Senegal's national dish thiéboudienne, a bold, hearty stew of fish, rice and vegetables simmered in unctuous tomato sauce; alternatively try yassa (spicy chicken or fish with rice) or mafé (meat in peanut sauce). If thirsty, slurp on delicious bissap juice, a kind of hibiscus iced tea, or attaya, a green tea sweetened with sugar and mint.

Vegetarians should look out for accara, crispy black-eyed bean fritters served on a baguette with a hot onion and tomato sauce (kaani). Everywhere you look there are stalls selling beignets (fried dough balls). Senegal was, of course, occupied by the French until 1960 and the influences linger on. And what to eat the morning after dancing the night away? Egg-filled breakfast baguettes and café Touba – coffee ground with black pepper to give it a kick. TJ

Where: Rue Sandinieri, Dakar
When: Daily 7.30 a.m. – 6.30 p.m.

DIBI

Recreate Senegal's favourite street food – grilled lamb with a mustard and onion sauce.

SERVES 4	1 onion, finely chopped
Preparation: 15 minutes	55 g/2 oz French grain mustard
Cooking time: 20 minutes	3–4 tbsp water
450 g/1 lb lamb chops	½ tsp sugar (optional)
4 ½ tbsp vegetable oil	Baguette or sweet potato fries
Salt and freshly ground black pepper	and salad, to serve

- Preheat the grill to high. Brush the lamb chops lightly on both sides with 1 tablespoon of vegetable oil and season with salt and pepper. Leave to marinate while you prepare the sauce.
- Combine the onion, remaining oil and mustard in a small, heavy saucepan and bring to a boil, stirring. Reduce the heat and simmer gently until the onion is soft and lightly browned, about 10 minutes, stirring frequently.
- Thin the mixture to a sauce consistency with 3 tablespoons of water, adding more if needed. Remove from the heat, taste for seasoning and add sugar if the sauce needs it. Cover to keep warm.
- Cook the lamb on the hot grill to taste, 6 to 8 minutes per side for medium. Spoon the mustard and onion sauce on top. Serve with a baguette or sweet potato fries and salad.

1 Fried chunks of wagashi (farmers' cheese), usually eaten with a spicy peanut powder.   2 Makola market stew.   3 A seafood stall selling fried and smoked fish and langoustines.   4 Baked tilapia.

MAKOLA MARKET

ACCRA

As an introduction to Ghanaian culture, Makola Market, in downtown Accra – one of the largest and busiest markets in West Africa – is as an intense and authentic 'first bite of the alasa' (Ghana's popular name for the African star apple) as you could hope for. Situated close to the Kwame Nkrumah Memorial Park, Makola is, at first, a bewildering expanse of improvised retail space, where you can buy just about anything your heart desires, from Kente cloth to mops. Although the ocean may only be a few blocks away, prepare to be bombarded and bamboozled by the smells and sounds of heady Ghanaian cooking: waakye, for example, a throw-everything-in stew of meat, tomatoes, noodles, rice and beans with the addition of shito, a hot sauce made from smoked prawns; kelewele (fried plantain) and abrikrakro, a fried cassava flour snack. Look out for chichinga, a kind of Ghanaian kebab and one of the country's most popular street foods.

Wash it all down, if you dare, with akpeteshie, a super-strong derivative of palm wine that will have your throat burning as hot as the Ghanaian sun. However, you can soothe it with succulent fruits such as pineapple, mango and soursop (a tropical fruit with a creamy, sour citrusy flavour).

Established in 1924 when Ghana was still a British colony (which it continued to be until 1957), the market is largely populated by female vendors and is governed by fearsome hereditary market queens, whose word is, in effect, law and who have seen Makola razed to the ground by fire and the government, only for it to rise phoenix-like from the ashes on more than one occasion. Head down first thing in the morning for an unforgettable experience, albeit one that is also a little more manageable than negotiating this labyrinthine market at its afternoon peak. Be prepared for a riot of colour, sound, smell and, most importantly, taste. TJ

Where: Kojo Thompson Road, Accra
When: Daily 7 a.m. – 7 p.m.

CAPE TOWN

Cape Town is simply brimming with a fusion of flavours from all over the globe in the many markets and from mobile food trucks. Street sellers have been a part of the South African city since before records began. Farmers travelled to Greenmarket Square in the seventeenth century to sell produce from wagons, which gradually transformed into a regular market. It was such a success that other markets sprang up all over the city.

There are lots of different cuisines on offer in the city – from Asian to Tunisian, but for a real taste of Cape Town you should try the local specialties. Unmissables include biltong – thin, dried, salted and spiced strips of beef or game (springbok, kudu and ostrich are common) traditionally eaten as snacks. Other delicacies include buttermilk or condensed milk rusks, which are a South African institution. Do as the locals do and dip one in your morning coffee. Or you can enjoy a tasty lunch of Boerewors – a traditional sausage made from beef, mixed with either pork or lamb and spices is usually made in a coiled shape and cooked on a *braai* (barbecue).

Another favourite is bunny chow, which surprisingly doesn't contain any rabbit. It's actually a hollowed-out loaf of bread filled with curry; locals never eat this with a knife and fork – it's meant to be eaten in your hands. Try chicken, pork or vegetarian varieties containing wholesome lentils and beans. Finish off with Cape Malay koeksisters – soft, warm doughnuts soaked in lightly spiced syrup and sprinkled with desiccated coconut. They just melt in the mouth and are best eaten as fresh as possible. Cape Malay koeksisters are very different from the twisted version, also popular among South Africans, which are less spicy in flavour and are dipped into an ice-cold syrup.

1   2

1   Funki Fungi grill gourmet mushroom kebabs at the Neighbourgoods Market in Woodstock's Old Biscuit Mill.
2   The glorious Victoria and Albert waterfront is a working harbour, as well as the location for Bay Harbour Market.

There are plenty of opportunities to sample the delicious street food on offer and discover the true taste of South Africa in Cape Town. Located in an old airplane hangar, Muizenberg's Bluebird Garage (see p.229) is where you will find incredible home-made food that is both authentically South African and international. On Friday evenings, a talented group of cooks and vendors offer gourmet treats ranging from Greek meze to Thai curries.

Bo-Kaap's Malay Quarter is one of the most multi-ethnic spots in Cape Town and the place to find traditional Malay cuisine. Bree Street offers plenty of terrific options and it's among the best places to experience Cape Town's unique culture. City Bowl Market on Hope Street also features global cuisine including paella, plus the famous Durban curries and more. Greenmarket

Square in the centre of old Cape Town and popular with locals and tourists alike, is today a regular stop for food lovers, offering everything from burgers to biltong.

The very busy Bay Harbour Market at the bottom of famous Hangberg Mountain is home to over one hundred traders. A wonderful destination for breakfast, lunch and dinner, this weekend market gets going with Friday Nite LIVE!, which offers live music and everything from Tunisian cuisine, ocean-fresh oysters and pizza to traditional Cape Malay dishes and more. The weekly Neighbourgoods Market in Woodstock's Old Biscuit Mill has an array of amazing food stalls at the back of the market. Also in Woodstock, Palms Market is another place for great food such as home-made pies, gourmet sandwiches and lots more.

1 Crispy spring rolls. 2 Stuffed wrap and pitta. 3 Charming market interior. 4 Food isn't fresher than when it is cooked right in front of you. 5 Fried swordfish steaks and salad. 6 Delicious pies, including Cornish pasties — especially popular in South Africa.

BLUEBIRD GARAGE

CAPE TOWN

Every Friday night, the Bluebird Garage food and goods market energizes the community of Muizenberg, a seaside suburb of Cape Town. Families, youngsters, old timers and artisans come together to eat, drink, shop and make merry in an unassuming yet beautiful old postal aeroplane hangar that retains much of its historical charm. The market has a bohemian, relaxed atmosphere.

Bluebird Garage was founded in 2010 by husband-and-wife team Dylan and Kim Speer, who set out to create a vibey space where small businesses and locals could gather, relax and have fun after a hard week's work. And they have achieved something a little bit magical. This is a *bona fide* neighbourhood market, authentic and unpretentious, where the forty-odd traders have been carefully chosen to create the perfect mix and showcase the very best of the district's specialist cooks, bakers and other creative talent.

Visitors flock here to browse through edgy artwork, vintage books and vintage dresses; trestle tables are loaded with a kaleidoscope of fabric, leather bags, stationery and hand-made jewellery. Even junior visitors are catered for: a Kids' Corner offers different craft activities each week while the adults get on with it. However, the real draw of this vibrant community hub is the freshly cooked food and specialty drinks: this is a place where people enjoy a wonderful meal with friends and family, to the soundtrack of live local music, laughter and chatter. Global-meets-local is the culinary theme, while craft beers and wines are also an intrinsic part of the mix. SQ

Where: 39 Albertyn Road, Muizenberg, Cape Town
When: Friday 4 p.m.–10 p.m.

7 The market sells an array of popular international street foods, from a Coney Island hot dog to pulled pork.   8 Spiced lentil curry.   9 Fresh pappardelle in tomato sauce.   10 Vietnamese rice paper rolls.

VENDOR SPOTLIGHT

The nosh at Bluebird Garage is truly eclectic, with authentic local dishes competing with delicious grub from around the world. Traditional bites include **potjiekos**, a South African stew traditionally prepared in a pot outdoors, and freshly sliced biltong, a dried, cured meat that's a regional specialty. **Debbie Herrmann** offers samoosas (samosas) – bursting with fillings such as Nguni beef (a cattle breed native to South Africa), bacon and three cheeses, and aubergine and mushrooms – that are a star attraction. Twenty-two-day-cured free-range steaks at **Lauden Kirk**, sourced from the Eastern Cape where he grew up, also have visitors drooling. You can also try dishes from further afield. Slow-cooked pulled-pork shoulder on rice from **Ragamuffin** and seafood tacos from **Tacos Locos** (below) have hungry visitors lining up, while there's also falafel, sourdough pizza, Indian curries, empanadas, gigantic organic burgers, gourmet wraps, sushi and dim sum. For dessert, there's a range of freshly baked goods, including brownies, cupcakes and tortes.

BEEF RENDANG
Ragamuffin's take on a tasty South East Asian classic.

SERVES 4
Preparation: 20 minutes
Cooking time: 2–3 hours

1 kg/2 lb 4 oz stewing beef, such as shin or chuck, cut into large pieces
2 thumb-sized pieces root ginger, finely chopped
10 garlic cloves, finely chopped
2 onions, finely chopped
½–2 chopped chillies, to taste
400 ml/14 fl oz coconut cream
1 tbsp tamarind paste
1 tbsp granulated sugar
2 tbsp soy sauce, plus extra to taste
1 cinnamon stick
1 tbsp peanut butter

For the spice blend:
4 kaffir lime leaves
1 tsp cumin seeds
1 tsp coriander seeds
4 cloves
1 star anise
3 cardamom pods
Crushed peanuts to garnish

- Preheat the oven to 200°C/400°F/gas mark 6. Grind all the ingredients for the spice blend in a spice grinder.
- Place all the ingredients, including the spice blend, in an ovenproof dish and mix well to combine. Bake for 2–3 hours, until the meat is tender, stirring every 30 minutes. The meat should be tender when done and the sauce dark brown and almost dry. If the sauce isn't ready, keep oven temperature high; if the sauce is ready, but the meat isn't, lower the temperature and continue cooking: the dish could take up to a further 3 hours. Add a little water – no more than 4 tablespoons – if the sauce is drying out.
- Serve immediately with crushed peanuts on top, and salad, if desired.

MIDDLE EAST

ISTANBUL BEIRUT
JERUSALEM DUBAI

2 The preparation of balik ekmek (translated literally as 'fish bread'): spiced and grilled mackerel fillets are carefully added to fresh buns, heaped high with crisp lettuce and tomato.

The wide-ranging cuisine of the Middle East preserves the glorious ancestral heritage of its peoples over many thousands of years. It evolved from the culinary styles of great civilizations including the Phoenicians, Egyptians, Persians and Mesopotamians. Wheat was first cultivated here, around 12,000 years ago, followed by barley, pistachios, figs, pomegranates, dates and other regional staples. The discovery of fermentation also led to the development of leavened breads.

In the middle of the seventh century, Arab conquerors of the Byzantine and Persian empires integrated their own culinary practices with local traditions. Arabs from Syria expanded to North Africa and reached the Iberian Peninsula in the early eighth century and remained there until they were expelled in the thirteenth century. They conquered Sicily in southern Italy and remained there for more than 200 years. As well as introducing their own culinary traditions and new crops, such as rice and citrus fruits, to these countries, unsurprisingly, they also assimilated the indigenous foods into their native cooking. Arab traders also introduced things such as exotic spices from India – cumin, turmeric and cloves; peppercorns and allspice from the Spice Islands; okra from Africa; and tomatoes from the New World, via the Moors of Spain.

The powerful Ottoman Empire dominated the Middle East and Eastern Europe from the end of the thirteenth century to the twentieth century and was centred in north-western Anatolia, in what is now present-day Turkey. Aspects of regional culinary practices from across the Empire were merged together, especially those of the Middle Eastern regions. During the Ottoman Empire the distinctive sweet pastries of paper-thin filo pastry, together with dense, sweet, strong coffee were introduced to the Middle East, where coffee remains the national drink.

3 The lively Machane Yehuda market in Jerusalem is home to a broad mix of vegetable, fruit, nut and meat stalls, in addition to traditional-style cooked fare – mostly Kurdish, Iraqi and North African cuisines – alongside more 'Western' stalls selling pastries and coffee.

Street markets have been a characteristic feature of the Middle East since the fourth century. Their first appearance was on the important trade routes, where the continual flow of foreign goods and travellers resulted in systems of haggling and trade within the cities. Designated areas of cities were allocated as areas of trade and thus the first markets came into existence. In the past, many people did not have domestic kitchens and sent out for their cooked food. Eventually markets also became social hubs where people met to drink coffee. Middle Eastern markets have maintained much of their historical and local identity – Machane Yehuda in Jerusalem (see p.251), for example, dates back to the Ottoman Empire.

A major influence on Middle Eastern cuisine was – and still remains – religion. Lamb, chicken and beef are the main meats eaten, as both the Jewish and Muslim faiths forbid the eating of pork. Foremost among the meat specialties in the region are a wide variety of kebabs, with many regional specialties and styles found in every street market.

Middle Eastern food is flavoursome and aromatic and a common factor throughout all the countries is the use of spices such as cumin, nutmeg and turmeric to achieve strong flavours that are unique to the cooking of a particular region. Typically, a stew will include a small amount of a spice mixture called baharat, which usually includes cinnamon, clove, cumin and coriander. Tradition differs from country to country and region to region, although there are obvious similarities in many dishes, with ingredients such as olive oil, olives, sesame seeds, chickpeas, mint, honey and pitta bread found throughout the Middle East, which belong to no single particular culture.

The region's ancient food markets, with their exotic sights and aromas, offer a diverse and exciting taste of history, culture and food at its authentic best. The sheer variety of colours, flavours and enticing scents of street food being prepared are astonishing. Falafel (deep-fried, spiced chickpea balls); kibbeh (a wheat crust stuffed with spicy lamb and deep-fried); world-famous doner kebab, the national dish of Turkey; kofta (fried meatballs); fatayer (pastries filled with chicken, tomatoes, cheese and honey); manakeesh (the pizza of the Arabic world); lokma (deep-fried dough in syrup); baklava (filo pastry, chopped nuts, sweet syrup and honey) and kanafeh (an indulgent cheesecake made with Nabulsi cheese, covered in sweet syrup scented with orange blossom water or rose water), which is common to Palestine, Syria and Lebanon, represent some of the remarkable dishes.

There is also a splendid fish culture, with countless restaurants and bars featuring different types of fish, often fried or grilled, or enclosed in parchment or a salt crust and baked. A typical Turkish dish is balik bugulama, a kind of fish stew. In many regions, fish is cooked or served with rice. Sayyadiya (or the 'fisherman's dish') is typical of the Syrian coast, in which pieces of fish are fried with onions and spices, then cooked with rice. Similar dishes are found all over the Middle East region. Shellfish are available in the coastal region but are subject to religious taboos among some Muslims and Jews. This isn't common to all Muslims and depends on particular clarifications of religious law. Shellfish are enjoyed in Istanbul, Alexandria and parts of Syria. A classic street food in Istanbul is mussels stuffed with rice, pine nuts and raisins.

Vegetables and pulses are everywhere – boiled, stewed, grilled, stuffed and cooked with meat and rice. The broad bean, which is ancient to the region, is eaten both fresh and dried. One of the most popular street foods is foul or ful, a hearty dish of broad beans, lemon and garlic, typically eaten for breakfast but excellent at any time of day as a dip, main dish or sandwich filling.

ISTANBUL

Istanbul has a rich street food culture, with a history stretching back thousands of years. The food here incorporates a blend of Turkish, Mediterranean and Eastern European flavours dating to when it was part of the Ottoman Empire. Some specialties such as boza (fermented millet drink) and simit (circular sesame bread) originated centuries ago and have remained virtually unchanged, whereas others such as salep (a milky, flower-infused beverage) have arrived more recently – a mere 300 years ago.

Vendors are everywhere in Turkey's largest city – setting up tables, selling from stalls and pushing carts. Eating out is part of daily life and street food is plentiful and cheap. Inviting aromas waft through the streets and alleys as skilled *ustas* (masters) cook their particular dishes. Inebolu Pazari (see p.240) opens at the crack of dawn on Sundays and is one of the best markets, with every type of food on offer. Both the city's top chefs and locals shop here for the freshest ingredients. The emphasis is on produce such as herbs, fruit, vegetables and fungi, but there are also tasty ready-to-eat foods, from köy ekmeği (village breads flavoured with herbs and cheese) to luxuriously thick, rich süzme (yogurt).

This fascinating city has other splendid markets. The Tarlabasi neighbourhood has a Sunday food market that meanders around the local streets. Among the many specialties on offer, simit is a favourite. Many stands give you the option to make your simit into a sandwich with tomatoes and cheese. You can also buy simit from the many vendors who wander throughout the city pushing carts. Listen out for the cries of '*Sıcak simit!*' ('hot simit!'). This molasses-dipped, sesame-crusted bread snack constitutes a tasty breakfast-on-the-go.

Established 500 years ago, the Grand Bazaar is the city's oldest market and the world's largest covered market. It has a huge number of vendors; stop for a breather and people-watch over a cup of coffee. Turkish coffee is more than a drink – it's an indispensable part of Turkish life and cultural heritage. Freshly roasted ground coffee is brewed slowly with water and sugar to produce a foam, then served in small cups with the grounds, which are allowed to settle at the bottom of your cup to preserve the full flavour.

Fatih Market – near Fatih Mosque in the historical area of the city – is the largest street market in Istanbul. It takes place every Wednesday and thousands of vendors line the streets. Favourites include gözleme (savoury hand-rolled pancakes) filled and cooked

to order. Thinly rolled dough is folded around a filling of your choice (chard, white cheese, vegetables or meat), then seasoned with butter as it cooks.

Chaotic Istiklal Caddesi is the city's main shopping thoroughfare. Midway along this well-known busy avenue you will see the Flower Arcade on the right with the Fish Market nearby. Try aromatic and spicy rice-stuffed mussels (midye dolma) sold by one of the many street vendors. Other popular snacks include deep-fried mussels served on skewers. Here, too, you'll come across kokoreç, a grilled offal delicacy of lamb's intestines wrapped around innards such as sweetbreads. They are then roasted, sliced and cooked on a grill with diced tomatoes, spices and herbs.

You can't miss the intriguing ice cream sellers in Istanbul. Each seller, wearing a red and gold fez, rings a bell and calls out to the crowds. They sell a thick, creamy, chewy ice cream known as salep dondurma. The mixture is churned regularly with paddles to keep it elastic and workable. This unique ice cream is resistant to melting as it is thickened with salep (a powder made from wild orchid tubers) and traditionally flavoured with resinous mastic (derived from an evergreen in the pistachio family).

1 Fish buns, or balik ekmek, provide the perfect roadside lunch in Istanbul. 2 Browsing produce. 3 Mackerel – a very popular fish in this region – is cooked in bulk and served with crisp salad. 4 Tea machine. 5 Sütlü nuriye – a milky dessert with layers of filo pastry.

İNEBOLU PAZARI

ISTANBUL

Kasimpaşa revels in its reputation as one of Istanbul's tougher districts. In place of the four-wheel drives and the five-star hotels found elsewhere around the city, there is a grittier reality of car accessory shops and watchful men sitting in smoke-filled tea shops. Every Sunday, however, a radical metamorphosis takes place. On a low, short anonymous road alongside the Kasimpaşa car pound, the İnebolu Pazarı thrums with glorious food life. This place is also known as Kastamonu Pazarı – both are towns in Turkey's Black Sea region that are synonymous with fertile soils, abundant produce, natural living, endless green views and a simpler way of life that feels decades away from the rush and hustle of Istanbul.

The clientele at this food market are a combination of the city's top chefs, quietly trendy locals cannily stocking up for the week ahead, taxi drivers, earnest civil servants, off-duty celebrities and families. In this wildly diverse metropolis, it is İnebolu Pazarı's food that brings them all together, and with it, the lusty, authentic flavours of the Turkish village. İnebolu Pazarı's main business is fresh produce, but its other function is to connect Istanbul's food lovers and homesick villagers to the world of pure contentment and clean air that lies far beyond the city. So from 7 a.m. on a Sunday, the Turkish countryside comes to town: willow baskets filled with fragrant straw and hens eggs; strings of renowned garlic from Taşköprü; glazed terracotta jars hefty with thick, white strained yoghurt; weird meaty mushrooms that smell like ceps and cost peanuts; plus a family shyly selling their dark, balsamic chestnut honey along with jars of pollen and grandma's home-made jams. Be sure to search out köy ekmeği, a specialty village bread that resembles sourdough in texture. Just follow the irresistible aroma. **KG**

Where: Küçük Piyale Mahallesi, Toprak Tabya Sokak, Kasımpaşa, Istanbul
When: Sunday 7 a.m. – 5 p.m.

6 Feasting on the catch of the day: fresh fish is a firm favourite, whether grilled, baked or deep-fried. While mackerel is served in buns of Turkish pide bread, anchovies are battered and served with slices of lemon and salad.   7 Fresh pollen at a honey stall.   8 Roast chestnuts.

YAYLA ÇORBASI

This traditional Turkish yoghurt soup, also known as meadow soup, is flavoured with dried mint.

SERVES 4

Preparation: 20 minutes

Cooking: 25 minutes

55 g/2 oz short grain rice

1.2 litres/2 pints water
   or vegetable stock

Salt to taste

1 egg

450ml/16 fl oz natural
   yoghurt

2 tbsp butter

2 tsp dried mint

Pinch of red pepper flakes
   (optional)

- Boil the rice in a covered pan with all the liquid until it is very soft. Add salt to taste.
- Beat the egg and add the yoghurt. Stir well and loosen with a tablespoon or two of the warm liquid.
- Slowly and carefully heat the yoghurt – too quick and it will curdle – stirring constantly. When it is warm (but nowhere near boiling), slowly pour the rice along with its cooking liquid into the soup, one ladle at a time. Stir each ladleful in very well until it is completely incorporated and the mixture is silky smooth.
- Slowly increase the heat until the soup is piping hot, but not boiling.
- Melt the butter in a small frying pan until it sizzles. Add the mint and cook briefly – until it releases its fragrance. Add the red pepper flakes, if desired.
- Serve the soup hot, with a drizzle of the buttery mint (and pepper) in each bowl.

FOOD HIGHLIGHTS

İnebolu Pazarı has around fifteen stalls, each sheltering under billowing tarpaulins to offer protection from rain and sun. Most sell fresh produce, although there's also a tea stall and peripatetic food sellers. There may be a **pirinç nohut** cart selling paper cones of rice and boiled chickpeas with scraps of chicken breast; in summer a travelling pickle seller or in winter a steaming cart of boiled and grilled **corncobs** and fat **roasted chestnuts**. Bag a stool at the tea stall and sip a glass of Istanbul's finest **çay**: the country's tea gardens are also in the Black Sea region. Shiny olives, fat tomatoes, crunchy, sweet cucumber and an award-winning slab of **white cheese** from the stall next door make this the *alfresco* breakfast of champions (above).

SOUK EL AKEL
BEIRUT

Souk el Akel, which literally means 'food market' in Arabic, is a melting pot of international foods and Lebanese cuisine – from hamburgers, pulled-pork and raclette to falafel, mixed grills and shawarma. With the gathering of such a diversity of cuisines, the market acts as a metaphor for the numerous influences brought by travellers and merchants to Lebanon throughout the country's long and vibrant history.

Every Thursday evening, a cobblestone alley in historic downtown Beirut is transformed into a bustling night market with appetizing scents wafting into the air. The weekly street food event is the brainchild of Anthony Rahayel, a dentist turned food blogger who wanted to bring European-style food markets to Lebanon. A lively, welcoming and friendly environment, it attracts people of all ages and backgrounds. It has something of a street festival atmosphere to it, with pumping music, bright lights and beautifully decorated stalls.

The market is a wonderful showcase for Lebanese specialties such as man'oushe (a pizza-like flatbread smothered with za'atar – a herby mix of oregano, thyme, sumac and sesame seeds – and olive oil) and shawarma (marinated spicy lamb or chicken from a rotating spit). If you're after lighter fare, look out for ful mudammas (stewed broad beans) or tabbouleh (bulgur wheat salad). There are around thirty vendors in all – many of these are regular, but there are new faces each week. An increasing number of stands are devoted to innovative international and fusion food, so expect to find all cuisines from Japanese and Chinese to French and Mexican. NS

Where: Foch-Allenby District, Beirut
When: Thursday 5–11 p.m.

1 An atmospheric food event. 2 Crisp, thin bread heaped with herbs, cheese, tomato and sumac. 3 Meat-stuffed flatbread. 4 Chocolate-dipped churros. 5 Up in smoke. 6 The Bros' teriyaki chicken burger. 7 Loaded ice lolly.

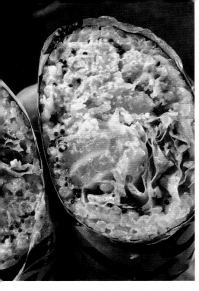

Waffle Bar

SHAWARMA

This Levantine meat dish is also known as a doner kebab or gyro.

SERVES 4

Preparation: 20 minutes, plus 2 hours marinating

Cooking: 1 hour 10 minutes

7 cardamom pods

2 cloves

4 pieces of miskee or mastic (resin)

1½ tsp salt or to taste

Boneless half leg of lamb, 1 kg/2 lb 4 oz

Freshly ground black pepper

¾ tsp ground cinnamon

1 good pinch allspice

2 tbsp lemon juice

½–1 tbsp cider vinegar

2 tbsp olive oil

1 onion, finely grated

1 tomato, finely chopped

5 bay leaves

- Place the cardamoms, cloves, miskee and half a teaspoon of the salt in a large bowl and gently crush them all together with a pestle.
- Cut the lamb into small to medium strips. Add all the other ingredients to the bowl with the strips of lamb and mix and rub them all thoroughly.
- Cover the bowl with cling film, place in the refrigerator and leave to marinate for at least 2 hours or overnight.
- Preheat the oven to 175°C/350°F/gas mark 4. Place the meat mixture in a roasting tin and bake for about 1 hour or until cooked through.
- Remove the roasting tin from the oven and place under a hot grill for about 2 to 3 minutes, until the meat is nicely browned.
- Serve with tahini sauce (tahini, crushed garlic, lemon juice and salt), chopped tomato, spring onions, pickles, fresh mint and parsley and radishes in a pocket of pitta bread.

VENDOR SPOTLIGHT

For a healthy labneh (Lebanese cheese) sandwich, go to **Mido's**. Their Lebanese-style beef sandwich (top) is also excellent, but it's somewhat heartier. **Suzanne Douaihy** sells the best kibbeh (croquettes made from bulgur wheat, onions and minced meat). **Sandwich w Noss** offer a delicious alternative to the traditional burger: a bacon and halloumi sandwich. Try **Ichiban** for a substantial sushi burrito or sushi burger (bottom). **Spot Crêpes** make outstanding savoury and sweet pancakes – the halloumi option, partnered with fresh tomato and mint, is particularly flavoursome. Visit the **Kung Pao** stall to construct your own individual spicy Chinese stir-fry.

15 Sizzling meat cooks on the grill. Beirut — with its energetic, friendly and timeless spirit — provides the perfect setting for the cosmopolitan food celebration of Souk el Akel.

MACHANE YEHUDA
JERUSALEM

Like the Western Wall and the Tower of David, the Machane Yehuda market is an icon of the timeless city of Jerusalem. Tasting food sold by the market's 250 vendors is a way of connecting with the city's 2,000-plus year history. Yet, unlike most tourist spots, this is one where Jerusalemites also like to indulge themselves. Nicknamed 'the shuk', it is the place locals regard as a symbol of their identity. The vibrant buzz of aromas, flavours and trading banter provides a heady backdrop to the most diverse selection of food in the city, defining it as Israel's street food capital.

Head to the market's two main aisles that fit between Agrippas Street and Jaffa Road. Look out for delis with olive mountains, valleys of spices and slabs of halva and falafel stalls all claiming the best recipe as well as endless offerings of hummus. Tantalizing aromas waft through the air: pitta breads and bagels are baked twelve hours a day. Yehuda's signature snack is Jerusalem mixed grill. Many city chefs claim to have invented it, but its origins are at this market. It uses just about everything edible from chicken, hearts, lungs, liver and spleens seasoned with spices, then seared on a griddle with onions and jammed into pitta bread. Other classics to look for are shakshuka (eggs poached in a spice-infused sauce of tomatoes, peppers, chilli and onions) and bourekas (flaky pastries stuffed with cheese, spinach or potato). A must-try is maqluba, an Arabic casserole of tomatoes, onions and rice heaped with lamb and falafel balls drizzled in tahini. This market brims with Middle Eastern delicacies and is a living example of how street food brings a city together, no matter what your creed. **AJ**

Where: Machane Yehuda Street, Jaffa Road and Kiach Street, Jerusalem
When: Sunday to Thursday 8 a.m.–7 p.m.; Friday 8 a.m.–3 p.m.

1 Busy market aisles.　2 Green kubbeh soup is a popular Kurdish dish – kubbeh are semolina dumplings with a flavourful meat filling, served here in a rich, hot broth.
3 Lemon and herb olives.　4 A bread seller at the shuk.

5 A vendor at a baklava and sweet stall serves the Levantine dessert kanafeh – a creamy cheese pastry soaked in bright orange syrup. 6 Time to meet friends, grab a bite to eat and sip a beer. 7 A pitta bread stuffed with chunks of grilled meat is a great snack on-the-go.

SHAKSHUKA

Eggs poached in a thick, spicy, tomato-based sauce is a staple breakfast dish in Israel.

SERVES 2

Preparation: 10 minutes

Cooking: 1 hour

2 tbsp olive oil

2 small onions, chopped

2 red peppers, chopped

2 yellow peppers, chopped

4 garlic cloves, finely chopped

2 tbsp ground cumin

1 tbsp ras el hanout spice blend

1 tsp paprika

2 tbsp tomato paste

Two 400 g/14 oz tins chopped
  tomatoes

2 eggs

140 g/5 oz zhoug or chilli sauce

To serve:

Seeds of ½ pomegranate

Feta cheese, crumbled

Pitta bread

- Heat the oil in a frying pan and cook the onions and peppers until they start to brown. Add the garlic, spices, tomato paste and tinned tomatoes. Bring to the boil, then reduce the heat and simmer for 45 minutes.
- Poach two eggs in the simmering tomato sauce for 2 minutes.
- Drizzle with zhoug (a Yemenite green chilli sauce) and sprinkle with the pomegranate seeds and crumbled feta cheese. Serve with warm pitta bread.

FOOD HIGHLIGHTS

For a self-guided tour of the market, grab a Shuk Bites card. This can be redeemed for six gourmet samples from traders within the market: choose from **kibbeh, baklava** (above)**, boureka** or **sambusak**, a deep-fried pastry filled with hummus and fried onions. So fervent is the city's passion for **hummus**, debate over which is best can be fiercer than politics. Many swear by the recipe at Azura, which is described as 'melt in your mouth bliss'. This kiosk is also legendary for Jerusalem's Arabic-inspired dishes, including **maqluba**, **oxtail stew** and **stuffed vegetables**. Less authentic but more progressive, Crave is the latest place to visit for kosher street food. American-influenced offerings include New York-style **brisket pastrami**, **burritos** with kosher bacon or kosher **kimchi**. One of the places where you can soak up the bustle of the market is at Manua Bah Shouk, which offers seats in the midst of the crowds. It is also a sure bet for Israeli classics such as **shakshuka** or **stuffed aubergine**.

SATWA CUTTING CHAI

Hailing from Mumbai in India, 'cutting chai' is a half portion of chai or tea.

SERVES 1
Preparation: 5 minutes
Cooking: 20 minutes
2 cm/1 in. root ginger, crushed
1 bay leaf

225 ml/8 fl oz/water
2–3 tsp black tea leaves
175 ml/6 fl oz milk
Sugar or jaggery (optional and
   to taste)

- Put the ginger and bay leaf into the water in a saucepan and bring to a boil for 4 minutes.
- Add the tea and simmer for a further 4 minutes. Then add the milk and simmer for 10 minutes. Add sugar to taste, if desired.
- Strain into a glass or cup and drink while hot.

AL DIYAFA STREET DUBAI

Thread your way on foot through Satwa's narrow streets at any time of the day and people will be walking, cycling or pulling up their cars in front of little eateries, some doorways no bigger than a cupboard. Between the towering Union Flag on the coast and the fourteen-lane Sheikh Zayed Road that carves its way through the middle of Dubai, this slightly ramshackle area is home to a concentration of expats from all over, and the food reflects the dishes of their homelands.

By law all cooking must be done inside kitchens, but many restaurants have used creative licence to achieve a genuine outdoor, street food experience. Along 2nd December Street (often referred to by its previous name of Al Diyafa), towering spirals of glistening chicken and lamb are carved into shawarmas, warm flatbread expertly wrapped around mayonnaise, salad, slivers of succulent meat, hot sauce and pickles. Whether you add chips inside your shawarma or not is a hotly debated question. An alternative filling is a freshly made falafel, hot from the oil. Peel back the paper and eat on the go while you witness people darting between shops that house armies of tailors, barbers, car mechanics and more. Satwa is also the place to try Filipino food and on cooler nights kare-kare – a peanut-thickened stew of oxtail (pork is regulated in the Emirates) and other offal, cooked until tender in a clay pot – is the fare of choice. Fresh lumpia is a type of spring roll made with a pancake-like wrapper packed with vegetables and tofu, for portable munching.

Trays of Arabic sweets keep warm over simmering barrels at Firas Sweets. Kunafah is a favourite, with crisp, shredded pastry, often in lurid colours, enclosing warm, oozing, gooey cheese and topped with crumbled pistachios. Tiny, perfect diamonds of baklava drenched in sugar syrup can be found there, too. Wander further and stop off for a chai. Look out for a never-ending queue outside a kiosk housing a man wielding an enormous teapot. Spiced, milky and sweet, cups of this steaming brew seem to fuel Satwa's relentless activity. **SP**
Where: 2nd December Street, Satwa district, Dubai
When: Varies but many open until the early hours of the morning. Most are closed on a Friday morning.

ASIA

MUMBAI DELHI KOLKATA COLOMBO KASHGAR
BEIJING SHANGHAI HANGZHOU XI'AN
HONG KONG TAIPEI SEOUL FUKUOKA TOKYO
LUANG PRABANG BANGKOK CHIANG MAI
PHNOM PENH SAIGON HANOI GEORGE TOWN
KUALA LUMPUR SINGAPORE JAKARTA MANILA

Among the world's oldest cuisines, Asian cookery is exotic, colourful and flavoursome. The ingenious use of ingredients and traditional cooking techniques have reshaped what were once lowly peasant dishes into culinary masterpieces that have achieved fame all over the world. Street food reigns supreme in this vast continent, a tradition that has lasted for thousands of years. From the second century BCE to the fifteenth century CE, the Silk Road was an important network of trade routes connecting Asia with the Mediterranean, North Africa and Europe. Trade on the Silk Road had a significant effect on the development of the continent's culture and, while silk was traded, it was only one of a wide range of products that was trafficked between East and West and that included spices, grain, vegetables and fruits.

The astonishing variety of dishes across Asia reflects a rich cultural history and diversity of flavours that is evident today in the street food sold by markets, vans, food trucks and carts. A combination of new and old dishes can be found, offering everything from breakfast to dessert. Two food stalls in Singapore made history by becoming the first street vendors to be recognized by the influential Michelin Guide. Singapore is the first South East Asian country in the world, and the fourth in Asia, to be rated by Michelin. It is also one of the safest street food cities in the world due to strictly enforced regulations and designated selling areas.

Regulations are in force throughout much of Asia, although it has to be said that these are often ignored. In China, for example, in an attempt to ensure food safety, vendors must obtain licences and operate within fixed locations and at designated times, with fines for violations. Government crackdowns on unlicensed street vendors regularly take place. Meanwhile, unlicensed street hawkers risk government persecution as they attempt to find

loopholes to continue operating. Similarly in Bangkok, Thailand, not all vendors comply with the rules and are licensed. It is recommended that customers stick to stalls that display a sticker of a smiling plate – a stamp of approval from health officials.

Modern Asian cuisine is experiencing a transformation – the result of combining ingredients and techniques from different regions into a new fusion style, created from Thai, Vietnamese, Indian and Chinese cuisines, together with a few French influences. Along with these, other Asian cuisines are also slowly being merged into hybrid dishes.

The huge continent of Asia incorporates many different cuisines, which can be divided into the south-west – India, Pakistan, Sri Lanka, Myanmar; the north-east – China, Korea, Japan; and the south-east – Thailand, Laos, Cambodia, Vietnam, Indonesia, Malaysia, Singapore, Brunei. The various regions each developed their own traditional cuisine as a consequence of history, environment and culture. Asian flavours can broadly be described as hot, sour, salty and sweet. However, these multilayered cuisines do have some foods and ingredients in common, such as rice, garlic, ginger and chillies. Rice was prepared by the continent's original hunter-gatherers, then cultivated and spread across the region before local cuisines began to develop. Chilli peppers, indeed all peppers, are native to the Americas and arrived in the region with European settlers in c. 1520.

Curries are prominent in the cuisines of the south-west and the south-east, but to a lesser extent in that of the north-east. South-western curries are typically based on yoghurt, while the curries of the south-east and north-east largely use coconut milk.

South-west Asian gastronomy has its roots in Persian-Arabian civilization and its associated customs and foods, such as the eating of naan (flatbread), mutton, kebabs (derived from Turkish

cooking) and the use of strong spices and ghee (clarified butter). In many south-western regions cows are used only for their milk and not for meat, due to Hindu beliefs. In addition to rice, chapati made from wheat or barley and other types of bread are also a major part of the diet and beans are a regular component of a meal. Many recipes use only olive oil and grilling and baking are common, with very few dishes being deep fried. Meals are centred mainly on vegetables, pulses such as lentils, split peas and chickpeas, and grains, and include only a small quantity of meat.

In north-eastern traditions and culture, ingredients, spices and seasonings are also regarded as medicines necessary for a long and healthy life. Korean traditional cuisine, for example, focuses on grilling or sautéing and the use of hot chilli spices. Food also became allied to many religious traditions, with food frequently used as symbolic offerings to venerate the ancestors. The north-eastern cuisines use soy sauce in a great many dishes and include noodles as well as rice. Vegetable oils are used for cooking, rather than ghee. The Japanese love using the freshest ingredients in their cooking and favour using seasonal foods. They are also renowned for their skill in arranging food so that it looks like a beautiful work of art on the plate. Japanese cooking often uses deep-frying for tempura (seafood or vegetables in a crisp batter) or, by contrast, raw foods such as sashimi (sparklingly fresh uncooked fish or seafood with soy sauce). The number five is significant in Japanese culture and this encompasses the country's food traditions, too. The five colours – white, black, red, green and yellow are included in every meal – a tradition since Buddhism arrived there from China in the sixth century.

The earliest cuisine of the south-east was almost certainly the peasant cookery of Thailand, which gradually spread its way into Laos, Cambodia, Vietnam, the Malay Peninsula and Indonesia.

Thai cuisine, in turn, was also inspired by the culinary contributions of these countries. Later on, European cuisines also had an impact on cooking in south-east Asia; Vietnam, Laos and Cambodia were all French colonies, Malaysia was a British colony and Indonesia was a Dutch colony. Only Thailand managed to avoid European colonization. The preference in this region is for fragrant, lightly prepared dishes that employ a subtle balance of stir-frying, steaming, and/or boiling, augmented with flavours such as citrus juices, basil, coriander and mint. Many cultural groups favour flavourings that are unique to the region, such as galangal (a hot ginger-peppery seasoning) and lemon grass. Indigenous spices and herbs include cloves, nutmeg and mace, as well as Thai basil, sweet basil and mint. Citrus flavours have a leading role in the region's cuisines, especially lime, which is native to Indonesia and Malaysia. Fish sauce is used liberally in the south-east, but not in south-western cooking.

Chinese cuisine has possibly become the most well known of all Asian styles of cooking. Two important Chinese thinkers – Confucius and Laozi – played a significant role in influencing their country's food. Confucius focused on well-balanced and proportioned dishes by blending ingredients, whereas Laozi – the founder of Taoist philosophy – was more concerned with the health benefits of recipes. In China there are several food styles based on region – the most basic difference being between northern and southern cooking. Southern dishes emphasize freshness and tenderness whereas in the colder north, dishes can be oily and the use of vinegar and garlic tends to be more prevalent.

The street food found in the bustling city streets and alleyways is one of Asia's primary attractions for locals and travellers alike. It remains a great low-cost way of exploring the exotic and exciting flavours of the diverse cuisines this great continent has to offer.

MUMBAI

The history of Mumbai's street food is intrinsically connected to its evolution from a fishing village to today's booming city. As immigrants came from all over India to work in the expanding metropolis, they brought their cherished culinary dishes with them. The result is a kaleidoscope of cooking styles and street food that defines Mumbai's food culture, with Muslim, Gujarati, Goan, Coastal, South Indian, Parsi and local influences.

A vital part of the city's culture, Mumbai street food is as exciting as it is mouthwatering. Wherever you go, you're sure to discover an infinite number of options when it comes to flavoursome foods to try. 'Khau galli' translates as 'food street' and you'll find numerous khau gallis throughout the city (see p.265). Carter Road khau galli near the Bandra promenade is jam-packed with street food hangouts and small diners. The stalls also offer a huge variety of snacks such as falafels, frozen yogurt and freshly made waffles. The khau galli at Mohammed Ali Road provides sizzling tikkas and succulent kebabs. It is also celebrated in the city for delicious Mughlai food, including phirni — a thick creamy milk-and-rice pudding with cardamom and saffron.

Mahim khau galli is a renowned street food destination for its choice of dishes. It is lined with stalls selling tasty meals and snacks such as khichda (meat, lentils, rice and spices) and

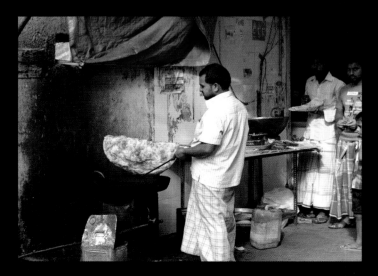

1		3
	2	

1 A street hawker perfecting masala dosa in Mumbai.
2 Deep-fried giant puri bread. 3 Eye-catchingly colourful falooda — lined up here on a fruit stall at Juhu Chowpatty beach — make for a sweet and thirst-quenching treat.

wonderful chicken tandoori. Then there is Princess Street, a foodie heaven with numerous stalls bursting with freshly prepared snacks and drinks. At night this street near the famous landmark Utsav Chowk in Kharghar turns into a hectic khau galli, where people flock to eat.

'Chaat' is a word used to describe an enormous variety of mostly savoury snacks and you're guaranteed to come across vada pav, one of Mumbai's favourite and widely available street snacks. There are countless vada pav stalls in Mumbai. A pav is a bread bun and it is stuffed with a fritter of spiced, fried, mashed potato (vada) inside it. These delectable snacks are accompanied by a plethora of different chutneys and spices. Bhel puri is another type of chaat. It is made with puffed rice, fresh raw vegetables and tamarind sauce. There are many variations, but the best are from any of the stalls on Mumbai's beaches. Pani puri (also known as puchka and goleganna) is popular everywhere. This

scrumptious dish consists of a small round, hollow puri (pastry shell) fried until crisp and then stuffed with a mixture of chickpeas, potatoes, spices, tamarind chutney and pani (spicy water).

Mumbai boasts an incredible variety of dosa (a thin pancake made of fermented rice and urad bean flour batter) that are traditionally filled with masala potatoes, served with sambar and coconut chutney. But there's a mind-boggling assortment of different dosas to choose from — Chinese dosa, Mysore masala dosa and jini dosa are only a few and all come with many different kinds of chutney. If you have a sweet tooth, you'll love the chocolate dosa.

A popular sweet dish, falooda is served cold in a glass and traditionally consists of milk, vermicelli, tapioca pearls, chunks of gelatine and rose syrup, but again there are numerous incarnations. Crawford market is especially renowned for its delicious and varied faloodas.

1 Customers enjoy plates heaped high with fresh fruit salad on a busy Mumbai street, from chunks of fresh watermelon to mango. 2 A chai stall by the roadside offers refreshments for locals and tourists. 3 Smaller bite-sized snacks and rolls.

KHAU GALLI

MUMBAI

Khau galli, literally translated, means 'treat lanes', and are essentially food stalls lined into haphazard rows, creating an explosion of vibrant colours, aromas and sounds that woo Bollywood actors and taxi drivers alike. These can be found across the city and the clang of pots, the sizzle of kebabs and the patter of naan bread kneading can go on for eighteen hours a day.

You'll find colours, textures and combinations of foods that are simply impossible to find anywhere else. That's down to the mix of cuisines that fuse here. Just one of the other-worldly offerings is Indian-Chinese pizza, which comes layered with cheese, berries and fruits, accompanied with a side of ice cream.

If you're still hungry late at night, head to the markets at the Muslim business district of Bohri Mohallah. The influences of Malaysia, Iran and Yemen all inspire the food here. One must-try dish for meat eaters is barah handi. It's a tantalizing mix of different meats simmered in twelve pots for twelve hours. This renders the fat to create a rich stock, and leaves succulent morsels of meat in a flavourful gravy, best mopped up with roti bread. And to finish – on your rounds look out for Taj Ice Cream. It has been handcrafting desserts for more than 125 years.

The sandwiches in Mumbai, like the Bombay sandwich, are unlike any other on the planet. The buttery white bread is stacked with beetroot, boiled potatoes, cucumbers, tomatoes, onion rings and mint chutney, to give a weirdly suprising taste sensation. There's also vada pav, an exotic bread roll filled with deep-fried mashed potato.

One place for meat lovers to go is Mahim's khau galli, situated along Mahim's Balamia Road. The enticing aromas of tandoors, grills and hot plates beckon with this market's twist on Mumbai favourites. Ones to watch for are the infamous butter chicken, biryani, shawarmas and every kind of kebab, from chicken to goat. Dare to attempt bheja, a curry made from goat brain. **AJ**

BHEL PURI

A classic puri street food recipe, layered for different textures.

MAKES 2
Preparation: 10 minutes
Cooking: 5 minutes

2 boiled new potatoes, cut in wedges
½ tsp chilli powder
½ tsp amchoor powder
Pinch of chaat masala
1–2 tbsp vegetable oil, for frying
450 g/1 lb puffed rice
125 g/4 ½ oz sev (chickpea noodles)
125 g/4 ½ oz chickpeas, fried crisp
55 g/2 oz pomegranate seeds
55 g/2 oz salted peanuts

6 papdi (round flatbreads), crushed
1 onion, finely chopped
2 green chillies, finely chopped
Squeeze of lemon juice

To serve:
125 g/4 ½ oz fresh coriander, finely chopped
Chilli powder, to taste
Pinch of masala powder
100 ml/3 ½ fl oz yoghurt, sweetened with honey (to taste)
2 tbsp tamarind chutney

- Toss the potato wedges with the chilli powder, amchoor powder and chaat masala. Fry in the oil until golden, then remove and set aside.
- Mix the remaining ingredients (except the yoghurt and tamarind chutney) in a bowl.
- Place the potatoes on a plate, spoon the mixed ingredients on top and add a squeeze of lemon juice.
- Garnish with chopped coriander, chilli powder and pinch of masala.
- Serve with the yoghurt on top and the tamarind chutney.

4 A typical Mumbai street food vendor selling mouthwatering fried snacks including puris, pakoras and samosas. Although found all over India, street food in Mumbai is particularly significant in that people from all economic classes eat on the roadside at all hours of the day.

1 Chole bhature (chickpeas and fried bread). 2 Gali Paranthe Wali, a lane famous for its abundance of fried bread. 3 Old Famous Jalebi Wala serves large, syrupy jalebi sweets. 4 Coal-roasted litti (dough balls of chickpea flour). 5 Skewered snacks.

CHANDNI CHOWK

DELHI

Head through India's capital and you'll find street food on offer everywhere, from train station floors to the sides of busy roads. A prime food spot is Chandni Chowk, one of the city's oldest markets, where alluring aromas fight for your attention amid a colour explosion of spice mountains, saris and flower garlands. In Delhi, families come to dine at markets instead of restaurants and they don't just eat one dish: they linger to enjoy a variety of different ones, satiating all tastes from spicy to sweet.

A classic is chole bhature – a crispy, waferlike ball that is served with a curry on the side. Although it is found all over India, Delhi's version is reputed to be the best, due to the reduced quantity of soda that goes into the mix. But the real pull of this snack is the chutneys that partner it. Many people will be familiar with the chutney trays that accompany poppadoms in Indian restaurants: the choice here is mind-boggling. Ask for recommendations, as vendors compete to offer the tastiest. The kebabs at Chandni Chowk are also said to be the finest in north India. Marinated in exotic spices from anise to turmeric, the best at the market can be found at Kakori Kebab, Galouti Kebab and Shami Kebab. Another snack that Delhi does especially well is golegappa. You'll find variations of these crispy parcels elsewhere in India: in Mumbai they call them pani puri, whereas in Kolkata they are known as puchka. These flavoursome snacks explode in the mouth, but unless you want a raging inferno on your tongue ask for extra mild.

Delhi street food takes 'hot and spicy' to the next level, even for hardcore chilli lovers. Relief comes in the soothing sweets on offer. Take the edge off even the most inflamed tongue with kulfi, a dense ice cream made from caramelized milk and dried fruit. Or seek out the exotic fruit chaat salads at Bishaam Corner, which are topped with various chanas (sweet and savoury chutneys). AJ

Where: A-17 Masoodpur Vasant Kunj, New Delhi 110006
When: Monday to Saturday 10 a.m.–6 p.m.

NEW MARKET
KOLKATA

Kolkata has a vibrant street food scene, with the roads around New Market awash with vendors selling typical Bengali snacks. Dating to the Raj era, New Market is a vast enclosed market for clothes and handicrafts, with a neighbouring area selling meat, fish, vegetables and all manner of foods. It is claimed that you can even get tiger's milk if you pay the right price. However, most people visit for Nahoum's; situated in the heart of the market, it's the city's last Jewish bakery and is renowned for its rich fruit cake.

Kolkata's best-known street food is the kati roll, a concoction of spiced meat and vegetables wrapped in a paratha flatbread. The kati began life in the New Market area at Nizam's Restaurant, which is still king of the Calcutta rolls. In Bengali, the word *kati* roughly translates as 'stick,' referring to how they were originally made. They are delicious and a far cry from your average kebab. The most ubiquitous street food stands are those selling puchka, a pastry shell (puri) stuffed with mashed potato and then dipped in spicy tamarind water and served in a tiny leaf bowl. Roadside stands piled high with mountains of upside-down puris covered in plastic are everywhere and although the quality of the water may be dubious, the salty mashed potatoes mingled with the watery crunch is hard to resist.

To experience the food scene around New Market, you'll have to navigate your way through a sea of moving people, stray dogs, cycle rickshaws and hand-pulled carts while being serenaded by a chorus of cars and taxis honking and hooting. Although chaotic, the atmosphere is friendly – and if it all gets too much, there are plenty of stands hawking steamed corn on the cob or fresh coconut milk to refresh oneself. You'll also find Punjabi, Tibetan and Chinese food vendors here, but to see why Kolkata is often referred to as the gastronomic capital of India, stick with the tangy Bengali snacks. For those with weaker stomachs, bhel puri – a mix of puffed rice, onion, tomato, coriander and chutney served in a cone of newspaper and eaten with a wooden spoon – is equally popular. **PS**

Where: Lindsay Street, New Market Area, Kolkata
When: Monday to Saturday 10 a.m. – 8 p.m.

8 Punjabi snacks are served alongside traditional Bengali street food.
9 Preparing paratha wraps for a customer.   10 Cooking up enticing
telebhaja (fried vegetables).   11 Stacked fruit cake boxes at Nahoum's
Jewish Bakery.   12 Fancy a break? Try tea and biscuits Kolkata style.

EGG KATI ROLL

This popular Kolkata-style street food is also known as a frankie.

MAKES 1

Preparation: 15 minutes

Cooking: 5 minutes

1 large egg

Salt

1 tsp vegetable oil

1 ready-made paratha

1–2 tbsp tomato ketchup,

plus extra for serving

2 tbsp onions, thinly sliced

2 tbsp cucumber, thinly sliced

1 tbsp fresh coriander, finely
   chopped

¼ tsp green chilli, finely chopped

Lemon juice

Chilli sauce, to serve

- Crack the egg into a small bowl, sprinkle with salt and beat lightly with a fork or whisk.
- Heat the oil in a frying pan. When hot, add one rolled-out paratha and cook on both sides by pressing and rotating gently with a spatula.
- Pour the lightly beaten egg onto the paratha and spread carefully with the spatula to cover the paratha completely. Cook until the egg is done.
- Place the paratha on non-stick baking parchment and then spread with the tomato ketchup.
- Add the onion slices and cucumber slices on one end of the paratha. Sprinkle with chopped coriander and chilli. Squeeze a little lemon juice on top.
- Use the parchment to help roll the filled paratha and tuck it in at the bottom to seal neatly.
- Serve with extra tomato ketchup and a dash of chilli sauce.

FOOD HIGHLIGHTS

Bengalis fry everything under the sun, so be prepared for an array of deep-fried treats. Fried snacks known as **telebhaja** include smoking, hot potatoes, cauliflower, aubergine and assorted other vegetables all dipped in gram flour batter. **Dahl bhajiya** (above) are deep-fried lentil balls. You'll also find **fish cutlets** and **mutton chops**. There is not much variety in colour – all the food looks a different shade of orange. Even the traditional Indian ice cream **kulfi** comes in mango and orange, although vendors also offer more unusual flavours including sitaphal (custard apple) and kesar pista (saffron and pistachio).

GOOD MARKET

COLOMBO

Good Market is Colombo's weekend dose of quirk. With sustainable, eco-friendly products, locally sourced produce and snack stalls, it is a must-visit destination if you're in the city. It draws a diverse crowd: young and old; locals and tourists; environmentalists and fashionistas. Stalls are set up every Saturday in the colonial racecourse complex in Colombo 7, under the shade of an ancient banyan tree. A carefully curated selection of vendors contributes to the market: the aim of the organizers is to showcase products that are 'good for people and good for the planet'.

Its green credentials aside, Good Market is a wonderful place to walk around in the afternoon sunshine, soaking up the good vibes while you sample some of Colombo's most exciting (and healthiest) street food. There is usually a selection of live acts or events on at the same time, from acoustic jam sessions to poetry readings. Tables are set up so that diners can sit down to eat their meals and enjoy the entertainment.

Stalls offer traditional village food such as curry, roti wraps and hoppers (crispy pancakes) and more recent imports, including tacos and brownies. The focus is on keeping things healthy — low-fat, low-sugar, gluten-free, egg-free and vegan options abound — and flavoursome. Diners can find satisfying snacks, substantial meals and cooling drinks. Good Market's star ingredient has to be the jackfruit: hailed by some as a vegan 'pulled-pork' substitute, the unappealing-looking fruit is found here fashioned into myriad different forms. The most popular is the polos (young jackfruit) cutlet — a savoury dish in which the superfood is tossed in spices and crumbs, then fried to a golden-brown blob of perfection. **KS**

Where: Nuga Tree Car Park, Colombo Racecourse, Colombo 07
When: Saturday 10 a.m. – 6 p.m.

1	2	6
3	4	
	5	

1 Fresh fruit pancakes.   2 Wandu appa: sweet steamed rice treats.   3 Spicy veralu achcharu (pickled olives).   4 Cheap Sri Lankan wraps, roast paan and roti are available from Jeewa's.   5 Pick up tacos from Taco Tekak.   6 Dining in style.

POLOS CUTLETS
Don't let the name fool you, these Sri Lankan cutlets are vegetarian.

MAKES 8

Preparation: 15 minutes

Cooking: 40 minutes

1 young ripe jackfruit

6 pieces goraka (tangy Sri Lankan spice); or use tamarind paste

¼ tsp turmeric

Pinch of salt

225 ml/8 fl oz olive or coconut oil, plus extra for deep frying

½ onion, finely diced

4 fresh green chillies, finely chopped

10 curry leaves

¼ tsp puréed root ginger

¼ tsp ground cumin

1 tsp puréed garlic

1 tsp chilli powder

¼ tsp freshly ground pepper

2 tbsp ground dried sprats or dried prawns

Juice of a fresh lime

8 tbsp plain flour

100 g/3½ oz breadcrumbs

Sweet chilli sauce, to serve

- Put the whole unskinned jackfruit in a large pan and cover with water. Add the pieces of goraka (or tamarind paste), turmeric and salt and bring to a boil.
- Cook for 10 to 20 minutes until the jackfruit is soft, then remove from the water and leave to cool.
- Strip the skin of the jackfruit, remove the centre pit and chop the fruit into small bite-sized pieces.
- Heat the oil in a frying pan, add the onion, chillies, curry leaves, ginger, cumin, garlic, chilli powder, pepper and sprats and fry over a low heat.
- Slowly add the jackfruit and stir without breaking up the pieces too much. Add the lime juice and set aside to cool.
- Gently mould the mixture into slightly flattened balls. Roll the balls in the flour and breadcrumbs.
- Deep-fry the cutlets in hot oil until golden brown. Drain on absorbent kitchen paper.
- Serve with sweet chilli sauce.

VENDOR SPOTLIGHT

Jeewa's and Kuma's Natural Foods specialize in jackfruit products, from burgers to jackfruit lasagna. They also prepare delicious wholegrain roti wraps – ask for the pol roti (coconut flatbread) to give your sandwich added flavour.

Achcharu Kadé sell the best rice and curry at Good Market, served on banana leaves in reusable coconut shells to reduce waste. Choose from beef, chicken, fish, prawn, cuttlefish, crab or a vegetarian option. To cool down the heat of your curry, afterwards try one of their natural ice lollies (left). The mango and kiwi option is the perfect balance of sweet and tart.

If you're looking to try a Sri Lankan hopper, go to **Chami Foods**. There, the bowl-shaped pancakes are served with manioc (cassava) and coconut sambol (spiced, grated coconut).

1 An Uyghur man in his winter hat, frying dumplings. 2 Kashgar's Sunday bazaar. 3 Rounds of hot, crisp hemek naan – traditional Kashgar bread. 4 Hearty soup made in large vats is ladled into bowls. 5 Uyghur men devour dumplings together at the bazaar.

SUNDAY BAZAAR

KASHGAR

Buying and selling at Kashgar's Sunday Bazaar is hungry work. When negotiations for carpets and copper pots get too heated, the crowds empty into the alleyways around the perimeter of the bazaar where hundreds of tiny eateries and street food sellers reside. It's a chaotic and colourful scene. Wafts of charcoal smoke greet you as you walk past men grilling long metal skewers of lamb kawap (kebabs), fanning the glowing embers and sending sparks into the air as they sprinkle cumin and chilli over the meat. Others pull flat rounds of naan bread from *tonur* pit ovens that give the bread a smoky, rustic flavour.

A Silk Road hub for centuries, the city of Kashgar, in Xinjiang in far western China, sits at a crossroads between Europe and Asia. The local cuisine, mostly influenced by the local Muslim Uyghur people, reflects tastes traditionally associated with the Middle East – cumin, chilli, saffron and sesame. Lamb and mutton feature heavily, cooked with peppers, tomatoes and aubergines, either slow braised or smoke grilled. Hand-pulled noodles are an Uyghur specialty, boiled and topped with a hearty stew of peppers, onions, aubergines and tomatoes for a satisfying dish.

Every corner of the bazaar is filled with food treasures. The lush fertility of the Kashgar oasis and the cool, dry climate combine to create some of the world's finest dried fruits and nuts – apricots, dates, sultanas in green, purple and black, raisins, walnuts and almonds. Imagine the most exquisite tiny dried figs the size of a marble, sweet and chewy with the crunch of tiny seeds, or freshly picked walnuts, the vendor's hands blackened by walnut oil. Eating at the Sunday Bazaar is an intoxicating experience not easily forgotten – the colourful crowds of women and men, their baskets piled high with quince and pomegranate, the wisps of smoke in the air and echoes of the Silk Road all around you. FR

Where: Corner of Binhe Bei Lu and Azirete Lu, Kashgar
When: Daily from 9 a.m.; Sunday is the busiest day

6 Eating on the go: grilled skewers of spiced sausage are a popular snack, consumed by visitors as they peruse the stalls.   **7** Kawap (lamb kebabs) are grilled on long skewers over an open fire.   **8** A vendor awaits customers at the livestock market in Kashgar, as onlookers lunch.

UYGHUR LAMB POLO

This satisfying pilaf usually features mutton, but lamb is equally good.

MAKES 4
Preparation: 15 minutes
Cooking: 45 minutes
600 g/1 lb 5 oz short-grain rice
2 tbsp vegetable oil
1 onion, finely sliced

200 g/7 oz lamb shoulder, cut into
   4 large pieces
4 carrots, julienned
Boiling water
1 tsp salt
10 dried apricots

- Wash the rice five times until the water runs clear, drain and set aside.
- Heat the oil in a deep wok and fry the onions and then the lamb over a high heat. Add the carrots and fry briefly. Cover the carrots with boiling water and cook uncovered over a high heat. Remove the meat from the pan and set aside.
- Reduce the heat to medium. Add the rice to the pan, distributing it evenly – it should be covered with a thin layer of cooking water. Add 1 teaspoon of salt. Place a lid on the wok and continue to cook over a medium heat.
- From time to time, gently turn over the top layer of the rice and gently pat it down so that it cooks evenly.
- Once the rice grains have a central hard bite but are soft on the outside, make a well in the centre and place the meat in it, then cover with rice.
- Bury the apricots in the rice. Replace the wok lid, reducing the heat to low. Steam for 20 minutes.
- The rice is ready when the grains are soft but still have a slight bite. Serve on a large platter, topped with chunks of the meat and the apricots.

FOOD HIGHLIGHTS

Start your lunch at the bazaar – smoky grilled lamb **kawap** (kebabs), great flat rounds of crisp **naan** bread, mounds of buttery **polo** (pilaf) or browned **samsas**, baked pastries filled with tender mutton. Watch, transfixed, as Uyghur-style, hand-pulled noodles – **laghman** – are made to order, the vendor pulling them like skeins of wool into finer and finer strands. Noodles come topped with a rich ragout of peppers, aubergine, onion, garlic and tomato. For dessert, you might try **maroji** (above), Uyghur hand-churned milk ice cream, or **matang**, sweet, chewy, nutty nougat made with local walnuts or almonds. Tell the vendor how much you want and he'll slice off a hunk with a sharp knife and chop it into bite-sized pieces.

GHOST STREET

BEIJING

Ghost Street (Gui Jie) in Beijing leads food trends in the Chinese capital. Open twenty-four hours a day, the 1.5-kilometre (1-mile) stretch of gastronomic delight is home to over 150 restaurants. It's a mecca for hungry locals and tourists alike, including inquisitive travelling dignitaries – there are many embassies nearby. Ghost Street was one of the first places in the city to feature privately owned Szechuan restaurants and that spicy legacy continues today with the peppery crayfish and invigorating hotpots on offer. The area is a veritable playground for the adventurous eater. Alongside classics such as Peking duck, you can also wrap your molars around spicy bullfrog, another Szechuan specialty – you must suck the toes apparently – and bao du, a

blanched and seasoned tripe dish. Then there's yang xie zi – lamb spine hotpot. And how did the street acquire its ghoulish name? Well, it may be due to the all-night traders who populated it during the Qing Dynasty (1644–1912) and whose lanterns created an eerie half-light. Or perhaps it's because it was once where the deceased were transported in and out of the city through the Dongzhimen Gate. Legend has it that the plethora of restaurants are there largely to service the needs of hungry ghosts. This does not put off the hordes of young people who descend on the street for the lively, open-all-hours atmosphere and fabulously spicy eats, although some visitors will be disappointed to know it is no longer lined with its famous red lanterns after officials deemed them a fire risk. Regardless, Ghost Street is still one of the most exciting street food destinations in China, perhaps even the whole of Asia. You just have to have the spine for it. TJ

Where: Tucked behind Dongzhimen Gate, Guijie Street, Beijing
When: All day, every day. Fridays and Saturdays are especially lively.

1 Dining in the warm glow of lanterns. 2 Cow stomach and seaweed for adventurous eaters. 3 Steaming hot dumplings.
4 Bao du (tripe) in bowls. 5 An architectural arrangement of skewered aubergine and enoki mushrooms ready for the grill.

SHANGHAI

The city's street markets can be traced back as far as the Zhou dynasty (1100–256 BCE) and they have remained a popular fixture of daily life here. Venturing into Shanghai's street food markets with their dazzling colours, captivating aromas, lively characters and general boisterous hubbub is a thrilling experience. At night, pop-up restaurants are set up on wheeled trestles and the streets are transformed into buzzing open-air dining spaces, complete with little tables and plastic seats.

The city's numerous markets, such as the heaving Chang Li Lu Food Market in the Pudong district, are the place to enjoy local specialties, especially at night. Stalls are packed together, with stools and tables on the streets. South Bund Fabric Market is known for its fabrics and tailors, but there is also plenty of street food on offer here. Zhangjiang Hi-Tech Park Night Market (see p.287) has around forty stalls with a wide choice of food to go. All these markets sell local specialties, many of which will be unfamiliar to Westerners who only know Cantonese food. Shanghai's sweet, oily cuisine is highly acclaimed for its use of freshwater fish (particularly river crabs), eels, seafood and water plants. Lotus root is a classic example. They are stuffed with sticky rice and pork or with sweetened rice, then bathed in flowery osmanthus blossom syrup until the lotus roots caramelize into a deep pinkish brown.

Mild and sweet puffy bread wrap jidan bing (the Chinese breakfast of champions) and crispy guo tie (pan-fried dumplings) are sold alongside local dishes such as shansi leng mian — fine wheat noodles served cold with a dash of vinegar and sesame sauce on top accompanied by hot eels in their sweet, unctuous, gingery, soy cooking liquid. Shanghai is famous for its eel dishes and shansi leng mian or 'eel thread cold noodles' is a number one seller.

Tofu (or bean curd) is also much loved here and comes in myriad forms. Look out for fermented tofu, stinky tofu, pan-fried tofu and thousand layer tofu (so-named because it has been frozen causing large ice crystals to develop resulting in cavities in the tofu that look layered). If you're feeling adventurous, try stinky tofu. You can't miss it – the smell is overpoweringly pungent. It is usually sold in golden, deep-fried chunks and served with a spicy chilli or sweet sauce, or sometimes both.

Sheng jian bao (dumplings) are stuffed with pork and shrimps, then steamed and fried until golden and crisp and served with soup. Locals will order a bowl of duck blood and noodle soup, but if this doesn't appeal, you can opt for beef vermicelli soup instead.

People queue for hours to buy crisp buttery spring onion and pork pancakes (cong you bing), which are made from a dough rather than a batter. Mouth-watering and filling they are not to be missed. Enormous sticky rice balls (ci fan tuan) are a typical Shanghai breakfast food, but don't be put off by their plain, bland-looking exterior. Fillings can include salted duck egg, fried breadsticks, chopped pickles, dried pork floss and pork sauce or sugar.

People in Shanghai love sweet foods and more sugar is used here than in any other part of China. Shanghai's scintillating selection of desserts and sweet cakes includes vivid green bean cake (which is surprisingly ultra sweet) and moon cakes, which date back to the great Tang dynasty (618–907 CE). Moon cakes come in a range of different flavours including green tea, red bean, sesame and chocolate. They are traditionally eaten during the Mid-Autumn Festival.

ZHANGJIANG HI-TECH PARK NIGHT MARKET

SHANGHAI

When you step out of Shanghai's metro into the night air, the first thing you'll notice is the smell of chargrilled meat and roasting chestnuts, and what looks like China's future — scores of young, hip, tech workers. They might be snacking on sheng jian bao, classic Shanghai soup dumplings, crispy on the bottom and soft on top; or shao kao, skewers of barbecued octopus or chicken. Shanghai's crackdown on unlicensed street food vendors has meant that downtown, impromptu corner gatherings of street food vendors are becoming a thing of the past. Nonetheless street food is an integral part of China's national psyche, and wherever there are people, street food will follow.

When the Zhangjiang Hi-Tech Park opened as a digital technology and biotech hub in the Pudong New Area, thousands of workers provided the critical mass of people necessary for a permanent night market to spring up and flourish. Sprawling from the exits of the Zhangjiang metro station, the market is like an enormous communal kitchen with forty regular vendors offering tastes from Shanghai and beyond. There's a vibrant energy coming from the tables crowded with young tech geniuses drinking beer and eating one of more than a hundred kinds of Chinese street food — xiaolongbao soup dumplings, noodles and regional specialties from far west China, Lanzhou and China's north. Don't miss the roujiamo, a Xi'an specialty of slow-cooked meat and green peppers in a grilled bun. To eat at Zhangjiang you won't need a lot of cash, or even a lot of Chinese — although knowing how to say *hao chi* (delicious) — always helps. You'll just need an enormous appetite. FR

Where: Zhangjiang Hi-Tech Park, Pudong New Area, Shanghai
When: Open daily, early until 9 p.m. (some vendors keep longer hours)

7 A roujiamo vendor preparing flatbreads.   8 Traditional Uyghur kebabs.   9 Vibrant colours, steaming pans and bubbling pots make for an atmospheric experience.   10 The distinctive aroma of roast chestnuts.   11 Shao kao – barbecued chicken.

SHANGHAI SHENG JIAN BAO

Steamed and pan-fried pork dumplings are a Shanghai specialty.

MAKES 12

Preparation: 25 minutes, plus
  40 minutes rising and resting

Cooking: 15 minutes

For the filling:

100 g / 3½ oz pork mince

50 g / 1¾ oz pork aspic

1 tsp Shaoxing wine

10 g / ¼ oz root ginger, finely diced

Pinch each of salt, white pepper

and sugar

For the dough:

1½ tsp dried yeast

1 tsp sugar

75 ml / 2½ fl oz warm water

150 g / 5½ oz self-raising flour

Vegetable oil for cooking

To garnish:

Sliced spring onions

Sesame seeds

- Combine all the filling ingredients.
- For the dough, mix the yeast with the sugar and warm water, add to the flour and mix to form a dough. Knead and set aside for 30 minutes.
- Roll the dough into a long cylinder and divide it into twelve equal pieces. Roll each one into a flat disc.
- Place 1 teaspoon of filling in the centre of each disc, pinch the edges closed and place in a frying pan, sealed side down. Set aside for 10 minutes to rise.
- Add 1 tablespoon of oil to the pan and fry the buns gently for 10 minutes; do not turn.
- Add water (enough to cover the bottom of the pan), cover and steam for 3–4 minutes. Garnish with sliced spring onions and some sesame seeds.

FOOD AND VENDOR HIGHLIGHTS

Zhangjiang Hi-Tech Park offers the greatest hits of Chinese street food. Spicy fried beef dumplings in flaky pastry, **niurou baozi** (left) are a specialty of China's Hui Muslim ethnic minority. At the **Auspicious Thousand Miles Dumpling Shop** you can choose from nine **hundun (wonton)** varieties, served in a steaming bowl of clear broth. At the **Pan Family Chive Pancakes** stall, Mrs Pan makes **jiucai hezi**, filling a soft pancake with egg and bright green jiucai (Chinese chives), which she fries on a griddle until crisp. No market would be complete without a **chao mian fried noodles** stall (where chow mein comes from). Choose your noodles and add-ins (meat and vegetables), and he'll turn it into a bowl of noodle goodness in two minutes flat.

吉祥千里香馄饨 水饺

素馅	小碗（12只）	7元	肉馅	青菜肉馅	7元	白菜肉馅	7元
	大碗（20只）	10元		香菇肉馅	7元	荠菜肉馅	7元
	粉丝鸡蛋豆腐	7元		韭菜肉馅	7元	大馄饨	7元
	豆腐韭菜鸡蛋	7元		三鲜肉馅	7元	小馄饨	6元
	鸡蛋韭菜	7元		芹菜肉馅	7元	凉拌水饺馄饨	

1 | 2
3 | 4

1 A traditional vendor sets up shop in the same place daily.
2 Photo opportunity: shopping under a canopy of crimson lanterns.
3 Sit to sample your food in the centre of the market aisles.
4 Enjoying street food with friends.

HEFANG STREET MARKET
HANGZHOU

Hangzhou's scenic West Lake in eastern China may boast elegant bridges, picture-perfect pagodas and delicate weeping willow trees, but it also has a distinct lack of eating options. So, after circumnavigating its 17-kilometre (10½-mile) shoreline, visitors would do well to head to nearby Hefang Street to sample typical Chinese street food, including Hangzhou specialties. This 500-metre-long (⅓ mile) food street has, like much else in China, an ancient history. Modelled on Song Dynasty (960–1279) architecture, the street was in use when Hangzhou was the capital of the Song emperors and many of the city's longest-established businesses still have a presence here. Three-

hundred-year-old Fang Hui Chun Tang sells traditional Chinese medicine and is one of the area's oldest stores. As well the touristy souvenirs on sale, there's a mind-boggling amount of food to sample, from beautiful 'dragon-whisker' candy and handcrafted nougat to all manner of things — meat, squid, crabs, spiralized potatoes — barbecued on sticks, to a seemingly endless supply of delicate cakes and biscuits, beautifully crafted and packaged, and delicately flavoured with red bean paste, fruits and aromatic flowers. TH

Where: Hefang Street (Wushan Square – Zhongwe Road), Hangzhou
When: Daily 8 a.m.–9 p.m.

STINKY TOFU

Don't let the pungent odour put you off – the taste is milder and more pleasant than you might believe.

SERVES 2–3
Preparation: 5 minutes
Cooking: 5 minutes

200 g/7 oz fermented tofu cut into thick slices (around 10 pieces)
150 ml/5 fl oz cooking oil
15 g/½ oz douchi (fermented black soybeans),
roughly chopped
10 g/¼ oz douban jiang (spicy broad bean paste)
Spring onion (to taste), roughly chopped
Root ginger (to taste), finely sliced
Water

· Wash the tofu thoroughly and drain off the water.
· Heat the oil in a frying pan or wok to a high heat. Reduce the heat and shallow fry the tofu on both sides until it turns golden brown. Remove from the oil and set aside (shown left).
· To the hot oil, add the fermented black soybeans, spicy broad bean paste, spring onion and ginger, and stir-fry briefly until the ingredients are combined.
· Add the tofu back into the pan along with a small amount of water. Turn up the heat, if needed, and simmer for 4 to 5 minutes until the sauce thickens.
· Remove from the pan and serve immediately.

1 Ready to grab and go: spicy tofu on a street cart. 2 Vendors obscured by stacks of potato twists and battered crabs. 3 Prepping spicy liangfen, a dish made from starch jelly that is usually served cold with savoury sauce. 4 Dumplings. 5 Snow fungus.

MUSLIM STREET

XI'AN

People come to Xi'an in Shaanxi province to witness ancient history in the shape of the Terracotta Army, but the Muslim quarter of the city is where you can literally taste the history. Xi'an is at the eastern end of the Silk Road and was the first Chinese city introduced to Islam. Arab and Persian merchants, who came here to trade, settled down and married. The locals called them the Hui people and many of the Muslims in Xi'an today are descendants of these original Silk Road travellers. The main food area, known as Muslim Street (Huimin Jie), stands in the shadows of the thousand-year-old Great Mosque of Xi'an. It is actually formed by ten streets – the most notable of which are Beiyuanmen, North Guangji and Dapiyuan streets. Here, you can explore the meeting of Middle Eastern spices with Chinese culinary arts.

Muslim Street is the ideal place to go to graze through a meal of many courses, starting with savoury morsels, filling up with mains and finishing with sweet treats as you saunter along. A row of quail eggs fried on a stick makes a convenient starter; they are often served with a spicy red sauce for extra kick. Juicy barbecued lamb kebabs (yang rou chuan), coated in chilli and cumin, are another excellent appetizer. Sheep skulls perched over a steaming vat indicate that the contents are mutton soup, which, served over crumbled bread, is a regional specialty (yang rou pao mo).

Persimmons are the symbol of the city: the bright orange fruits are peeled, flattened and dried, and can be found piled high at many stalls. They are at their most enticing when pounded with flour, sugar and dried osmanthus flowers, then deep-fried in oil like doughnuts. Known as shi zi bing, persimmon cakes are a Xi'an street food staple. Walnuts are another key feature at the market – whether roasted or encased in sugar as a walnut brittle. **SM**

Where: Muslim Quarter includes Beiyuanmen Street, North Guangji Street, Xiyangshi Street and Dapiyuan Street, Xi'an

When: Open daily until late

6 A flame-throwing stove provides a dramatic display.   **7** Striking sugary snacks.   **8** Muslim market chefs in action. As well as food, there are ancient architectures of the Ming and Qing dynasties along the street.   **9** Quail eggs are carefully cracked and added to long sticks.

SNOW FUNGUS AND PEAR SOUP

Long used in Chinese medicine, snow fungus is a nutritious ingredient. Eat the pear, snow fungus and dates and drink the soup.

MAKES 6
Preparation: 30 minutes
Cooking: 1 hour
1 snow fungus
3 Asian pears, peeled,

cored and halved,
  to serve
10 jujubes (red dates)
30 g/1 oz rock sugar
1 litre/1¾ pints water

- Cut the snow fungus into several pieces and soak it in cold water for 30 minutes.
- Place all the ingredients in a saucepan, cover and bring to a boil. Simmer for 1 hour.
- Serve by putting half a pear in a bowl and adding a ladleful of the soup liquid and some of the snow fungus.

VENDOR SPOTLIGHT

Noodles come in all shapes and sizes in Xi'an, but the best are the thick, hand-stretched, ribbon-shaped type (biang biang mian – below). The noodles are topped with vegetables or stewed meat, mainly beef or mutton. **Lóubĕilóu Fànzhuāng**, located at the north end of Beiyuanmen Street, serves the best. Buns stuffed with juicy braised meat (roujiamo) are the original hamburgers. Usually baked in a furnace oven, these delicious snacks can be found throughout Xi'an. Go to **Wang Kui Lazhi Roujiamo** on Changlefang Street for the most flavoursome meat filling. If you are looking for a good breakfast food, try some rice and date cake (zenggao) from **Dongnanya Zenggaowang**, which can be found at the crossroads of Xiyangshi Street and North Guangji Street.

SHAM SHUI PO HONG KONG

In the heart of Kowloon – within the boundary of Lai Chi Kok Road, Yen Chow Street, Tai Po Road and Boundary Road – is the relatively poor, working-class area of Sham Shui Po. Although known primarily for its abundance of cheap electrical goods, many of which may not last the journey home, it is, like any other neighbourhood in Hong Kong, home to an assortment of *dai pai dongs* – street food hawkers churning out deliciously simple noodle dishes, succulent dumplings, fresh seafood (some of it still swimming) and a plethora of meats on skewers, ready to be grilled to perfection. The food here is, in short, electric.

You'll find deep-fried squid and beef balls dripping in curry sauce, a variety of dim sum and the famous cow offal stew for those who are brave of heart and strong of stomach (both of which, incidentally, you'll probably be eating). The pungency of food is a virtue here. Stinky bean curd (fermented tofu) is deep-fried and served with a hot chilli or sweet sauce to take the edge off the rancidity, while possibly the most famously belligerent

fruit of them all, the spiky and foul-smelling durian, is also popular here for its rich, creamy texture – dare you give it a try?

Refresh your palate at the assorted juice bars as you wander Sham Shui Po's busy, themed streets, each dedicated to the sale of a specific kind of goods. If you're still peckish, why not try French toast with kaya, a type of coconut jam very popular throughout South East Asia. So revered is this neighbourhood for its food that there are organized food tours you can join if you wish. However, as a solo explorer there's really only one tip you need: join the longest queues full of locals, or covet the busiest tables (sharing of tables is usual and expected), for they are a sure sign of quality. TJ

Where: Sham Shui Po District, Hong Kong
When: Daily 10 a.m. until 8 p.m. – 10 p.m.

1 Meat on skewers is brushed with flavourful sauces.   2 These spherical waffles – known as eggettes and egg puffs – make perfectly chewy snacks.   3 Shiny brown chestnuts ready for roasting.   4 Meat cooked in thick broth.   5 The evening rush – Pei Ho Street fills up.

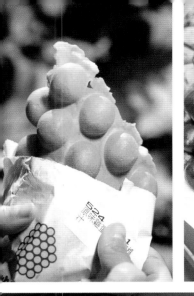

6 Hawkers selling chestnuts and sweet potatoes in the middle of a busy street.   7 Sticky cooked chicken can be dipped in a multitude of mouth-watering sauces or eaten plain.   8 Not a stall for vegetarians: an abundance of meats from dried and cured to cooked and fried.

SALT AND PEPPER TOFU

The crispy salt, pepper and spice coating gives tofu a heavenly texture.

MAKES 4–6

Preparation: 5 minutes

Cooking: 10 minutes

480 g/1 lb 1 oz firm tofu	Potato starch, for coating
½ tsp salt	1 tbsp vegetable oil
½ tsp ground white pepper	1 onion, diced
¼ tsp five-spice powder	2 tsp garlic, finely chopped
2 tsp caster sugar	2 red chillies, finely chopped
	2 tsp Shaoxing wine
	2 tsp light soy sauce
	1 spring onion, thinly sliced

- Cut the tofu into bite-sized pieces and blanch in salted water for five minutes, then drain and pat dry using kitchen paper.
- Mix the salt, pepper, five-spice powder and sugar together well. Sprinkle some of the mixture on both sides of the tofu, then lightly coat with potato starch.
- Heat half the vegetable oil in a frying pan over a medium-high heat. Fry the tofu until lightly browned. Set aside.
- Add the remaining oil to the pan. Sauté the onion until transparent and then push it to the sides of the pan.
- Sauté the garlic in the middle of the pan until softened and add the chillies.
- Toss in the browned tofu and sprinkle over the wine.
- Pour in the soy sauce and stir in the remaining salt, pepper, five-spice powder and sugar mix. Stir to combine.
- Add the sliced spring onion and serve.

VENDOR SPOTLIGHT

Start at **Pei Ho Street Market**, a collection of *dai pai dongs* serving not just Cantonese food, but flavours from all across South East Asia. If you need a further noodle fix, seek out **Cheong Fun Wang** on Heard Street, for delicious thick rice noodles slathered with peanut sauce, sesame seeds and spice (above), if you want it. For dessert, head to **Kwan Kee** on Fuk Wah Street for rice pudding, sugar cake and black sesame rolls – this humble spot even gets a mention in the Michelin Guide!

SHILIN NIGHT MARKET TAIPEI

Northern Taipei is home to Shilin Night Market; large, sprawling and diverse, it is also the most revered on the island. Adored for its iconic food stalls, fashion outlets, shoes and accessories, this is an eclectic, gaudy, buzzing destination. It is possible to buy snacks to eat on the go or perch on a stool and eat something more substantial like beef noodle soup. From small handheld spring onion pancakes and chive pockets (pastry filled with seasoned meat) to bowls of shaved ice with mango or aiyu lemon jelly (a local specialty), the choice is overwhelming.

The food on offer spans Chinese regional cuisines, Japanese influences (dating to the occupation from 1895 to 1945) and local indigenous. Teppanyaki stalls with their sizzling hot plates are popular – watch chefs flamboyantly splash Shaoxing rice wine on their dishes, creating an intoxicating alcohol-fuelled atmosphere. Oyster omelettes, a Taiwan specialty, are produced by dedicated chefs who combine eggs, potato starch, green onions, seasoning and fresh oysters. Dispatched onto searingly hot pans and doused in a famous red sauce (ketchup, soya sauce and miso), this dish is defined by the gelatinous texture the potato starch creates and its sweet accompaniment.

This is a market of two parts: inside, there is the more modern area, where legal vendors sit; outside, lining the surrounding streets, are the illegal vendors. Hawkers selling illicit wares have to be ready to relocate their carts as soon as their lookout begins whistling, alerting them to the arrival of the police. These vendors offer some of the best treats: steamed or fried pork buns, potsticker dumplings (similar to gyoza), Taiwanese sausages on sticks (sweet, garlicky and meaty) or candied olives and tomatoes that have been dipped in the thinnest, crunchiest caramel. If you are in Taipei, this is an experience not to be missed. SP

Where: Shilin, Taipei (Chientan MRT on the Tamsui/Hsintien line)
When: Daily 5 p.m.–11 p.m. but to midnight at weekends

7 Pepper and pork buns ready to be bagged up and handed to customers: rounds of dough are stuffed with marinated pork and green onions, wrapped in a bun and cooked in the round barrel oven. 8 The Hot-Star Fried Chicken stall sells ultra-large deep-fried chicken steaks and is incredibly popular – worth the wait in the inevitable queue.

SEOUL

Wandering around the tumultuous streets of Seoul, the overwhelming number of carts and stalls offering a myriad of tempting snacks and cooked dishes is mind-blowing. Street vendors have been a long-standing tradition in South Korea's capital since the fourteenth century, when markets sprang up around the city's walls and gates, with merchants offering a huge range of goods, including foods to be eaten on the go.

Part of the whole experience of Seoul is visiting the boisterous markets. The narrow alleys of Seoul's oldest and largest market, Namdaemun (see p.307), are lined with food stalls, their rich aromas percolating the air. At nightfall, the market is lit with colourful neon lights and takes on a life of its own. Just by Namdaemun Gate two (one of eight) is the city's famous hotteok food cart. Hotteok is a type of doughnut usually filled with sugar

honey, nuts and cinnamon. Here, in addition to the sweet kind, there's a curious version stuffed with sesame and soy glass noodles, carrots and spinach, basted with a fruit-seasoned soy sauce. Gwangjang Market (see p.311) is mainly for locals, so prices are really low. With food stalls as far as the eye can see offering a huge choice of foods, you'll be spoilt for choice when eating here.

A fashionable modern shopping area popular with locals and tourists is Myeong-dong. At night, numerous street food vendors appear with all sorts of delicious specialties to feast on, including desserts and sweet treats. Bbopgi (also known as dalgona) is a toothsome Korean candy made from sugar and baking soda, that was once very easy to find on the street. Myeon-deong is now one of the few places left to find this delicacy.

Today stalls and tented vendor carts (*pojangmancha*) sell a host of foods from delicious dumplings to unique local favourites such as silkworm pupae. If you're feeling adventurous, try beondegi, or steamed silkworm larvae; sold in pots, they look like small brown bugs and are munched like popcorn. Locals snack on them as they walk around. Tteokbokki (spicy rice cakes) are essential to street food and easy to find. Be warned, these small rice cakes or sticks, coated in an explosively fiery red sauce, aren't for the faint-hearted

Everyone who comes here should try Korean barbecue-grilled beef, pork ribs and liver served with sides of spicy red kimchi (fermented vegetables, chillies and anchovies.) Other unmissables include the large variety of tasty dumplings found throughout the city (the best are reputedly from the street right next to the Ssamziegil building) and spicy, juicy Korean fried chicken.

Anyone with a sweet tooth will be in heaven in the streets of Seoul, as sweets and desserts are everywhere. Koreans adore bungeoppang, which translates as 'carp bread' although it contains no fish. It is a sweet, fish-shaped cake typically filled with sweet red bean paste, cream or sweet potato. Other local favourites include breakfast waffles filled with whipped cream, ice cream, fresh fruit and sauce served like a taco; traditional egg bread (gyeranbbang) – small, vanilla-flavoured breads topped with a baked egg; and melt-in-the-mouth kkultarae – the Korean equivalent of dragon's beard candy (candy floss). This dessert is made from a block of honey, stretched and pulled into thousands of strands, dipped into cornflour, then wrapped around ground nuts. It is fascinating to watch street vendors pulling the strings of honey and shaping the finished kkultarae into small white, pink or green pillows of sweetness.

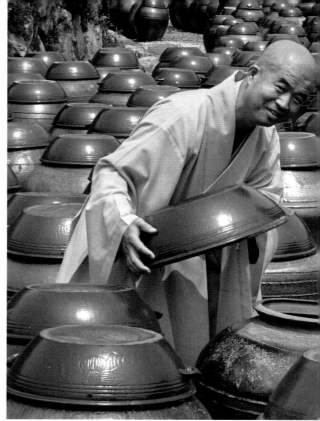

NAMDAEMUN MARKET SEOUL

Namdaemun is one of the oldest and most famous markets in Korea, named after the Great South Gate it neighbours in the centre of the capital, Seoul. Since the 1400s traders have been hawking their goods in this vast market, which boasts more than 10,000 stores and street stalls, and stretches over 6 hectares (16 acres). It's a real labyrinth to navigate, and buzzes with activity twenty-four hours a day.

Order a bowl of boribap, barley rice topped with a smattering of vibrant vegetables: yellow crunchy bean sprouts, tart pickled radish, earthy bracken roots, exotic mountain vegetables, crispy lettuce and sweet leeks. Mix this medley together with a dollop of moreish gochujang (fermented chilli paste) sauce to create a symphony of bold flavours. Venture around the corner and discover a dimly lit passageway dedicated to kalchi jorim, a stew made from silver hairtail fish. As you walk through, the odour of this fiery red dish consumes your senses, and you'll soon see why. Every shop front dons steel bowls set over open flames bubbling vivaciously, enticing customers inside. These mini cauldrons flaunt chunks of fresh fish simmering happily with slices of Korean radish, soy sauce, garlic and plenty of gochugaru (red pepper flakes). It's a simple, but hugely satisfying bowl – salty, spicy and packed with flavour. The real highlight, however, is hotteok – a cross between a crispy pancake and a chewy doughnut, filled with molten gooey brown sugar and decadently fried in butter. Hotteok are found all over Korea, but Namdaemun has the best – and even boasts a savoury version, japchae hotteok, stuffed with sweet potato noodles.

It's best to visit Namdaemun in the evening when the street food stalls open, just outside exit 5 of Hoehyeon station (line 4). These sell tteokbokki (fiery hot rice cakes), bungeoppang (fish-shaped pancakes filled with sweetened red bean) and eomuk (fish cakes). JJ

Where: 21 Namdaemunsijang 4-gil, Namchang-dong, Jung-gu, Seoul
When: Daily 6 a.m.–9 p.m.

6 Varieties of blood-red kimchi – traditional pickled vegetables – make for an arresting display plated up on a stall.   7 Steaming spicy soups and stews with kimchi fermented in bright red chilli flakes.   8 A vendor surveys crowds filtering through the market, ready to beckon customers.

MIXED SEED HOTTEOK

These sweet pancakes are a popular Korean street food, particularly during the bitterly cold winter months.

SERVES 10

Preparation: 40 minutes,
   plus 3–4 hours rising
Cooking: 25 minutes

For the dough:

350 ml/12 fl oz whole milk
2 tbsp white sugar
7 g/¼ oz instant dried yeast
½ tsp salt
250 g/9 oz strong white bread flour,
   plus more for dusting
150 g/5½ oz sweet glutinous
   rice flour
20 g/¾ oz cornflour

For the filling:

125 g/4¼ oz light muscovado
   sugar
75 g/2¾ oz mixed seeds
   (golden linseed, sunflower,
   pumpkin and sesame seeds)
1 tbsp ground cinnamon
¼ tsp sea salt
240 ml/8½ fl oz vegetable or other
   mild-flavoured oil for frying

- For the dough, in a small saucepan, warm the milk slightly and whisk in the sugar and yeast, making sure they are dissolved completely. Stand the mixture in a warm place to activate, about 3 to 5 minutes, or until bubbly.
- In a large bowl combine the salt and all three of the flours. Slowly pour in the warm milk and yeast mixture. Mix gently with a wooden spoon until a uniform, but slightly sticky dough forms. Shape into a ball and cover the bowl with a damp cloth. Allow to rise in a warm place, until doubled in size, about 1½ to 2 hours.
- Knock the dough back and allow it to rise again until doubled in size, another 1½ hours.
- After the dough has risen the second time, dust a clean surface with flour and knock the dough out onto it. Knead it a couple of times.
- Shape the dough into a fat log. Divide into ten even pieces and roll into balls. Cover with sheet of cling film, to prevent a skin forming on the surface.
- For the filling, mix together the muscovado sugar, seeds, cinnamon and salt.

- Dusting with flour as necessary to prevent sticking, press a dough ball into a 10-cm (4-in.) diameter disc. Place the disc in your hand and cup it slightly.
- Scoop up about 1½ to 2 tablespoons of the sugar/seed mixture and place in the centre of the disc. Seal by pinching the edges together at the top, wrapping the dough around the filling. Once sealed, reshape gently into a round ball.
- Place with the seam side down on a well-floured surface. Cover again with cling film. Repeat, forming pancakes with the remaining dough and filling.
- Place a large, non-stick pan over a medium heat and coat generously with oil, about 3 to 4 tablespoons.
- Working in batches of three, place the pancakes seam side down on the hot frying pan and immediately flatten them gently with a spatula. Fry over a medium to low heat for about 3 to 4 minutes on each side, until the dough is golden crispy brown and slightly springy to the touch. Transfer to a wire rack.
- Wipe your pan clean with kitchen paper in between batches and use fresh oil with each batch. Allow the pancakes to cool slightly before eating.

FOOD HIGHLIGHTS

Look for a nondescript plastic door that hides famed Kalguksu Alley. For decades, this narrow lane has housed the best **kalguksu** (knife noodles) soup vendors in all of Seoul. Fiercely competitive, the second you enter all the *ajoomas* (older ladies) aggressively beckon you to sit down at their stall. Kalguksu consists of a steaming bowl of savoury anchovy broth full of handmade noodles, finished with crispy tofu, roasted seaweed, fresh spring onions and crushed sesame seeds. In true Korean tradition, you also receive a few side dishes gratis: two types of **kimchi** (fermented spiced veggies) and **bibim naengmyeon** (spicy cold buckwheat noodles).

1 | 3
2 | 4

1 Bowls of hot food are distributed to marketgoers. Don't be put off by the busiest areas or outlets – these often have queues for a reason. 2 Smaller stalls with visitors on benches. 3 Dakkochi (chicken skewers) cooking over hot coals. 4 Korean egg bread.

GWANGJANG MARKET SEOUL

Located in the Jongno area of Seoul, Gwangjang is a massive indoor market. Shaped like a large 'X', there are four entrances, with two long corridors criss-crossing at the centre. During the day, these corridors flood full of shoppers seeking bargains on silk, linen and *hanboks* (traditional dresses). At 6 p.m. these stores close and give way to hungry diners looking to fill their bellies with some of the best street food in Seoul. The heart of the food market lies in the centre of the 'X' where suddenly you're hit with a torrent of noise and the tantalizing smells of foods filling the air.

The centre of the market features bindaetteok stalls, each with a large deep griddle frying up the mung bean pancakes for which Gwangjang is famed. Most stalls exhibit an old-school stone pestle grinding up mung beans and water to make a thick paste. This paste is then mixed with bean sprouts, pork, kimchi and spring onions, and then ladled onto sizzling griddles to create big, round crispy pancakes — a cheap and truly irresistible treat. Gwangjang is also renowned for its mayak gimbap and yukhoe, with certain alleys dedicated to these delights. Mayak gimbap are mini seaweed rolls stuffed with rice, pickled radish, carrots and spinach. The sweet, tangy soy and mustard dipping sauce they are served with are what makes gimbap so moreish, hence its name. *Mayak* means 'narcotic', describing just how addictive these little bites are.

The stalls down Yukhoe Alley monopolize the Korean steak tartare trade. Vastly different in flavour from their French counterpart, this satiating fragrant dish is comprised simply of julienned strips of raw beef, lightly seasoned with soy, sesame oil, pine nuts and sweet Korean pear, and topped with a raw egg yolk for creaminess. In addition to these alleyways, there are around 200 stalls selling a wide array of foods, including soondae (Korean blood sausage, often served with heart, liver, salt and pepper), boribap (barley rice served with vegetables and spicy sauce), hwe (Korean sashimi), jeon (savoury fritters) and mandu (Korean dumplings). **JJ**

Where: 88 Changgyeonggung-ro, Jongno-gu, Seoul
When: Daily 9 a.m.–11 p.m.

YANAGIBASHI MARKET FUKUOKA

At just 120 metres (425 ft) in length, Yanagibashi Market is not a huge place. However, it is one of the most popular fish markets in Fukuoka prefecture. Renowned for its ramen, the air is permeated with the smell of charcoal, fish and meats, as well as the umami scent of broths. With an impressive selection of fish and seafood, the auctions at Yanagibashi start at 3 a.m. Surrounded by street food vendors offering everything from chargrilled squid and eel to candied fruits on sticks, this lively market is significantly cheaper than its Tokyo counterpart.

From humble beginnings in 1916 when one vendor sold his seafood wares, this is the second busiest market in Japan, after Tsukiji in Tokyo. With over 400 stalls and footfall of around 8,000 visitors daily, Yanagibashi Market is a thriving hub and offers street food of all shapes and forms. In autumn and winter the warming smell of chestnuts roasting (tenshin amaguri) can be found from every corner as vendors tempt hungry shoppers. **LB**
Where: 1-5-1 Haruyoshi, Chuo, Fukuoka-shi, Fukuoka
When: 8 a.m. to 6 p.m.; fish auctions from 3 a.m.

PORK AND SHOYU RAMEN
Shoyu ramen is a classic Japanese dish.

SERVES 6
Preparation: 25 minutes
Cooking: 3 hours 30 minutes
For the kombu dashi:
20 g/2 large pieces dried kombu
500 ml/18 fl oz water
For the shoyu base:
225 ml/8 fl oz soy sauce
2 tbsp dry sake
1 tbsp mirin (rice wine)
For the pork stock:
680 g/1½ lb boneless pork shoulder

Salt and pepper
2 tbsp vegetable oil
450 g/1 lb pork spare ribs
2 bunches spring onions, chopped
2 carrots, grated
1 head garlic, halved horizontally
2.5 cm/1 in. piece ginger, sliced
35 g/1¼ oz bonito flakes
For the ramen and garnish:
3 packs dried/6 packs fresh ramen
3 large soft-boiled eggs
6 spring onions, thinly sliced

- Make the dashi by soaking the strips of kombu in the water until it softens and opens up, about 15 minutes. This will leave a thickened and salty broth.
- Make the shoyu base by combining the ingredients.
- Season the pork shoulder and roll it up, tying with string every 5 cm/2 in. Brown in a large saucepan over a high heat, for 10 to 12 minutes. Add the ribs, spring onions, carrots, garlic, ginger and bonito flakes.
- Remove the kombu from the stock and set aside. Add as much of the dashi as will fit in the pan containing the pork. Bring to the boil, then reduce to a simmer. Skim to clarify. Add more dashi as the liquid reduces, until the

pork is tender – about 3 hours.
- Remove the pork from the stock and leave to cool, then chill. Strain the liquid through a fine-mesh sieve and chill.
- To assemble, bring the strained stock to the boil in a pan, then reduce to a simmer. Cook the ramen separately, as per packet instructions.
- Thinly slice the pork. Layer up the bowls by piling meat on to the hot noodles and ladling stock with shoyu base over the top. Add half an egg and spring onions to each portion before serving.

TOKYO

Japan's hectic, mammoth capital city is a fascinating blend of ancient and modern, especially when it comes to its diverse street food. Shopping streets in Japan date back more than 500 years and were first recorded during the period when the samurai warriors relaxed commercial regulations in order to stimulate the economy in the areas they controlled. Mobile food carts (*yatai*) were present in the city in the 1600s, but they became more popular and increased greatly in number during the late nineteenth and early twentieth centuries. They probably originated with the food stalls that sprang up outside Buddhist shrines to feed hungry pilgrims from the fifth to the seventh centuries.

There are many places in this lively city where you can sample excellent Japanese street food. Tsukiji Market (see p.316) is the world's biggest fish market and is rightly renowned for its fabulous fish and seafood, but here you can also sample outstanding local delicacies. Experience yumcha – the brunch-style tradition of eating dim sum dishes such as steamed, meat-filled dumplings along with Chinese tea.

Ameya-yokocho Market (see p.320) in the Ueno district translates as 'candy shop alley' and while you'll encounter many sweet vendors selling Japanese favourites such as the charming fish-shaped taiyaki pancakes filled with creamy custard or sweet red beans, there's much more besides to feast on. Snacks range from fresh sushi rolls to takoyaki (octopus pancakes).

Umeyashiki Shopping Street in Ota-ku is a significant shopping street with over 140 stores. Grab a tasty lunch from Tempei, who sell freshly fried tempura in bento (traditional lunch boxes). Japanese business districts also attract bento *yatai* that open at lunchtime on business days. Alternatively, for an inexpensive but

1	2
	3

1 A stall owner at Tsukiji Market prepares samples in front of dishes of fresh fish and seafood. 2 Tantalizing okonomiyaki, sometimes known as the Japanese pancake. The word loosely translates to 'what you like grilled'. 3 Vibrant Tokyo streets.

filling lunch, buy kare pan (curry bread), a large crispy, curry-filled doughnut. Plenty of places sell these, including the takeaway around the corner from Shimokitazawa station in Setagaya.

Bright neon lights up the narrow entrance to Ebisu Yokocho. This bustling food arcade is crammed with stalls, separated by plastic curtains, where customers sit on crates and soapboxes to relish hotpot or barbecue with a glass of umeboshi sours (salted plum with shochu rice spirit and soda). It tends to become packed in the evening, so go early to find a seat.

Wander along the street leading up to Sensōji Temple in the Asakusa neighbourhood, where vendors sell snack-sized portions of goodies such as mochi (sweet, chewy rice cakes), ningyo-yaki (red bean paste filled cakes) and sembei (rice crackers). It's fun to stand and watch sembei puff up as they're cooked over hot charcoal. Or sample okonomiyaki, Japanese-style omelettes filled with vegetables, seafood and noodles. Omoide Yokocho in Shinjuku is a street food nirvana. This tiny lane is host to restaurants and stalls that sell time-honoured favourites and is enormously popular with locals. Fill up on yakitori (skewers of grilled meat and vegetables), bowls of hot noodles and fried tempura vegetable balls in broth (kakiage).

Food trucks are some of the best places to find street food in Tokyo. Known as 'kitchen cars' in Japanese, their menus include Western, Chinese and ethnic food as well as Japanese. Yaki imo (baked sweet potato) trucks and carts fitted with wood stoves are easy to spot all over the city. The trucks drive around slowly intoning 'yaki imo . . . yaki imo . . . yaki imo' on a loudspeaker. Look out for the Plus Spice truck with an Indian flag at the window. They attract large crowds and serve curries – mild to cater for Japanese taste – together with hot, fresh naan bread.

1 Grilled squid sticks cooked to perfection are piled up on trays, ready to be bought at Tsukiji Market. 2 Delicate and delectable: griddled scallop with roe, sea urchin and crab meat. 3 This vendor keeps an eye on the grill at his stall, which sells oysters and seafood.

TSUKIJI MARKET TOKYO

The world's largest fish market, Tsukiji has been a popular tourist destination for a number of years now. Busy and traditional, while the market welcomes tourists, it does not stop for them and it pays to have your eyes open to avoid being knocked over by flurries of fish carts. Following the great Kanto earthquake of 1923, the market was moved to Tsukiji from its former space at Nihonbashi. Originally selling offcuts unused by the Edo Palace, the booming market now trades over 1,676 tonnes (1,847 tons) of fish and seafood every day. Many visitors come early in the morning for the tuna auction whereas others arrive later for a wander and a sushi breakfast or fresh egg omelette (be prepared to queue for the latter, as it is very popular with the locals). The tuna auction is a real highlight and it is worth booking as tickets for visitors are limited. The massive tuna fish have been hollowed out and frozen before being laid out in rows on the floor for inspection by potential buyers. Then the serious business of bidding begins. Elsewhere you can watch fish being cleaned, gutted and filled with a scoop of rice right in front of you.

Street food is a memorable part of Tsukiji's attraction, with everything from yakitori to ramen and sushi offered on its outskirts in the Jōgai-Shijō area. Surrounding the central market are striking rows of professional sashimi knives, multicoloured Wellington boots and other food-related goods. Honing in on the centre of the market, bright red suckers from octopuses can be seen. Huge tuna hang from hooks, crabs are stacked up on end and a rainbow of fish cuts tempts passers-by. LB

Where: 5 Chome-2-1 Tsukiji, Chuo, Tokyo

When: Outer Market: varies by shop, typically 5 a.m.–2 p.m. The wholesale area is open to visitors after 9 a.m. Check the online market calendar before you visit, as it is sometimes closed on Wednesdays. The tuna auction is open to visitors from 5.25 a.m.– 6.15 a.m. (restricted to 120 visitors per day).

CRAB AND SHIITAKE GYOZA WITH PONZU DIPPING SAUCE

A citrusy dipping sauce partners crab and shiitake dumplings.

MAKES 30

Preparation: 30 minutes

Cooking: 10 minutes

For the gyoza:

200 g / 7 oz Chinese cabbage, shredded

200 g / 7 oz fresh, white crab meat

4 large, fresh shiitake mushrooms, chopped

2 spring onions, finely sliced

2 tsp grated root ginger

2 garlic cloves, finely chopped

1 small chilli, finely diced

1 tsp light soy sauce

¼ tsp sesame oil

Oil for frying

125 ml / 4 fl oz water

30 gyoza skins (wrappers)

For the sauce:

125 ml / 4 fl oz soy sauce

50 ml / 2 fl oz yuzu (Japanese citrus fruit) or alternatively use fresh orange juice

2 tsp lemon juice

1 tsp sugar

- For the gyoza, blanch the cabbage in a pan of boiling salted water for 20 seconds. Drain and refresh in cold water, then drain again.
- Combine the remaining ingredients, except for the gyoza skins, and mix to create a sticking paste.
- Put a little crab mixture in the centre of a gyoza skin. Trace a half moon around the edge of the wrapper with a wet finger. Fold in half, over the filling, and pinch in the centre.

- Keeping hold of the middle, make a pleat in the top of the wrapper, and continue folding small pleats from the middle out. Finish by turning and repeating the process so that the whole edge of the gyoza is pleated. Repeat until all 30 skins are full.
- Heat the oil in a frying pan and fry gently, pleated side first, for about 2 minutes per side.
- For the sauce, mix together all the ingredients and serve with the gyoza.

VENDOR SPOTLIGHT

Strolling around the outer market, you will see all manner of street food – and typically for Japan, it is always prepared fresh. Everything from delicious grilled oysters, hot ramen with pork, okonomiyaki and curry rice to tasty gyoza and dipping sauce or squid yakitori can be found, with nothing costing more than about 700 yen (£5). **Dai-Ni Tsukiji Seimenjo** sell excellent gyoza with a variety of fillings and fresh sauces; this small stall is always busy with salarymen from nearby Ginza and the side streets of Tsukiji. Grilled eel (unagi) on sticks is popular the length and breadth of Japan and this Tsukiji specialty can be found at **Nisshin Tasuke**. **Ajino Hamato** have over eighty years' experience selling fish-based snacks to market visitors. They concoct a special fish paste that is used to enhance all snacks on sale here. Almost every flavour of fresh delicious dumpling can be found at **Suga Shoten** and people travel for miles to try the steamed dumplings stuffed with black pork, which is sourced from the Kagoshima prefecture.

AMEYA-YOKOCHO TOKYO

It is not clear exactly how Ameya-Yokocho (or Ameyoko) market in Ueno in central Tokyo got its name. Some believe Ameya-Yokocho can be literally translated as 'sweet shop alley', so named because of the large number of sweet stores in the area post-World War II, when sugar was scarce and it was the location for a bustling black market. Others believe Ameya refers to the US army surplus stores that sprang up alongside the market, which runs next to the elevated train tracks between Ueno and Okachimachi stations.

Whatever the truth of the semantics, there is a US legacy of sorts in the delicious street foods found here, due to relief efforts post war, when America flooded Japan with wheat flour. So alongside ubiquitous ramen, you can still buy small crêpes known as issen-yoshoku, which roughly translates as 'one-penny Western food'. Ameyoko is, in fact, a veritable snack heaven: feast on takoyaki — fried dough balls containing octopus, green onions and ginger and topped with mayonnaise, katsuoboshi (dried tuna flakes) or takoyaki sauce; yakatori (chicken skewers); and

okonomiyaki, commonly known as Japanese pizza, a savoury pancake of batter and cabbage served with various toppings. Try them with the umami-packed sauce of the same name, made from soy and shiitake mushrooms.

Also worth a mention is grilled tuna collar or kama, which is served in many of the eateries in the streets around the market. Although considered by some to be cheap scraps, it is well worth the visit alone: cooked on the bone, the tuna — crispy on the outside, tender on the inside — has incredible flavour. Head to the market at dusk for the best bargains — Ameyoko is one of the few places in Tokyo where bartering is actively encouraged. TJ

Where: 4 Chome Ueno, Tokyo 110-0005
When: Daily 10 a.m.–8 p.m. (note some stores close on Wednesdays)

1 Visitors gather on street corners in makeshift dining areas for the authentic experience. 2 Some stalls have room for hungry customers to sit and feast. 3 Vendors sell a variety of dishes. 4 The crowds speak for themselves.

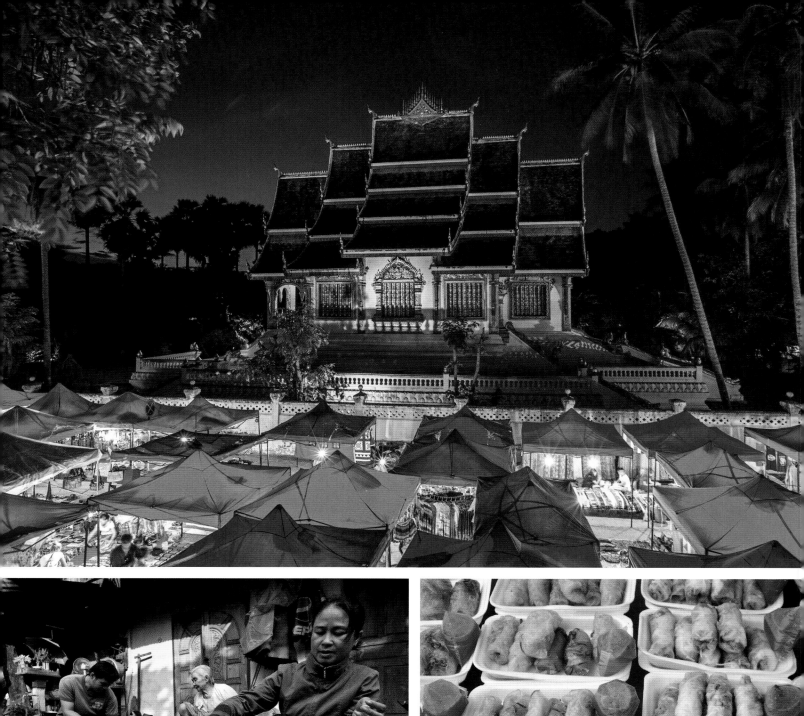

LUANG PRABANG NIGHT MARKET

LUANG PRABANG

Every evening at dusk, rows of red and blue tents fill Luang Prabang's main street, Sisavangvong Road, as hundreds of vendors set up their stalls for the city's famous night market. The stalls, lit by strings of bulbs, glow like large, colourful lanterns against the night sky. Renowned as the best place to buy locally made handicrafts in Laos, Luang Prabang Night Market is also an excellent showcase for Laotian cuisine. Food sellers are clustered at the end of the market, where Sisavangvong Road meets Settathilat Road. More stalls are tucked away down a narrow alleyway that comes off the main street, the entrance to which is obscured by smoke pouring from barbecues. Diners eat at rickety folding tables, perched on plastic stools.

There is a diverse choice of local foods on offer, including the national dish, laap (also spelled larb, larp or lahb) – a minced meat (or fish) salad served with fresh vegetables and herbs. The meat in laap is traditionally raw and it 'cooks' in a marinade of acidic lime juice and spices. More foreigner-friendly versions will use cooked meat. Barbecues – often shared by several vendors – grill meat and fish in front of you. Tilapia, freshly caught from the Mekong, is stuffed with lemongrass, then skewered, salted and cooked. Laotian sausages, which use real intestines as casing, are eaten with a spicy dipping sauce. There is plenty of vegetarian food, too: spring rolls and vegetable dumplings; steaming noodle soups; and Thai-style vegetable curries. Dishes are accompanied by khao niao (sticky rice), which is steamed and served in bamboo baskets.　NB

Where: Sisavangvong Road, Luang Prabang
When: Daily 5 a.m.–11 p.m.

5 A wealth of variety: delicious meals ready to be scooped up and served. Do ask if you need more information or would like to try – most vendors will be happy to help.   6 Tilapia fish cook over hot coals.   7 Lacquered roast chickens and marinated kebabs.

SPICY BUFFALO LAAP

Feel free to substitute any other meat, fish or tofu for the buffalo.

SERVES 2

Preparation: 15 minutes

Cooking: 5 minutes

For the laap:

1 tbsp vegetable oil

4 shallots, sliced into thin rounds

5 spring onions, thinly sliced

1 hot red chilli, sliced into thin rounds

1 tbsp fresh galangal or ginger, finely chopped

4 garlic cloves, finely chopped

150 g/5½ oz minced buffalo meat

½ tsp salt

1 tbsp fish sauce

1 tsp granulated sugar

Juice of 2 limes

2 tbsp roasted rice powder (khao khua) for binding

For the salad garnish:

1 small handful of beansprouts, sliced (soak briefly in hot water to soften)

2 long beans or 5 runner beans, sliced

1 handful of fresh coriander, chopped

1 handful of fresh mint, chopped

1 tsp chilli powder

1 stalk lemongrass, white section sliced into thin rounds

Optional

4 sawtooth leaves, finely chopped

1 small handful of banana flower, finely chopped

Sticky rice and greens, to serve

- For the laap, heat the oil in a pan and add the shallots, spring onions, red chilli, galangal (or ginger) and garlic. Lightly cook on a medium heat for a few minutes, stirring until golden brown.
- Add the minced buffalo meat, salt, fish sauce and sugar. Gently cook over a medium heat until the meat is well cooked.

- Remove the buffalo meat from the pan and place in a deep bowl. Mix in the lime juice and roasted rice powder.
- Mix in all the salad garnish ingredients (plus the sawtooth leaves and banana flower, if desired).
- Serve with steamed sticky rice and greens.

FOOD HIGHLIGHTS

Dotted around the market, there are several stalls selling **tam maak hoong** (spicy papaya salad). It is made from green papaya, which has a cucumber-like consistency, and accompanied with plenty of lime juice, chilli and fish sauce. If you are craving more familiar foods, seek out friendly sandwich lady Noi (left), whose stall is emblazoned with appreciative notes written by tourists from around the world. She sells delicious stuffed baguettes – opt for the **khao jie pate** (Lao sandwich), stuffed with pork pâté, salad and chilli paste. The best desserts are **khanom krok** – small, disc-shaped cakes made from coconut milk, sugar, sticky rice and flour. Look out for sellers making them in special cast-iron pans over a hot charcoal brazier.

BANGKOK

Cooking and selling food on the streets is traditional in South East Asia and is deeply ingrained in the region's cultures. Street food in Thailand's bustling capital dates back to at least the sixteenth century, when food was sold from floating markets and Bangkok was known as the 'Venice of the East'. The arrival of Chinese immigrants, particularly in the nineteenth century, saw an increase in the diversity of food on offer. Today, everywhere in the city there are clusters of stalls on street corners and in alleys; vendors can be seen on tricycles and motorcycles or pushing mini-kitchens

on metal carts. Some open around the clock, though in many areas they're closed during the day on Mondays for official street cleaning. Some vendors work on foot, carrying filled baskets balanced on bamboo yokes. Along the *khlongs* (canals) and waterways, sellers paddle their wares offering 'boat noodles', curries and vibrantly coloured kanom (sweetmeats and snacks). The streets are a hive of activity, with vendors enthusiastically stir-frying in well-worn woks, grilling meat skewers or boiling noodles. The choice can seem bewildering. All over Bangkok, you can easily find affordable and delicious Thai food with its trademark flavours of sweet, sour, spicy and salty thanks to local ingredients such as coconut milk, lemongrass, basil, chilli and fish sauce.

Or Tor Kor (see p.332) is probably the best-known market in Bangkok, renowned internationally for its outstanding fresh

2
3

1 Banana leaves hold a host of local fresh and cooked ingredients ready for preparation.   2 Khao Gaeng means 'cover rice with a topping' – just point to what you fancy for a quick delicious meal.   3 Grilled pork skewers (mu ping).

produce as well as its street food. Another essential stop for food lovers in Bangkok is Chinatown or Yaowarat (see p.329), which is regarded as the birthplace of Thailand's street food and remains its epicentre. Yaowarat Road's stalls present a dizzying variety of specialties, many of which retain a strong Chinese identity.

Another must-visit is Bang Rak, an ancient district of Bangkok with many immigrant inhabitants, who brought their own food cultures with them. These gradually amalgamated with traditional Thai cuisine to produce dishes such as roast duck, rice porridge, pork dumplings and green curry with roti.

In Bangkok's Old Town you'll encounter traditional Thai street food specialties that are difficult to find anywhere else. Legendary eatery Prachak Pet Yang, for example, is celebrated for its Chinese-style roast duck served with a dark, spicy sauce over rice. Around Khao San Road and Soi Rambuttri in the old district of the city, you'll find lots of options serving everything from fried rice to tom yum soup. Among the cheapest places to eat are the Khao Gaeng shops. Khao gaeng (curry rice) is an institution on the capital's streets; it is a selection of curries and stir-fries, any combination of which can be piled on to a plate of rice. Popular choices include gang kiew wan gai (green curry with chicken) and gaeng som goong (sour curry with shrimp).

Satay – meat threaded on bamboo sticks, grilled over an open flame and served with peanut sauce and ajad (pickled cucumber salad), shallots and chillies in sugar syrup – can be found everywhere you go. There's four key noodle varieties available: thick or thin rice noodles, bouncy egg noodles and mung bean noodles. A local version of Japanese sukiyaki, a wok-fried mixture of glass noodles, egg and seafood with chilli sauce abundantly pepped up with pickled garlic, is a Thai favourite. One of the city's most talented street cooks, Jae Fai on the Mahachai Road specializes in stir-fried noodle dishes; guay tiew pad kee mow (drunken spicy noodles) is especially recommended.

If you fancy something sweet, look out for lod chong, bright green rice flour noodles floating in glasses of chilled sweet coconut milk. Other delicious treats include khao niew mamuang (mango sticky rice) – a widely available and sublime combination of sweet, juicy mango with sticky rice and coconut cream – and – for the ultimate sugar hit – tong yord (round egg yolk tart). Egg yolk, sugar and flower water are boiled in sugar syrup and formed into small balls to create these lusciously sweet yellow snacks.

CHINATOWN BANGKOK

Yaowarat Road, the main thoroughfare that weaves through Bangkok's Chinatown — one of the city's most vibrant and lively neighbourhoods — is said to resemble a dragon's back, arching up to the head where 'heaven and earth meet'. And what an incredible, colourful, frenetic creature it is. Chinese traders settled here during the eighteenth century, and with easy access to the river for unloading their junks into warehouses, they quickly prospered. Today, Chinatown has grown into a hugely popular shopping and food destination for locals and visitors from across the globe.

The best way to experience Chinatown is to plunge into the network of narrow lanes that radiate out from the main streets. In the alleys of Trok Itsaranuphap, for example, shouting porters are laden with fish balls and huge ash melons. Elsewhere, street vendors proffer a profusion of edibles, from dried Chinese meats and waxed sausages to dried jujube (Chinese date) and persimmons. In Yaowarat, where fruit is a major attraction, imported cherries abound alongside the finest durian. The area is densely packed with vendors selling a host of different edibles: crab noodles, prawn wontons and fried rice; crunchy guava and green mango sold with sticky nam plaa waan sauce. Chestnuts roast in giant twisting cauldrons.

Chinatown is at its most enthralling at night. Pulsing neon signs illuminate the food stalls, woks ablaze along the entire length of the strip. Late in the evening, visitors seek out restorative soups such as kway chap, served with rolled rice noodles, blood cake and pork. And young Thais converge here for sweet treats including grilled bread rolls stuffed with fillings such as green pandan jam, peanut satay sauce or Thai tea-flavoured custard. LF

Where: 6 Yaowarat Road, Samphanthawong, Bangkok 10100
When: Daily, but the street food scene truly comes alive after sunset

1 Dried shrimp stall. 2 Crab noodles and prawn wontons.
3 Scabbard fish. 4 Spring rolls. 5 Shop selling goon chiang (Thai dried pork sausage). 6 Fruit, dried prawns, chilli, and fish sauce. 7 Array of dumplings. 8 Noodle soup to order.

RAAT NAR MUU

A popular Thai dish of noodles with pork and thickened gravy.

SERVES 2

Preparation: 10 minutes plus 2 hours marinating

Cooking: 10 minutes

For the pork:

1 tbsp soy sauce

1 tbsp oyster sauce

1 tbsp cornflour

85 g / 3 oz lean pork shoulder, sliced

For the rest of the dish:

3 tbsp vegetable oil

½ tbsp garlic, finely chopped

½ red chilli, sliced, to taste

A handful of torn Chinese kai lan or kale

1 tbsp soybean sauce

1 tsp fish sauce

2 tbsp oyster sauce

1 tsp caster sugar

250 ml / 9 fl oz water

30 g / 1 oz cornflour

2 large handfuls of fresh wide rice noodles

2 tbsp dark soy sauce

White pepper, to serve

- For the pork, mix together the soy sauce, oyster sauce and cornflour in a large bowl. Add the pork, stir well to coat and cover with cling film. Marinate in the fridge for at least 2 hours.
- In a large saucepan, heat 2 tbsp of the oil and add the garlic and chilli. Fry until fragrant, then add the pork. Stir-fry until almost cooked through, then add the kai lan, soybean sauce, fish sauce, oyster sauce, sugar and water. Slowly pour in the cornflour mixture (mixed with a little water to form a thin paste), stirring, until the sauce is thick and glossy.
- Heat a wok over a high heat. Spread the noodles over the base and up the sides, and cook without stirring until charred at the edges. Add the remaining oil and the dark soy sauce, then use a wok scoop or large spoon to turn and scrape the noodles off the bottom of the wok or pan. When brown and slightly dry, add to the pork mixture. Sprinkle with a dusting of white pepper.

9 Refresh and restore with medicinal tea.   10 Stall owner Pa Jeen.
11 Yaowarat by night.   12 Stewed goose with coriander, rice, steamed vegetables and chilli sauce.   13 Giant prawns.   14 Bread stuffed full of Thai jam.   15 Glazed suckling pig crackles over a *tao* (charcoal burner).

FOOD AND VENDOR HIGHLIGHTS

Try these Chinatown favourites if you can:

Hoy Kraeng Pa Jeen, Soi Texas road, has been running for more than forty years, winning acclaim for delicately boiled blood cockles and green-lipped mussels. Owner Pa Jeen and her son cheerfully dispense dipping sauces.

Lau Tang Lueh Chue Han Palo, 467/1 Yaowarat Road, is famous for goose, which is served stewed and sliced in a broth full of woody spices such as cassia and star anise. A sauce made with chilli, vinegar and lime juice refreshes the palate.

Nai Mong Hoi Tod, 539 Phlab Phla Chai Road, serves oyster omelettes (below) cooked over a charcoal fire fanned with a desk fan. Each omelette is cooked to order, soft or crunchy, with the saline pop of the freshest oysters.

Also not to be missed:

Khao man gai ivory white boiled chicken, jasmine rice and soup with dipping sauce

Patongko fried dough sticks with green pandan custard

Durian the king of fruits with a formidable aroma

Bami mu daeng wheat noodles with red roast pork

Bua loy nam king black sesame-filled dumplings in ginger broth

Satay chicken or pork skewers grilled and brushed with coconut cream

Gung ob wunsen aromatic baked prawns and glass noodles in a clay pot.

OR TOR KOR BANGKOK

Arguably Bangkok's finest fresh food market, Or Tor Kor is brimming with a dazzling selection of fresh produce brought in from the provinces of Thailand, as well as a squeaky-clean food court at one end. The main draw of the wet market is the incredible selection of live seafood: scallops in their shells, stacks of crab and huge bright blue river prawns chilling on ice are only a few examples of what you might find. Beautiful fruit and extremely fresh vegetables are abundant, with entire stalls dedicated to different cultivars of mango, fanned out from pale green to yellow and deep orange. This is nirvana for home cooks: neat bundles of ingredients such as lemongrass, galangal and kaffir lime leaves are available, ready to drop into classic dishes such as Tom Yum Soup.

Locals come here to buy gourmet gifts, too, such as premier cru fish sauce or pastel pink shrimp paste, the tiny black dots of the shrimp eyes an indicator of quality. Closer to the food court, past towering mounds of curry paste, there are cooked offerings: grilled prawns or pre-prepared blue swimmer crabs sold with dipping sauce, to sit and eat at the tables further on. There are plenty of snacks: tiny pastries, painstakingly crimped, with pineapple jam inside, as well as sticky purple rice steamed in bamboo canes. Or you can choose from an array of spicy nam priks (chilli sauces and pastes) featuring ingredients such as dried fish, chilli, crab and tamarind to eat with rice or vegetables. **LF**

Where: Kamphaengphet Road, Bangkok
When: Daily 6 a.m.–8 p.m.

HOI LAI PAD NAM PRIK PAO

Sweet, tangy and spicy with a hint of smokiness, the roasted chilli paste nam prik pao intensifies these clams with holy basil.

SERVES 2
Preparation: 10 minutes, plus
  20 minutes soaking
Cooking: 5 minutes
2 large handfuls clams or mussels, cleaned
1 tbsp vegetable oil

2 tbsp nam prik pao (chilli paste), plus 1 tbsp oil from the jar
1½ tbsp garlic, finely chopped
3 bird's-eye chillies, finely sliced
1 tbsp soybean sauce
1 tbsp fish sauce
A handful of fresh holy basil leaves

- Soak the clams or mussels in cold water for 20 minutes, then drain and rinse.
- Heat the vegetable oil and 1 tablespoon of nam prik pao oil in a large saucepan, then add the garlic and chillies. Cook until fragrant.
- Add the soybean sauce and clams. Stir-fry gently for one minute.
- Add the fish sauce and the rest of the nam prik pao and stir-fry for one more minute over a high heat, adding a splash or two of water to prevent sticking.
- Add the basil and cook until wilted. Serve immediately.

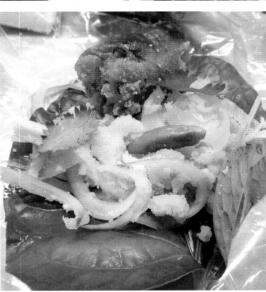
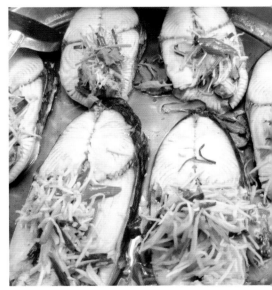

GAT LUANG MARKET

CHIANG MAI

In Chiang Mai, Thailand's northern capital, Gat Luang (which means huge market) encompasses Warorot and Ton Lam Yai markets, as well as the commercial market and a wholesale market selling ethnic clothing. It was once the centre of northern trade, attracting merchants from Burma, India and China, and trade to Bangkok began here, the packed barges making the long journey down the Ping River to the capital. Gat Luang has a great buzz: gossiping shopkeepers and porters dash between the markets and the river, at odds with the sleeping rickshaw drivers parked along the lanes.

It would be unthinkable for a Thai to return home from visiting Warorot without a giant sack of northern Thai delicacies: crispy pork rinds (kaab moo), relishes such as nam prik num made from roasted green chilli pounded with garlic and fermented fish sauce, and the crimson 'bolognese' sauce of roasted red tomatoes and minced pork. Dam Rong is perhaps the most famous of these altars to northern Thai food, with fat coils of herby Chiang Mai sausage (sai oua), fermented pork sausage (naem) and awesome flattened fried pork chops. Pass down rows of cellophaned dried fruits and giant discs of pressed chrysanthemum flowers for tea and you emerge among the fresh fruit. Ton Lam Yai sells all manner of culinary equipment, from sticky rice steamers to teak spoons. To the side is a long strip of wet market where you pass benches stinking with dried fish, then you emerge onto a street where fresh coconut milk is made. If you get there early enough in the morning, a vendor fries Chinese doughnuts (crullers) in the shape of dragons, dinosaurs and elephants. **LF**

Where: Chiang Moi Road, near the Ping River, Chiang Mai
When: Daily 5 a.m.–6 p.m.; the outside market stays open later, until 11 p.m.

1 Sweets and coconut juice – but don't be tempted to try as these are religious offerings.   2 Son-in-law eggs in tamarind sauce are a takeaway favourite.   3 Preparing a gigantic stir-fry with plently of colourful veg.   4 Order up!

5 Braised in wild honey, these meats are certainly fit for royalty.
6 Vibrantly coloured curries and stews lined up on a stall – be sure to ask which are mild and which spicy, unless you'd rather be surprised! 7 Bright lights and busy tables create a lively atmosphere.

NAM PRIK ONG

This popular northern Thai spicy dip pairs pork and tomato with chilli.

SERVES 2–3
Preparation: 20 minutes
Cooking: 20 minutes
For the nam prik:
12 dried long red chillies, deseeded and soaked in water until soft
1 tbsp sea salt
2 tbsp chopped lemongrass (white inner stem)
5 tbsp garlic, chopped
5 tbsp shallots, chopped
2 discs of tua nao (fermented soybean cake), roasted over an open flame until slightly darkened (some shrimp paste can be used instead but check for saltiness)
150 g/5½ oz minced pork
650 g/1lb 7 oz cherry tomatoes (sour or unripe ones are better)
4 tbsp vegetable oil or lard
Tamarind juice, if needed

To serve:
Steamed duck eggs
Pork rinds
Vegetables
Coriander leaves

- Using a pestle and mortar, pound the chillies and salt until they form a smooth paste. Add the lemongrass and continue pounding. Add four tablespoons of the garlic, the shallots and fermented soybean cake and pound until fine. Mix in the pork and tomatoes.
- Add the oil or lard to a frying pan and fry the remaining garlic on medium heat until golden. Add the nam prik mix and fry over a low heat. Continue stirring for about 20 minutes until it is sticky and a deep, dark red; add a little water if it dries out too much. It should just start to separate. It should taste a little sour; if not, add a little tamarind juice.
- Cool and serve with steamed duck eggs, pork rinds and a selection of vegetables such as cucumber, fresh coriander leaves and boiled pumpkin.

FOOD AND VENDOR HIGHLIGHTS

Pork rinds – **kaep muu** – come in great puffy tangled strips, ending in crunchy curls with a cheeky nub of fat hiding underneath. Dip them in **nam prik num**, a green chilli relish. The frying process can be observed taking place in giant bubbling woks in the darkest section of Ton Lam Yai market. Northern Thai food uses lots of dry spices, particularly in the minced meat dish known as **laap**, which differs from the laap found elsewhere in Thailand. The dry spices are sold neatly presented in wooden boxes and pre-mixed laap powder can be bought featuring the elusive Thai long pepper **dee-plee**, papery dill seed and the lemon-scented pepper **makwan,** a cousin of Sichuan pepper.

About halfway down the centre aisle in Warorot market, a lady sells **roasted pork ribs with wild honey**. These roasted ribs are so famous that Thai Airways occasionally fly them down to the palaces in Bangkok at royal request.

Every morning a stall on the corner of Wichaynon Road sells soy milk and deep-fried Chinese crullers (doughnuts, below) in the shape of dinosaurs and various animals that are a breakfast favourite. Get some regular chromosome-shaped ones to dip into wobbly pandan custard and condensed milk while you wait for your preferred animal.

1 Bright and bustling: the high ceilings and many windows are part of the experience at Central Market. 2 Food is on sale alongside souvenirs, clothing, shoes and a diverse range of wares. 3 Delicious pastries sprinkled with sesame seeds.

CENTRAL MARKET

PHNOM PENH

The ziggurat pyramid structure of Phsar Thmei is a paean to art deco architecture and provides an unlikely home to Phnom Penh's busy Central Market. Centrally located in Cambodia's capital, it feels more like a cathedral than a market in one of South East Asia's poorer cities – when it opened in 1937, it was believed to be the largest market in Asia. A renovation programme by the French Development Agency was completed in 2010. The domed central building is home to a vast warren of stalls, from which four branches of market space radiate outwards. It feels light and airy inside, thanks to the high ceilings and numerous windows.

Pushing through crowds of shoppers, it's easy to spot clusters of pink stools in the centre of the market, where Cambodians crouch as they slurp bowls of hot fragrant noodles. Hawkers line the square around Phsar Thmei, providing relief for shoppers to rest their feet and fill up on snacks. Shoppers trade Cambodian rial for small plastic carrier bags filled with soup stock to carry home, while bouquets of seasoning – chopped limes, sliced chillies, smashed lemongrass and galangal tied with an elastic band and ready to throw into a bubbling soup – are sold ready made. Fast food at its freshest – everything from avocados to deep-fried crickets – is slurped, gulped and chewed by a crowd of Cambodians on the go.

Ruled by the French from 1863 to 1953, Cambodia's food bears more than a passing resemblance to Gallic cuisine. Numpang pâté is like Vietnamese banh mi – meat or egg in a baguette, doused with chilli sauce, crunchy cucumber and fish sauce. Frogs are widely eaten (thanks to the country's network of freshwater rivers and lakes) and snails scooped up in a bowl, drenched in fragrant garlic sauce are a delicacy. **ER**

Where: Neayok Souk, Phnom Penh 855
When: Daily 7 a.m.–6 p.m.

KUY TEAV

This aromatic beef noodle soup is a breakfast dish in Cambodia.

SERVES 4
Preparation: 20 minutes
Cooking: 2 hours
For the broth:
2 litres/3½ pints beef stock
1 onion, peeled and quartered
1 tbsp coriander seeds
1 piece cassia bark (or a cinnamon stick)
3 star anise
1 tbsp sugar
1 tbsp soy sauce
5 tbsp fish sauce
1 chilli, including seeds
To finish:
4 tbsp vegetable oil

4 garlic cloves
200 g/7 oz sirloin steak, thinly sliced
1 tbsp fish sauce
4 leaves pak choi or Chinese cabbage, shredded
2 spring onions, finely chopped
Juice of 1 lime
Sugar, to taste
1 tbsp sriracha (or quality hot chilli sauce)
To serve:
Cooked rice noodles
Beansprouts
To garnish:
Lime slices
Handful of chopped fresh coriander

- For the broth, put all the ingredients into a pan and bring to the boil. Cover, and simmer on a low heat for 1 to 2 hours. Taste and season with more fish sauce, chilli or sugar as needed.
- Press the broth through a sieve and reserve the liquid.
- Heat the oil in a wok or deep frying pan, add the garlic and cook until golden. Add the steak, fish sauce, pak choi, spring onions, lime juice, sugar and sriracha and fry until cooked.
- Ensure the broth is hot, and add a portion of rice noodles and beansprouts to the bottom of each bowl. Top with the beef mixture, and pour over a ladleful of broth. Garnish with lime and coriander.

1 A butcher sells various cuts of meat. 2–3 Baby squid impaled on sticks make an eye-catching snack. 4–5 Roasted and stir-fried meats sprinkled with peanuts and coriander. 6 Mouth-watering aromatic pho. 7 Giving fast food a new meaning!

VAN KIEP STREET SAIGON

Saigon, Vietnam's biggest city, is a ravenously hungry one. It is so obsessed by food that it is best thought of as one huge alfresco food court. Street after street of food hawkers create aromatic dishes from grilled quail to sautéed basil leaves. Van Kiep Street perfectly captures the spirit of the city's food lanes. It is currently *the* fashionable place, oozing a shabby cachet not dissimilar to London's Camden Market or Bangkok's Khao San. At Van Kiep Street you can explore Vietnamese cuisine from around one hundred different outlets. From early in the morning vendors start firing up their hobs ready to feed street food junkies.

There are few places to find a better local breakfast of op la. The dish is made cowboy style in a metallic pot with an array of ham, pork, caramelized onions and topped with an egg, which is then mopped up with baguette. By evening you're likely to see street performers descend on Van Kiep, crooning out karaoke. Neon lights up crowds hunching over plastic tables gobbling up street food specialties. They include Saigon's signature pork patties, similar to a mini burger, grilled over a mesh. Grilled quails and chicken are also prevalent, although the current on-trend dish is grilled octopus – this is best found at the Quán Út Lang stall. A wave of stalls sell bun mam (fermented fish noodle soup) at the intersection of Phan Xich Long. Locally, the dish is known as 'Mekong in a bowl' because it crams in just about every food that comes from the river delta – prawns, noodles, fish cakes and pork compete for your taste buds, with a side of greens. Another classic local fish dish is banh canh cua, a hearty broth made from udon noodles and shrimp that will fill you in one sitting. This is best found at 63 Van Kiep. Other curious delicacies include ca kho to, a dish of catfish braised in a caramel sauce that is served in a clay pot. Delicious gui coan (summer rolls) and myriads of pho (soups) and banh mi (Vietnames baguette) are also in abundance in this thrilling exhibition of Vietnamese street food. AJ

Where: Van Kiep Street (border of Phú Nhuan and Bình Thanh districts)
When: Daily 7 a.m.–11 p.m.

CENTRAL MARKET HANOI

Vietnam has rapidly become an epicentre of international cuisine. Influences from Japan, France and China converge here in a culinary explosion of street food and Hanoi's Central Market (known locally as Cho Hoi An) is the ideal place to come and enjoy this country's wonderful flavours. The market became a street food hub after the old quarter of Hanoi was declared a UNESCO World Heritage Site in 2010. The city's side-street noodle carts then moved here in a bid to 'clean up' the city, much to the dismay of food lovers who thought it less authentic.

Yet the market remains authentic enough and reveals a behind-the-scenes slice of Vietnam's gastro culture. There are live fish, giant shrimps and crabs in tanks and basins, squawking live hens and ducks. Bamboo baskets are loaded with spices, pulses and noodles. It's a herb lover's dream: the aroma of freshly picked basil, aniseed, coriander and Vietnamese lemon mint perfume the air. There are five main street food dishes to look out for. The undisputed champion is cau lao – *al dente* noodles served in a

pork broth, topped with crispy noodle squares. It's a Hanoi specialty and the market is legendary for creating the best. Another is gourmet baguette banh mi, reputed to be the world's best here. The pork-filled white rose dumpling (banh bao banh vac) is a must-try local delicacy, as are the sticks of BBQ chicken or pork. Another Hanoi classic is the ginger chicken rice dish, com ga.

A few insider tips: go to the market early in the morning. It is more chilled, there is space to take pictures and traders are less aggressive. More importantly, the food is fresher; noon is the best time for lunch. Wear shoes, not flip flops, as it is not uncommon to be in line of a splash of chicken blood. **AJ**

Where: Tran Quý Cáp, Minh An, Cho Hoi An, Quang Nam
When: Daily 8 a.m.–7 p.m.

1 The distinctive bright yellow market facade.   2 A variety of rice noodles on sale.   3 Local snacks sandwiched between banana leaves.   4 A vendor bagging up Vietnamese pickles.
5 Prawns and noodles in translucent rice wrappers.

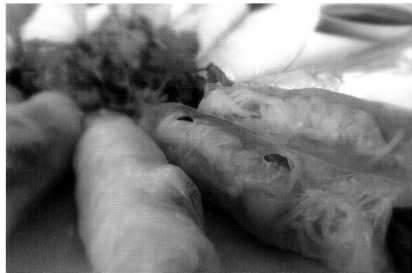

6 7 8

6 Flavourful fresh herbs and leafy vegetables are an integral part of Vietnamese cuisine.   **7** Some sell from bicycles, others from baskets on wooden supports, carried over the shoulder.   **8** Banh tet on sale – cylindrical sticky rice cakes, rolled in banana leaves and boiled.

BANH XEO

The recipe for these crispy pancakes is from chef Jonathan Villar.

SERVES 2

Preparation: 15 minutes, plus
  30 minutes standing

Cooking: 15 minutes

For the pancakes:

350 g/ 12 oz rice flour

1 tbsp baking powder

2 tbsp turmeric

50 ml/2 fl oz sunflower oil

450 ml/16 fl oz water

1 tsp chilli powder

4 eggs

For the filling:

150 ml/5 fl oz vegetable oil

100 g/3½ oz shallots, finely chopped

3 garlic cloves, chopped

1 carrot, grated

300 g/10½ oz prawns, minced

2 lemongrass stalks, grated

3 kaffir leaves, finely chopped

2 tbsp grated galangal

1 tsp chopped fresh mint

2 tbsp chopped fresh coriander

4 tbsp Thai fish sauce

3 tbsp brown sugar

4 red chillies

1 tbsp tamarind paste

Chopped peanuts, to garnish

- For the pancakes, whisk all the ingredients together to form a smooth batter. Set aside for at least 30 minutes.
- Heat a little oil in a non-stick frying pan and fry a quarter of the batter at a time to make four thin pancakes. Fry until golden and crispy. Set aside.
- For the filling, heat the oil in a pan, add the shallots and garlic and cook gently for 3 minutes. Add the remaining ingredients and stir-fry until the prawns are cooked. Spoon the prawns on to each pancake, fold over and secure with a skewer, topped with a red chilli. Drizzle cooking liquid and top with tamarind paste and chopped peanuts.

VENDOR SPOTLIGHT

Vendors are constantly hustling visitors to sample their food, with the expression, 'You want cau lao?' (the market special). Most vendors have the same menus and are found in the middle aisle. Gastro legend Anthony Bourdain has proclaimed that vendors here offer the best in the world. Stalls that consistently stand up to such acclaim include: **Pho, Cao Lau, Hu Tieu, Kinh Moi** (look for the blue-and-white sign; pork noodles, below, are recommended); **Miss Thuy's** is one of the latest favourites, and she also runs cooking classes. **Be Na Café** has great English explanations of the kind of foods on offer and fantastic spring rolls. Less hectic is **Liet's**, located on the outer rim of the market. Barbecued meat sticks are exquisitely grilled at **Bale Well**. For banh mi, visit **Tiem Banh Mi Phuong** – meats are prepared fresh and a 'secret sauce' added. Expect queues.

KIMBERLEY STREET HAWKER STALLS GEORGE TOWN

The original pearl of the orient, Penang is a fantasia for food lovers. The history of the island is one of abundant wealth. As a major hub for maritime trade down the Strait of Malacca (gold, spices, rubber, opium and the island's crops of nutmeg and areca or betel nut), it attracted merchants the world over. This faded glory can be seen most vividly in the capital of George Town — in its colonial mansions, incense-clouded Chinese clan houses and Hindu temples. Street names such as Lebuh Armenian and Lorong Ceylon are a reminder of the ethnic mix. Special mention must go to Penang's Babas, Chinese middlemen made wealthy as go-betweens for the colonial British and Malay labourers, who took local wives (plural) or Nyonyas. Each wife would compete for the husband's affection with evermore complicated dishes using Chinese cooking techniques together with Thai and Malaysian ingredients like pink torch ginger flower and lemongrass. Baba-Nyonya rituals and discerning standards are still gloriously manifest in the food of Penang today.

The main cultures today are Chinese, Malay and Indian, and food can be a melding of the homeland's respective provinces. It is normal to have a Cantonese chee cheong chok — thick rice porridge with pork and chitterlings for breakfast; fragrant nasi lemak, Malay coconut rice wrapped in a banana leaf for lunch; and a Tamil-style fishhead curry for dinner. Kimberley Street is a good starting point to get an insight into George Town's complex cuisine; centrally located in the UNESCO heritage zone, hawkers pop up at all hours. Evening is the best time to go — a pyrotechnic display of wok wizardry, twisting curls of satay and a tangle of plastic stools under neon. ER

Where: Kimberley Street, 10100 George Town, Penang
When: Varies but most daily (some close on Thursday) 4 p.m. until late

6 Sticky and succulent char siu (roast pork), ready to enjoy. 7 Rojak is a fruit and vegetable salad liberally dressed with sweet sauce and peanuts. 8 Pork offal porridge is prepared, known locally as chee cheong chok. 9 Appetizing pork satays. 10 Radish cakes, served in banana leaf.

CHEE CHEONG FUN

These simple rice noodle rolls are served for breakfast in the hawker centres and dim sum joints of George Town.

SERVES 3

Preparation: 10 minutes

Cooking: 5 minutes

3 ready-made rice rolls (available in the chilled section of Chinese supermarkets)

For the sauce:

2 tbsp petis udang (prawn sauce)

2 tbsp kicap manis (sweet soy sauce)

Water (to thin consistency to a thick pourable syrup)

For the garnish:

1 handful of red shallots, shallow fried until crisp

1 tbsp dried shrimp, dry fried until firm, then blended or pounded to a fine powder. Alternatively crumbled dried salted anchovies

3 tbsp light soy sauce mixed with sugar for drizzling

Good quality chilli sauce (to serve)

- Follow the packet instructions for steaming the rolls. Combine the ingredients for the sauce and stir well. Thin with a little water if necessary.
- Loosely arrange and unfurl the steamed rice rolls on a plate, generously cover with the sauce and top with crispy shallots and dried shrimp powder or crumbled dried anchoves. Finish with a spoonful of chilli sauce.

FOOD HIGHLIGHTS

It's getting quite hard to find **ban chiang kuih** made the traditional way with charcoal, but you can find these delicious griddled pancakes (below) on the corner of Kimberley and Cintra streets every morning. Toppings include crushed peanuts with sugar, sweetcorn and egg. The long-serving auntie and uncle tending to the charcoal are fascinating to watch. It is hard to miss **duck koay chap** as the long queue at Restoran Kimberley snakes through the plastic tables and chairs of the hawker stalls at night. The dish uses home-made, flat rice noodles that roll into wobbly straws in the rich duck meat broth. They were originally designed to resemble pork intestines, which is what this dish is traditionally made from. Packed full of duck meat, it is delicately salty with soy and fragrant from woody spices such as anise and cinnamon. You can find two types of **fresh nutmeg juice** here – red and white. It is often served with a dried salted plum when iced and is the perfect foil for oily food. Two hawkers sell the fried rice cake known as **char koay kak** both day and night on Kimberley and Cintra streets. They manically flip cubes of shredded daikon (winter radish) and tapioca flour, mixed with dark soy sauce, beansprouts, chilli sauce and egg, in giant flat pans. It is only made tastier by the smoky lard and woodsmoke.

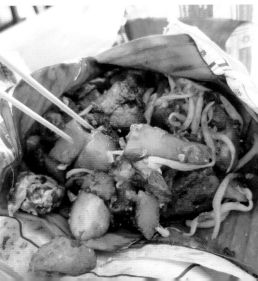

JALAN ALOR

KUALA LUMPUR

Stepping on to Jalan Alor is to encounter the beating heart of Kuala Lumpur's vibrant and diverse street food life. It's a bustling street with heaps of character and packed tight with hawkers selling all sorts of delicious snacks – from choose-your-own skewers and fragrant noodle dishes to exotic dishes such as frog porridge and pungent fresh durian fruit. Locally dubbed 'Wai Sek Kai', which means 'Glutton Road', you'll need to bring a mighty appetite in order to try it all. Jalan Alor is located right next to another favourite hangout spot called Changkat Bukit Bintang, which draws the local and tourist crowds with its selection of trendy bars, clubs and restaurants. After having one too many drinks it's almost a tradition for Changkat nocturnal party animals to head down to Jalan Alor to cure their hunger wants and needs. Once better known as the Malaysian capital's red light district, now, when the lights go down on Jalon Alor, it's the best place in town for all sorts of Malay street food. It originally began with a humble chicken wing stall but has burgeoned into one of the world's busiest food destinations. As well as Malay delicacies, you'll also find Chinese, Thai and Indian cuisines: from sticky sweet, well-charred chicken wings to butter prawns, lala soup (clam soup) and all manner of seafood and fruits. After sunset the entire street becomes one giant open-air restaurant with stalls and restaurants providing seating that dominates the entirety of the roadsides, while lanterns cast a genial glow on the proceedings. Rival vendors will call out to you as you stroll along the street as you decide what takes your fancy in Kuala Lumpur's food haven. **JW**

Where: Jalan Alor, Bukit Bintang, 50200 Kuala Lumpur
When: Daily until late; best to venture there after 5 p.m. for the stalls but restaurants are open regular hours

1 Lanterns lead the public to this street food hub. 2 Hungry customers. 3 Cooking with a naked flame. 4 Look out for chicken rice, famously cooked in clay pots, so that the bottom layer of rice forms a layer of crispy, fragrant crust.

VENDOR SPOTLIGHT

One of the most beloved eateries on Jalan Alor is **Wong Ah Wah** (below), famed for their mouth-watering barbecued chicken wings, which can't be missed thanks to Mickey Mouse sitting proudly on the signage. Their wings are chargrilled until the skin is blackened and crispy and the meat moist and juicy. You'll find variations of these marinated, grilled chicken wings in most parts of the street, but these are the only ones you must try. A not-to-be-missed noodle eatery on Jalan Alor is **Uncle Lim Pan Mee**, which has operated for more than thirty years. Tease your taste buds with a bowl of this traditional Malaysian dish cooked with hand-made noodles, mushrooms, fried dried anchovies and vegetables. Run by the second generation, the fish ball noodles stall nestled in **Chua Brother Coffee Shop** has been around for more than fifty years. Locals like to flock to this stall for its delicious noodle soup with fish balls, fish cake slices, fish dumplings, bean sprouts and fried pork lard. The bouncy fish balls are hand made by the owner using high-quality fish hand picked at the wet market daily.

MALAYSIAN CHICKEN WINGS

These sticky, sweet wings are a Jalan Alor institution.

SERVES 3–4 (10–12 WINGS)
Preparation: 10 minutes, plus
   12 hours marinating
Cooking: 25 minutes
For the marinade:
5 shallots, finely chopped
5 cloves garlic, finely chopped
5-cm/2-in. piece of root ginger, peeled and chopped into small pieces
1 tsp dark soy sauce
5 tsp regular soy sauce
3 dashes white pepper
3 dashes sesame oil
Sugar and salt (to taste)
10–12 chicken wings

- Combine the ingredients for the marinade and coat the chicken wings, ideally leaving for up to 12 hours.
- Preheat the grill or oven to 150°C/300°F/gas mark 2.
- Cook under the grill until cooked through or for 25 minutes in the oven.

1 The food hall beckons. 2 Breakfast of fried bee hoon, made with rice vermicelli noodles. 3 Swing by Zhen Zhen for authentic local cuisine. 4 Wok hei, or 'breath of the wok', is a taste sensation. 5 Order up! Plating Hainan chicken and bok choi.

MAXWELL ROAD HAWKER FOOD CENTRE SINGAPORE

The Maxwell Road Hawker Food Centre in Singapore's Chinatown is a favourite haunt of foodies for its enormous variety of delicious and affordable dishes, especially its celebrated Chinese meals, which are rarely found in other markets in the surrounding area. The site was originally established in the 1950s as a wet market. In the 1980s, the market was converted into a temporary hawker centre. The site was then renovated in early 2000 and finally reopened in May 2001 as a food centre.

Start the day at Maxwell Road with a breakfast of roti john (bread fried with egg, beef or mutton, served with chilli sauce) or roti prata (fried Indian pancake with curry). Fish – particularly the esteemed fish-head curry – is hugely popular here. However, the most renowned food to be found on this street is Hainan chicken rice, which is also probably the most famous dish in the country.

The best is reputed to be from Tian Tian Hainan Chicken Rice (stalls 10 and 11), which local foodies have voted the best Hainan chicken rice stall in Singapore. Tian Tian has even attracted the attention of internationally known chefs such as Anthony Bourdain and Gordon Ramsay. The stall is open from 11 a.m. to 8 p.m. (closed on Mondays) or until they sell out. Be prepared to queue, however. MQF

Where: 11 South Bridge Road, Singapore 058656
When: Varies by each stall, so best to check sources locally

6 Fare for adventurous eaters — braised pig's trotter and pig's tail soup.
7 Local delicacies including century eggs — preserved in a clay mixture, they turn a dark green colour. 8 Help yourself to cockles. 9 Chicken is the star dish here. 10 Asian 'Western food' is popular in food courts.

HAINAN CHICKEN RICE

This Chinese dish has become a much-loved Malaysian culinary staple.

SERVES 2

Preparation: 20 minutes

Cooking: 1 hour

1 chicken, about 1.25 kg/2 lb 12 oz

10 g/¼ oz root ginger

6 spring onions, chopped

For the sauce:

150 ml/5 fl oz water

1 tsp sugar

2 tsp dark soy sauce

2 garlic cloves, finely chopped

1 chilli, finely chopped

2½–3 tsp root ginger, chopped

For the rice:

1 tbsp vegetable oil

250 g/9 oz rice

2½–3 tsp root ginger, chopped

1 tbsp water

½ cucumber, peeled and sliced, to serve

- Rub the chicken skin with the ginger and season with salt.
- Pour enough water into a large pan to cover the chicken. Add 2 spring onions and the ginger and bring to the boil.
- Put the chicken into the pan, reduce the heat to a simmer, cover and cook for about 25 minutes until cooked through.
- Remove the chicken and immerse it in cold water for 5 minutes. Drain the chicken in a colander (reserving the stock) before cutting into serving pieces.
- For the sauce, put the water and sugar in a pan and slowly bring to the boil. Add the soy sauce and boil until thickened. Add the garlic, chilli and ginger.
- For the rice, heat the oil in a pan and add the rice, remaining spring onions, ginger and water. Cook for 5 minutes. Add the chicken stock, bring to the boil and cook for 15 to 20 minutes.
- Spoon the rice onto serving plates and top with the chicken pieces and sauce. Serve with cucumber slices on the side.

VENDOR SPOTLIGHT

Must-try stalls at Maxwell Street Hawker Food Centre include **Zhen Zhen Porridge** (stall 54), where the legendary thick porridge (above) is packed with chicken, fish or vegetables and century egg. The latter is a preserved egg with a translucent, jelly-like, dark greenish-black white and creamy bluish-green yolk, with a slightly cheesy flavour. Another bestseller here is yu sheng rice porridge, which is garnished with raw fish slices. **Hua Sliced Fish Bee Hoon** (stall 77) sells a crowd-pleasing favourite — Cantonese-style fish-head bee hoon soup with chunks of tasty fried fish that soak up the thick soup. The Fuzhou oyster cake is rapidly becoming a rarity, so don't miss sampling this crunchy peanut-topped, crisp fried snack with a filling of oysters and minced pork from **Maxwell Fuzhou Oyster Cake** (stall 5). Another very popular eating place is **China Street Fritters** (stall 64), who offer a wonderful variety of deep-fried prawn fritters, fish cakes, five-spice pork rolls (ngoh hiang) and more. It's well worth stopping by.

囻豬脚
Braised Pig's Trotter
$4.00

猪尾汤
Pig's Tail Soup
$5.00 / $6.00

五香
MEAT ROLL

皮旦
CENTURY EGG

豆子
BEAN CURD

豬干卷
LIVER ROLL

魚
FISH

CHICKEN
WHOLE $24

ROASTED CHICKEN
半只 HALF $12

HAWKER
FOOD

鲜·鲜蛤
H & COCKLE

B

曬嗳·尤魚·油條·豆卜
ROJAK · CUTTLEFISH · YOU TIAO · TAU PO

$3/$5/$7/$8

SELF-SERVICE THANK YOU
自助服務

鲜 蛤
COCKLE
$3/$5

1 Master of the coals – chargrilled chicken satays.   2–3 Perfecting a laksa broth is a fine art, use coconut milk to thicken.   4 Roast pork belly with preserved vegetables on rice.   5 You'll be back for seconds of local specialty fish-head curry.   6 Moreish kebabs.

EAST COAST LAGOON MARKET SINGAPORE

Singapore is a country where small indulgences are often taxed or banned, but when it comes to food, it is all about hedonism. Street food even has its own official place of worship – the hawker centre. Most scenic of all is East Coast Lagoon, perhaps the only street food market on the planet that is located on a beach. The main draws are the bargain prices and variety: you can eat your way through the cuisines of the world here. Although it is packed at weekends, there are more than 120 vendors and you are guaranteed to find a dish you've never heard of before.

The fish-head curry is more delectable than it sounds. The head of a snapper is stewed in an Indian-style broth with aubergine and okra. Try the booth at Eastern Red Seafood, which has twenty years' experience perfecting this culinary art form. Local crowds also flock here to munch their way through a seemingly endless rotation of chicken wings and satay. Haron Satay serve home-made peanut sauce and are generous on the chargrilled meat. For chicken wings try Ah Hwee, which is famed for its crisp, charcoal-blackened skin, yielding to tender meat. The stall has operated since the market opened in 1978 and is also rated for barbecue pork noodles.

More unusual curiosities include oyster omelette and fried oyster dishes, of which this market promises the best in town. Song Kee Fried Oyster Bar has perfected the tricky balance of texture. Top of the most wanted list for many visitors, however, is Char Kway Teow, a flavoursome mix of noodles, cockles and bean sprouts in a special sauce. If you're a fresh fish lover, barbecued stingray – a slab of chargrilled fish smothered in sauce and served on a banana leaf – is the top treat at East Coast BBQ booth. You'll leave hooked on a dish you'd never ever tasted before. AJ

Where: 1220 East Coast Parkway, Singapore, 468960
When: Daily 8 a.m.–9 p.m.

JALAN PECENONGAN JAKARTA

When dusk falls, culinary adventures commence at Jalan Pecenongan. The side-street dining areas start to set up shop. Mobile dining carts move in and the stoves and charcoal grills are fired up. Jalan Pecenongan is a designated area for *wisata kuliner* (culinary tourism). There is an emphasis on fish and Chinese-influenced dishes, but you'll also find national delicacies here like nasi goreng (Indonesian fried rice), of which there must be getting on for about one hundred different versions, as well as rarities. Among them is martabak, an Indonesian pancake stuffed with unusual sweet buttery fillings. There are abundant seafood grills and a curious type of Chinese rice porridge that is surprisingly tasty, despite some of the unexpected additions such as raw eggs, tofu and fish.

This is one spot in the Muslim capital of Jakarta where you can grab pork. Grill stations charcoal sate babi (pork satay) to perfection, along with tasty pork ribs. Other meats that end up skewered on a satay include goat (sate kambing) and all manner

of animal guts. There is a fascination here with using all kinds of innards in meat dishes. Jakarta is the birthplace of beef soto betawi, a rich beefy broth, but you can request it without (or *tanpa babat*). Soto betawi is surprisingly addictive, especially when topped with fried shallots that give a crunchy texture, to be mopped up with clumps of sticky rice.

When it comes to eating food at Jalan Pecenongan, always ask for less spice. Otherwise your server will assume you can handle it like the locals, who have a titanium-proof resistance to even the fiercest chilli. **AJ**

Where: Between Jalan Pecenongan, Kebon Kelapa, Gambir, Kota Jakarta Pusat and Daerah Khusus Ibukota, Jakarta 10120

When: Daily open 24 hours

1 Tending to banana fritters in a giant wok.   2 Kari bihun medan (rice noodle curry).   3 Deep-fried sweetmeats.   4 Nasi goreng served with crunchy fish crackers.   5 Preparing traditional Indonesian fruit salad.

6 Sweet treats are a welcome dessert after a meat feast of rich satay.
7 How can you possibly choose just one dish with food this succulent?
8 Indonesian egg curry – order sambal goreng telur to flavour this dish.   9 Vendors are barely visible over stacks of plated fried meats.

NASI GORENG

This staple dish, meaning 'fried rice', is synonymous with Indonesia.

SERVES 1

Preparation: 15 minutes

Cooking: 5 minutes

1 tbsp vegetable oil	175 g/6 oz cooked
1 small onion, finely chopped	basmati rice
½ tsp chilli powder, or to taste	1 tbsp fish sauce
2 garlic cloves, crushed	1 tbsp soy sauce
1 carrot, grated	Salt and pepper, to taste
½ small Savoy cabbage, shredded	1 large egg
	1 tsp chilli sauce
	1 lime wedge
	2 tbsp crispy fried shallots

- Heat the oil in a wok on high heat. Add the onion and chilli powder and cook for 3–4 minutes until softened and lightly caramelized. Stir in the garlic for 1 minute.
- Toss in the grated carrot and shredded cabbage, stir-frying for 1–2 minutes. Add the cooked rice and stir to heat through thoroughly. Pour in the fish sauce, soy sauce and some salt and pepper. Create a well in the middle of the wok and crack in the egg. Fry until the white is almost set.
- Serve the rice in a large bowl, with the egg on top. Drizzle with chilli sauce and a squeeze of lime juice. Sprinkle with the crispy fried shallots.

VENDOR SPOTLIGHT

The many Chinese-influenced eateries at Jalan Pecenongan ease you in gently to Indonesian cuisine. **Garden Ayam Kodok** has specialties of grilled fish or seafood fried rice that far surpass the Western takeaway equivalent. Or perhaps be more adventurous with deep-fried frog legs.

Nasi Uduk Sri Rostika is the best bet for finding classic dishes like nasi uduk and nasi goreng, plus a variety of satays (above). The place described as legendary for satay (although pricier than most) is **Kedai Sate Babi Krekot**. The main items offered here are lean meat satay, pork skin satay and a pork bone tea soup. What distinguishes this place is the tender meat and the bizarre, yet tasty, additional cuts of meat. The champion is a pork liver satay. Liver is wrapped with a thin, fatty tissue, giving it a succulent moist texture contrast to the charred crispiness. No peanut sauce here, however.

For the signature dessert of Indonesia, martabak, head to number **43 Pecenongan** for sweet pancakes with malted chocolate and other favourites. You'll find 24-hour dining at the city's favourite Chinese porridge house, **Bubur Kwang Tang**. Unlike any other porridge, these bowls come with just about every add-on, from eels to eggs.

10 Intriguing and eye-catching fruit desserts are neatly lined up, promising welcome refreshment to marketgoers.

JALAN SABANG JAKARTA

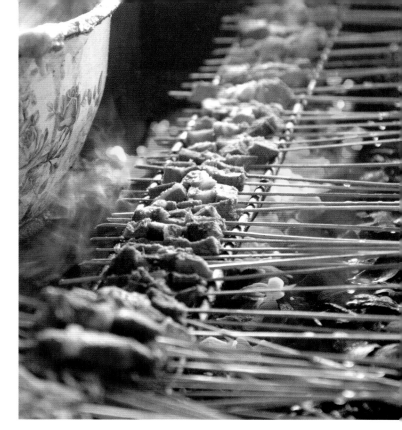

Street food dining is probably one of the most authentic ways of mingling with the locals in central Jakarta, not to mention the tastiest. The area known as Jalan Sabang is probably the Indonesian capital's finest example of this social experience, where tastes, beliefs and appetites meet over unpretentious plates of edible joy twenty-four hours a day. Eating out at a street stall is as common here as eating at home. At Jalan Sabang, you're sure to rub shoulders with locals as you tuck into endless skewers of satay chicken. Jalan Sabang is a street that is fast becoming renowned for grilling the best meats in town and competition to serve the best peanut sauce is fierce. Originally a dish from Java, the art of satay has been mastered in Jakarta, and if white meat seems too commonplace, goat satay kebabs offer a heartier alternative. The other dishes you're guaranteed to find here are nasi uduk (rice cooked in coconut milk), pecel lele (deep-fried catfish), ayam bakar (chargrilled chicken), mie goreng (fried noodles) and nasi goreng (fried rice).

One street plate oddity that's been refined in Jakarta is the peculiarly named brain brain fish (otak-otak). Essentially it's a 'brain texture' fish cake wrapped in banana leaf then grilled over charcoal to impart a smoky flavour. When matched with the local peanut sauce, it creates a taste explosion. Another lesser-known specialty is nasi padang, essentially a meze-style mix of dishes that come served with rice together with gulai hati (cow liver) and udang balado (chilli shrimp) for a mini banquet. Sabang does Jakarta's best street stall version at Rumah Makan Garuda.

Some fear that Sabang's street food culture could soon die out as it is becoming more difficult for hawkers to acquire licences to trade on the city's pavements. Added to this, upwardly mobile locals believe it is more modern to head to overpriced shopping malls rather than eat on the streets of Jakarta. The time to go there is now and hopefully the tradition will continue. AJ

Where: Jalan Sabang, near Sarinah department store, Jakarta

When: Hours vary, but most stalls open all day, every day

1 Glutinous rice-stuffed suckling pig satisfies any appetite.   2 On Friday nights the market buzzes with activity.   3 Takoyaki balls are filled with minced octopus or tempura scraps.   4 Mixed grill shawarma is served in this international market.   5 Try one or more of these salty snacks.

MERCATO CENTRALE MANILA

Right in the centre of the business district is perhaps not where you would expect to find Manila's most popular night market, but Mercato Centrale is completely at home beneath the soaring skyscrapers of Bonifacio Global City (BGC). The market has been filling the bellies of eager patrons from all over the metropolis of Metro Manila since 2010, although it has only been at its current BGC location since 2015. The rules have remained the same since day one: home-based businesses only and no duplicates. Expect lovingly cooked, distinctive dishes as a result.

With an influential Filipino food blogger at the helm, Mercato Centrale's following was instant and has been growing ever since. Local office workers and Manileños from all over the city spill into the open-air plot to devour everything from Hungarian hot dogs

to Indonesian fish cakes and a chocolate churro or three. Here you'll find global food from Mexico to Japan. Be warned, spare seats can sometimes be scarce – particularly on Friday paydays. Thankfully, in true Manila style, Mercato Centrale is a late-night affair (closing time is 3 a.m.), so you can afford to sip a San Miguel beer on the sidelines and scout out a prime spot.

If the brightly lit vendor canopies and live bands aren't enough of a giveaway of where to find this urban haunt, look out for the giant astronaut mural (by Los Angeles art duo Cyrcle) that hovers overhead. Mercato Centrale's success has seen it expand from its flagship BGC location into pop-ups all over Metro Manila. LH
Where: Corner of 25th Street and 7th Avenue, Bonifacio Global City
When: Thursday to Saturday, 6 p.m. – 3 a.m.

AUNTIE MAY'S BEEF SALPICAO
This original family recipe, which uses Aberdeen Angus beef, has been voted the best home-made salpicao in Manila.

SERVES 4
Preparation: 15 minutes
Cooking: 15 minutes
900 g/2 lb Aberdeen Angus beef tenderloin, cubed

Salt and pepper, to taste
50 ml/2 fl oz Worcestershire sauce
50 ml/2 fl oz oyster sauce
6 garlic cloves, chopped
2 tbsp olive oil

• Mix the beef, salt and pepper in a bowl and leave to stand.
• Meanwhile, combine the Worcestershire sauce and oyster sauce in a small bowl, stir and set aside.
• For the crunchy garlic bits, heat 1 tablespoon of olive oil in a frying pan. Add 3 cloves of chopped garlic and cook until golden brown. Drain on absorbent kitchen paper.
• Heat another tablespoon of oil in the pan and add the remaining garlic. Stir regularly and cook until the garlic begins to brown.

• Increase the heat to high and add the beef. Sear each side for 1 to 2 minutes. Add the Worcestershire-oyster sauce mixture and continue to cook for 3 to 5 minutes.
• Serve immediately, with a sprinkling of crispy garlic bits on top.

1 Prepared before your eyes: a street vendor at the Queen Victoria Market in Melbourne serves up chargrilled octopus and other seafood hot from the grill to marketgoers.

AUSTRALIA AND NEW ZEALAND

MELBOURNE SYDNEY AUCKLAND WELLINGTON

The first inhabitants of Australia, the Aborigines, were hunter-gathers who ate a wide variety of plants, fruits, insects and animals. Much of their expert knowledge of indigenous foods was disregarded by the first white settlers (mostly convicts, many of them Irish) who arrived in around 1788 to the British colony of New South Wales and who brought with them their own familiar foods such as bread, cheese and salted meat. Some governors encouraged these first settlers and 'dungaree settlers' (freed convicts) to start smallholdings to supply agricultural produce for Sydney's early markets.

Immigrants and gold prospectors began to arrive from the 1830s and they were more open to accepting native foods, particularly kangaroo. A common dish of the time, the kangaroo steamer, became very popular. A recipe for this kangaroo stew was included in *The English and Australia Cookery Book* published in 1864 and is widely regarded as the first truly colonial Australian dish. Unfortunately, colonial cooks lacked culinary skills, although this wasn't entirely a disadvantage, as people wanted substantial plain food and plenty of it. Early colonists improvised cooking methods, with food cooked over an open fire or in the ashes. The cooking was rather unimaginative with meat, roasted, grilled or boiled and vegetables boiled in large amounts of water.

Pies originally brought by English and Irish settlers became so popular that they could be described even today as Australia's national dish. Today the Aussie meat pie has many variations and can be found in every street food market. Sold from street carts in early colonial days, pies were the first real takeaway food. Pie carts were sometimes accompanied by coffee stalls and from the 1870s, these were established in Sydney, Melbourne and Adelaide

By 1838 Australians were relishing American tomato ketchup with their pies. In Adelaide and other areas, pie carts also served

Cornish pasties, introduced by Cornish miners journeying to quarry and mining towns in Australia. One Cornish immigrant who moved to Adelaide in the 1880s is believed to have instituted the pie floater – 'a mince-pie floating in a soup-plate of thick, dark-green pease gravy'. Pie carts became even more popular during the Depression of the early 1930s, as they offered hot, cheap food.

At the start of the twentieth century, subtle changes began to take place and cooking relied less on native foods and ingredients. The advent of refrigerators led to a multitude of chilled dishes and ovens encouraged the cooking of satisfying casseroles. These changes in eating and cooking styles led to outdoor picnics and barbecues. Australians love a 'barbie', a tradition that probably began in the 1920s, when it almost certainly developed from the 'chop picnic'. The name came from the West Indies and was associated with a large outdoor event where a carcass was roasted.

Around the same time, Australian women developed an enthusiasm for baking and cookbooks of the time gave far more recipes for pies, cakes, puddings and biscuits than for savoury dishes. National specialties were created such as lamingtons – sponge cubes dipped in melted chocolate and coated in desiccated coconut. Both Australia and New Zealand lay claim to having invented the pavlova – a large meringue filled with fresh fruit and cream – named in honour of the famous Russian ballerina Anna Pavlova, who visited New Zealand and Australia in 1926.

Australian cuisine changed enormously after World War II, when increased affluence coincided with a growing interest in food and eating out, which in turn led to more restaurants. Travel and a wave of immigrants from Europe and Asia introduced new foods and cuisines. Asian vegetables and fruits thrive in the Australian climate and these factors combined to encourage a distinctive contemporary Australian cuisine. Asian cooking

QUEEN VICTORIA MARKET

techniques such as stir-frying are now as common as grilling. More recently there has been a revival of native foods (bush tucker) such as wattleseed, macadamia nuts and emu meat. These, along with specialized food enterprises, farmers' markets, artisan products and food carts, have revolutionized Australian street food.

The Maori, descendants of the Polynesians, arrived in New Zealand around 800 CE and found plenty of birds, seafood and plants to eat. They brought with them the taro plant and kumara (sweet potato), which flourished in the New Zealand soil and became a staple of their diet. Food was cooked in pits dug in the earth (*hangi*), similar to a New England clambake. Like the Aborigines, the Maori cooked over fire or in the ashes. European settlers brought new foods with them and the Maori were particularly enthusiastic about pork, mutton and potatoes. And, as they did in Australia, the British often tried to replicate typical British dishes using native fish and birds. The arrival of Italian and Greek immigrants in the nineteenth century, along with the introduction of deer and rabbits and the discovery that fruits like the kiwi flourished in the New Zealand climate, transformed the culinary scene. From the late 1950s the joint influence of New Zealanders returning from abroad and new migrants, particularly Asians, led to a more cosmopolitan food culture and a café scene. Asian food is hugely popular and there's a wide choice from street food vendors.

Street food has a long history in New Zealand and fresh produce markets have great importance. Harbourside (see p.389), the oldest market in Wellington, has been trading since 1920, in the days when vendors sold their wares from caravans and carts. The street food scene has since grown rapidly due to rising demand from consumers. The increasing number of food trucks and pop-up stalls offer a range of foods including Mexican, Italian and Asian, plus native favourites such as plump, juicy, green-lipped mussels.

QUEEN VICTORIA MARKET

MELBOURNE

Queen Victoria Market sits at the heart of Melbourne, both physically and as an embodiment of the city's food culture: edgy global offerings made with quality local ingredients. Its colourful history began in 1957, when plans were floated to establish a fruit and veg market to deal with overcrowding at nearby Eastern Market (which closed in the 1960s). The idea was unpopular due to the proposed location beside Old Melbourne Cemetery (now the market's car park). As a result, the site was used as a market for livestock and hay, and then meat, for the next two decades. Vic Market, as it is known in Melbourne, has since grown into the southern hemisphere's biggest open-air market.

Today, it sprawls across almost 7 hectares (17 acres). The Deli Hall, dripping with Art Deco charm, offers up everything from local cheeses to cured meats, including kangaroo jerky. The Meat Hall is a carnivore's dream, stocking many cuts of meat and fish hard to source elsewhere in Melbourne. Victorian wines, including organic blends, can be sampled and paired — for those who like eccentric combinations — with hot jam doughnuts from an authentic 1950s food truck.

An impressive scope of international cuisine can be found when the food pop-ups appear. In a few short strides you can pass Sicilian barbecue and Sri Lankan koththu roti, Hawaiian 'Big Island' smoked pork and an Aussie twist on tapas. Although a popular food truck rally takes place every Sunday, it is the night markets that draw the best vendors, which change with the season. BP

Where: Corner of Elizabeth and Victoria Streets, Melbourne
When: Tuesday and Thursday 6 a.m. – 2 p.m.; Friday 6 a.m. – 5 p.m.; Saturday 6 a.m. – 3 p.m.; Sunday 9 a.m. – 10 p.m.

6 Stir-fry from The Vegan Collective, which offers delectable meat and dairy-free options to visitors.   **7** Sumptuous Vietnamese fried chicken, light, tasty and ready to eat from The Brass Coq.   **8** Families dine on makeshift wooden crate tables at the Wednesday night market.

THE BRASS COQ'S GREEN PAPAYA SALAD

A vibrant salad from a Vietnamese-inspired Melbourne eatery.

SERVES 1–2

Preparation: 10 minutes

½ large fresh green papaya, very
  thinly sliced

A handful of mixed South East
  Asian herbs, such as mint, basil
  and coriander

½ red onion, thinly sliced

1 carrot, very thinly sliced

1 long red chilli, thinly sliced

½ Ruby Red grapefruit, cut into
  small cubes

A handful of dried shallots and crushed
  peanuts, plus extra to serve

125 ml/4 fl oz Vietnamese
  dipping sauce

- Place all of the ingredients in a mixing bowl — the amount of chilli can vary according to taste and heat tolerance.
- Gently mix the ingredients together by hand, ensuring everything is combined and coated in dressing.
- Serve immediately, garnished with extra shallots and peanuts if desired.

VENDOR SPOTLIGHT

For a sweet market treat with an Asian twist, try **Butterlake Pancakes**, which serves up its own versions of the Japanese dessert imagawayaki. It has replaced the usual red bean paste filling with a selection of gooey options, including Tim Tam chocolate biscuits, peanut butter and coconut, and hazelnut spread and banana (left).

Another example of Melbourne's contemporary twist on Asian classics can be found a few footsteps away at **OK-Nomi**. Okonomiyaki — a savoury pancake that varies between regions — might be Osaka soul food, but would be awkward to eat on the go; OK-Nomi solve the problem by wrapping it around chopsticks.

The **Cassava Chip Man** can usually be found somewhere between the two, dishing up piping hot cassava chips loaded with Caribbean gravy and cheese. Despite the considerable amount of meat on offer at Queen Victoria Market (sausages, porchetta, souvlaki and more), **The Vegan Collective** attracts its fair share of carnivores, no doubt due to tasty dishes such as rich yellow lentil and coconut curry.

SYDNEY

Australia was colonized in the late 1700s and many settlers arrived in the ensuing years each introducing their own food, mainly British, Asian and Middle Eastern. All culinary cultures are here on the Sydney streets, often with a modern Australian twist. Although street food has emerged only in the last twenty years or so, the scene in the city has recently seen impressive changes. Food markets and food trucks are flourishing and there's plenty of choice when it comes to freshly cooked street food. Today's cuisine is as varied as its landscape; there is an extensive range of world foods, but it is also worth seeking out Australian specialties. Pies are a popular snack to eat on the go – classic Aussie meat pies filled with minced meat, gravy, mushrooms, onions and cheese. Or tasty Anzac biscuits – Anzac stands for the Australian and New Zealand Army Corps that fought together during World War I – made with coconut, golden syrup and oats.

Some of Sydney's finest street food can be found at its markets. The award-winning Carriageworks Farmers' Market (see p.383) has a huge following of regulars every Saturday. Enjoy a wide choice, from free-range bacon and egg rolls and steamed Chinese dumplings to Chinese and Australian-Chinese dishes using native ingredients like yabbies (crayfish), as well as exceptional coffee.

The Rocks Friday Foodie Market, held at Jack Mundey Place, offers a great choice of world foods – French, German, Japanese and, of course, Australian. Enjoy gourmet wraps, burgers, barbecued salmon and Turkish gözleme (stuffed flatbreads with fillings such as feta and spinach) as buskers provide a colourful musical backdrop with guitars and banjos.

Kopi-Tiam on Spice Alley, a new outdoor street food market on Central Park's Kensington Street development, is situated in a series of connecting courtyards and its stalls offer a delectable choice of Thai, Singaporean, Malaysian, Hong Kong, Vietnamese and Japanese dishes. The stalls, run by old hands from some of Sydney's popular South East Asian restaurants, sell street food staples at affordable prices. The four permanent stalls are joined by occasional pop-ups, so there's always something new on offer.

When you're out and about, remember that some of Sydney's finest street food is from the food trucks. Here you can enjoy a dazzling variety of dishes and snacks to suite every taste, from some of the most appetizing vegetarian food you'll ever eat to outstanding organic, seasonal produce like wagyu beef burgers.

1 Carriageworks Farmers' Market in full swing.   2 Harry's Café de Wheels parked in sunny Woolloomooloo, Sydney. Beginning life as a caravan café in 1938 it is famous for its traditional pies and pasties. 3 Browsing specialty cheese stalls at The Rocks Foodie Market.

1	3
2	

CARRIAGEWORKS FARMERS' MARKET SYDNEY

Every Saturday, more than seventy farmers and artisan producers from across New South Wales pack up their goods and head to Sydney's premier fresh food market, a much-loved treasure in the city's glittering food scene. Part of the heritage-listed Carriageworks development, a former railway yard that has been transformed into a thriving cultural hub, the market is held in a beautiful hangar-like space that was once a blacksmith's workshop.

From the crunchiest carrots and radishes to artisan loaves, cheeses and bowls of fragrant pho, fresh seasonal food is the name of the game here. Australian chef and passionate foodie Mike McEnearney uses his expert eye to curate the stalls, creating a mix that offers something for everyone. Look out for Kylie Kwong, chef, restaurateur and television presenter, who is often found manning the pork bun steamers at her stand. Buy a loaf from the

Bread and Butter Project, a social enterprise run by Sydney's renowned Bourke Street Bakery, or try indigenous food products from Currong Comestibles, including chutneys and shrubs made from native Australian plants, herbs and fruits.

In the summer, slake your thirst with a freshly pressed juice and a seat in the shade while listening to live music. Or, in winter, warm the cockles with a bowl of steaming porridge and a cup of some of Sydney's best coffee. SQ

Where: 245 Wilson Street, Eveleigh NSW 2015
When: Saturday 8 a.m.–1 p.m.

1 Wild mushrooms on sale. 2 Carriageworks visitors strolling in the sunshine. 3 Pork buns in progress at Kylie Kwong's stall: Billy Kwong. 4 Free samples of handmade Australian butter on offer – try it with Sonoma bread.

GLENFIELD AUCKLAND

On any given Sunday evening, when you'd expect many to be winding down from the weekend and contemplating the days ahead, there is a feast taking place in Auckland, New Zealand. Up to 10,000 people head to a large car park under the Westfield Mall in Glenfield for delicious cheap food from around the globe and a carnival atmosphere for all the family.

In a city with over 200 different ethnic groups, roughly a quarter of whom identify as Asian, there is naturally a strong Asian bent to the food choices, with dishes such as Filipino BBQ ribs, Japanese takoyaki and, of course, a vast array of dumplings to whet the appetite. For the more adventurous eater, there is the Chinese specialty, cow offal stew. You'll also find Chinese doughsticks or crullers known as youtiao, and for those with a sweet tooth, halo-halo, the Filipino ube, or yam-based, ice cream with a vibrant purple hue.

However, there's not only Asian food: look out for deliciously sticky Turkish baklava and gözleme (savoury, filled pastry pockets),

Hungarian lángos – a kind of deep-fried flatbread – and churros among the global offerings from over one hundred food stalls.

Glenfield is one of seven weekly night markets (each taking place on different evenings) – six in Auckland, one in Hamilton – with the first opening in Pakuranga in 2010, and later Glenfield in October 2011. The brains behind it is Chinese businesswoman Victoria Yao, who was looking to revive Auckland's nightlife and develop a real night-time economy. With Glenfield it looks like she has achieved her goal. Plus, it is all under cover, so nothing can spoil this food party, apart from, well, the end of the weekend – but there's always next week. TJ

Where: Glenfield Mall level one car park, Auckland
When: Sunday 5.30 p.m.– 11 p.m.

1 Bustling crowds.   2 Lángos – fried bread topped with tomato and feta.   3 Delicious ice cream.   4 Hot churros and chocolate dip.   5 Towering and striking twisted potato sticks.   6 Dumplings.   7 Raclette melts over vegetables.

HARBOURSIDE MARKET
WELLINGTON

Every Sunday Wellington's sprawling waterfront plays host to the capital's biggest weekly food event, the open-air Harbourside Market. Swaying yacht masts and turquoise water create a stunning backdrop to the market, where up to 25,000 people weave around a section of the harbour's promenade and the large vacant car park opposite the Museum of New Zealand Te Papa Tongarewa. Eleven trucks of Kapiti coast growers arrive at dawn and unpack towers of crates brimming with vibrant, fresh produce: tender asparagus, bright citrus, crisp brassica and exotic Asian greens. Nearby, food vendors line the water's edge offering goods that celebrate New Zealand's diverse culinary history: Indian murtabak stuffed with chicken curry, Indonesian BBQ, Chilean calzones rotos (fried pastries) and custard doughnuts. A retro, lime-green caravan pumps out fair-trade, organic espresso. Among the artisan stalls one offers a pungent array of fine French cheeses, another native honey. A small fishing boat moors off the wharf unloading a variety of fresh fillets and whole fish. There's plenty of space to sit and eat, or to watch the tides of people drift by. A popular spot is on the long concrete ledge facing Waitangi Park's native plantings and the Chaffers Marina. Markets have operated here since the 1920s and the current incarnation dates from 2011. Market curator Fraser Ebbett believes passionately that community is central to its ethos. He provides an area for community groups to fundraise, and Kaibosh, a food redistribution programme, rescue any leftover food and distribute it through a network of local charities. Performers are also warmly invited. PM

Where: Corner of Cable and Barnett streets, Wellington
When: Sunday 7 a.m.–2 p.m. in summer, 7 a.m.–1 p.m. in winter

1 Visitors enjoy the view by the water's edge.   2 Pastries are dusted with sugar at The Greek Food Truck.   3 Stalls sell fresh produce.   4–5 Delicious poffertjes from Montfoort's stylish white caravan.   6 A scenic way to sample street food.

LAMB TAGINE STUFFED PITTA WRAPS

Zaaffran's Moroccan-inspired wraps use tender New Zealand lamb.

SERVES 6

Preparation: 10 minutes

Cooking: 1 hour 40 minutes

1.5 kg /3lb 5 oz lamb shoulder, cut into large pieces

1 large onion, chopped

4 garlic cloves, crushed

1 tsp salt

½ tsp ground black pepper

1 tsp of ras el hanout spice blend

1 tsp paprika

6 tbsp olive oil

125 ml/4 fl oz water

200 g/7 oz soaked prunes

6 large flatbreads or tortillas

200 g/7 oz chermoula paste

250 g/9 oz quality mayonnaise

1 fancy lettuce, leaves separated

½ red cabbage, finely shredded

100 g/3½ oz black olives, chopped

250 g/9 oz carrot, grated

60 g/2 oz flat-leaf parsley, chopped

1 onion, finely sliced

Olive oil, for brushing

- Mix together the first eight ingredients in a tagine or wide, deep, heavy-based saucepan. Add water, cover and bring to the boil on a medium heat. Reduce to simmer for 90 minutes or until the lamb is tender. Add more water as needed to ensure it doesn't dry out. Once thick and caramelized add the prunes. Simmer for 10 minutes.
- Divide the lamb tagine and remaining ingredients evenly between the flatbreads or tortillas; place the filling one third in from the bottom edge of the bread to allow for wrapping. Spoon mayonnaise and chermoula to taste. Add salad and roll into wraps. Brush the tops of the stuffed pittas with olive oil. Heat in a sandwich press or gently fry in a pan until lightly coloured.

VENDOR SPOTLIGHT

Harbourside Market provides ravenous punters with an eclectic array of brunch snacks and delectable sweets. Some are regional Kiwi cuisine. **Food for the People** offers up a classic Golden Bay mussel fritter served simply on white bread, or a hot, free-range bacon and egg butty (above) — food described by the owner as 'almost gourmet local street food'. **House of Dumplings** do an interesting twist on traditional dumplings, with each plump, fried morsel lovingly hand made from scratch with local ingredients. Flavours include prawn and garlic chive, Nepalese spiced lamb and vegan Japanese six mushroom. **Montfoort** have sweet tooths covered with traditional Dutch desserts. Their specialties are poffertjes, soft, pillowy bite-sized pancakes served with powdered sugar and butter, or the equally indulgent, chewy stroopwafels (caramel waffle sandwiches).

GLOSSARY

COOKING TERMS

Al dente – an Italian term for food that is cooked until it is 'firm to the bite'. It is often used to describe pasta.

Baste – to spoon juices or marinades over food that is being roasted or baked to prevent it from drying out and to glaze the surface.

Blanch – the process of plunging ingredients, usually vegetables and fruit, into boiling water briefly, then draining and refreshing them in cold water in order to stop the cooking process.

Blend – to thoroughly combine two or more ingredients with a wire whisk or spatula.

Braise – to slowly cook food in liquid in a tightly sealed pot on the stovetop or in the oven.

Bruise – to partially crush an aromatic food such as garlic and spice pods to release flavour.

Crimp – to press two pastry edges together, sealing them and forming a raised, decorative pattern around the edge, creating a diagonal ridge on the rim.

Curdle – caused by overcooking, too much heat or agitation. An egg- or cream-based mixture will separate into a liquid that contains small, solid particles.

Deep-fry – to rapidly cook foods by submerging them in a deep pan of very hot oil. It is essential to use oils that can be heated to a high temperature without smoking, for example, corn, grapeseed, sunflower and peanut oil.

Infuse – to steep an aromatic ingredient in hot liquid until its flavour has been extracted and absorbed by the liquid.

Knead – to mix and work dough into a smooth, elastic mass. Kneading causes the gluten strands within the flour to stretch and expand, enabling dough to hold in gas bubbles formed by yeast; this allows it to rise.

Marinade – to soak food in a seasoned liquid mixture for a certain length of time. The purpose of marinating is to add flavour and/or tenderize the food.

Poach – to cook gently in simmering liquid so the food (fish, steak, chicken, vegetables, eggs) retains its shape.

Reduce – to decrease the volume of a liquid by boiling it rapidly to thicken it and intensify flavour. The resulting richly flavoured liquid – called a reduction – can be used as a sauce or as the base of a sauce.

Simmer – to bring liquid by itself or with other ingredients to the point just below boiling over a low heat. Small bubbles rise slowly, bursting before reaching the surface.

Steam – to cook food on a rack or in a basket placed above boiling liquid in a covered pan.

Stir-fry – to quickly cook a combination of meat and/or vegetables in a hot frying pan at a temperature below smoking point. Stir-fry food in small quantities, taking care not to crowd the pan. Cook quickly, stirring constantly in a minimal amount of fat or liquid.

INGREDIENTS

Allspice is not a blend of spices but a spice in its own right. It has a highly aromatic flavour often described as a combination of cinnamon, clove, nutmeg and pepper. It is available as whole dried berries or ready ground.

Amchoor is a powder made from dried unripe green mangoes and is used as a citrusy seasoning.

Black pepper is aromatic and invaluable for seasoning.

Buckwheat flour is milled from buckwheat. It is not related to wheat and is gluten-free.

Caraway seeds have a warm, pungent aroma and sweet tangy flavour.

Cardamom has a rich sweet, slightly lemony fragrance. The tiny black seeds are enclosed in green pods and should be lightly crushed before using to release the flavour.

Cayenne pepper is a red, fiery hot spice ground from the pod and seeds of dried chillies and should be used sparingly. A pinch is all that is usually required.

Chaat masala is a tangy Indian spice blend.

Chanterelle is a golden yellow fragrant mushroom with a fleshy cap and curly edge with an aroma of apricots.

Chermoula is a spicy paste blend of coriander, cumin, preserved lemon and chilli.

Chickpea (gram) flour is made from ground chickpeas. It is pale yellow and powdery with an earthy flavour.

Chickpeas are one of the easiest legumes to digest; the small, light golden peas have an appetizing flavour and keep their shape well when cooked. They are popular in Middle Eastern countries and India (known there as gram).

Cinnamon has a warm sweet fragrance and is sold as sticks (quills) or powder. It is difficult to grind your own cinnamon fine enough from the bark. Buy it ground in small quantities as the flavour quickly disappears.

Cloves are the dried flower buds of a tree in Indonesia. Pungent and spicy in flavour, they should be used sparingly.

Coconut cream is very similar to coconut milk but contains less water. It has a thicker, more paste-like consistency.

Coriander has a warm aromatic, slightly nutty flavour with a hint of citrus and pepper.

Cumin is sold as whole seeds or ready ground and imparts a warm, slightly sweet spiciness to chutneys.

Easyblend dried yeast is usually sold in sachets. It is added directly to the flour, not mixed with the liquid like fresh yeast and the dough usually needs only one rising.

Fennel has a strong aniseed flavour and is available as the bulb and leaves, or dried seeds. Look for small white bulbs with bright feathery tops. Slice off the root and shoots and peel off the tough outer layer if necessary.

Filo is paper-thin sheets of pastry commonly used in Greek, Eastern European and Middle Eastern cuisines. It is brushed with oil or butter and layered.

Ginger can be used as the fresh root or dried and ground, and crystallized or candied in syrup. Ground ginger is the dried, powdered root and has a quite different flavour to that of the fresh root. Ginger adds a touch of heat and a warm fragrant aroma and flavour.

Gum mastic is a popular ingredient in North African and Mediterranean cuisines. The yellow gum mastic crystals are a natural resin from the Chia tree and have delicate pine-resin and balsamic aromas.

Haricot beans are small, oval and creamy white in colour. They are familiar to us as baked beans in tomato sauce but are also used in soups and stews.

Jackfruit tastes similar to a mango but with notes of banana, peach and pear.

Jaggery is an unrefined sugar made from sugar cane juice or palm sap that is cooked down and set into blocks.

Juniper berries have a bittersweet, slightly resinous pine flavour and should be lightly crushed before using to release the flavouring oils. Use sparingly as their flavour is pungent.

Kofta is a meatball or meatloaf dish found in South Asian, Middle Eastern, Balkan and Central Asian cuisines.

Kombu is dehydrated, edible kelp seaweed.

Marionberries are blackberries native to Oregon, USA; they are sweeter and juicier than other blackberries.

Mung bean flour is a ground white starch made from mung beans. It may have a green or pink tint when wet.

Mustard: English mustard is yellow and is the hottest. **French** mustards include Dijon, which has a sharp fresh taste; Bordeaux, which is mild and the grainy Meaux. **German** mustard has a strong flavour but is milder than English. **American or yellow** mustard has a sweet mild flavour good for liberal use. **Wholegrain** mustard contains mustard seeds and is good for stirring into sauces and dressings.

Mustard seeds have a fresh clean aroma and pungent, sharp flavour.

Nutmeg is warm, aromatic and fragrant. It adds interest to sweet and savoury dishes, and is best freshly grated.

Papaya (pawpaw) is a tropical fruit that may be pear-shaped, cylindrical or nearly round. When ripe, its skin is a deep yellow or orange, with similar coloured soft, sweet, fragrant flesh and black edible seeds.

Paprika is milder than cayenne pepper. It is ground from dried red peppers and its flavour varies – mild, sweet, hot or pungent, but never fiery.

Pistachios are small bright green nuts with a mild, sweet flavour and a slightly chewy texture.

Puy lentils are regarded by gourmets as the best of their kind. These small green lentils, which come from the Velay region of France, keep their shape well after cooking and can be added to dishes for texture.

Ras-el-hanout is a classic spice mixture used in Moroccan cuisine with a heady sweet aroma. The name means 'top of the shop'.

Red kidney beans have an attractive rich red colour, mealy texture and earthy flavour.

Red lentils are bright orange and usually sold split, so they don't need soaking before cooking. They cook quickly to a soft golden beige mass and are one of the easiest legumes to digest, with a bland, pleasant flavour.

Sea salt is obtained by evaporating seawater and its mineral content gives it a different flavour to table salt, which is usually refined from mined rock salt.

Sesame seeds are tiny cream-coloured or black seeds with a subtle nutty flavour. Toasted sesame seeds have a more distinct flavour.

Shaoxing is wine made from fermented, glutinous rice.

Snow fungus is a species of mushroom with lacy, clusters and a 'snowball' appearance. It is usually available in the dried form, which needs to be reconstituted in water before cooking. When soaked in water, the fungus expands, turns white and takes on a wobbly, jellylike texture.

Star anise is the star-shaped fruit of an evergreen shrub indigenous to southern China and Vietnam. Both the fruit case and seeds have a strong aniseed flavour and may be used whole (remove before serving) or ground.

Tahini is a thick paste made from ground sesame seeds.

Tomatillos look similar to small green tomatoes and have a white inside. The exterior papery husks should be removed before eating.

Turmeric is the root or rhizome of a member of the ginger family; it adds a pungent flavour and deep orange-yellow colour. It is usually sold ready ground.

Vinegar: Balsamic vinegar is rich and syrupy and has a smooth sweet-sour flavour. **Sherry** vinegar has a rich sweet taste and can be used in the same way as balsamic vinegar. **Cider** vinegar has a golden colour and delicate flavour. Use in marinades and salad dressings.

White pepper is hot but not as intensely aromatic as black pepper.

Zest is the grated outer peel of citrus fruit (excluding the bitter white pith just under the surface). It is used as a flavouring in sweet and savoury dishes.

FOOD TRUCK TWITTER HANDLES AND RECIPE CREDITS

Austin
@BBQRevolt
@EastSideKingATX
@UGonnaEatOrWhat
@traileralliance
@BatonCreole

Boston
@RoxysGrilledChz
@cloverfoodlab
@bonme
@Redbones
@zinnetruck

Los Angeles
@RoamingHunger
@Border_Grill
@grlldcheesetruk
@CMLobster

@CantersTruck
@CoolhausLA

New York
@mrbingnyc
@VeganLunchTruck
@elolomega
@SnowdayTruck)

Washington DC
@RoamingHunger
@foodtruckfiesta
@los_wingeez
@okbibija
@captaincookiedc
@crepelovetruck
@AstroDoughnuts

Berlin
@TapiocariaBln

London
@Luardos
@jhalmuriexpress
@bleeckerburger
@trumanbrewery
@motherclucker
@blutopicecream
@goodpropertea

Paris
@LeCamionQuiFume
@LeRefectoire
@CantineCali
@LaBrigadeFT
@LeCamionBOL
@Bugelski

18 Tara Lee, credited to Eric Pateman of Edible Canada **21** Valentine Lechevallier **25** Monica Schwartz **31** Anthea Gerrie, credited to Bar Moruno **32** Anthea Gerrie, inspired by Border Grill food truck **37** Jolyon Webber **38** Jolyon Webber **45** Alex James, credited to Janet McGowan **52** Alex James, created in collaboration with Thomas Alexander from Cantina Del Ponte **55** Nikki Spencer, credited to Quincy Market's Walrus and the Carpenter Oyster Bar **69** Sue Quinn **70** Jolyon Webber **82** Connie Law **85** Isabel Hood **88** Maria Rieger and Reynaldo Melgar **92** Tom Jenkins **96** Eleanor Ross **100** Jake Primley **106** Laura Barnes **111** Jolyon Webber **123** Carol Wilson **129** Carol Wilson **131** Graeme Taylor, credited to Aye Love Real Food **133** Arlene Kessly, credited to Raclette Raclette **138** Victoria Stewart **46** Kayleigh Rattle, credited to Mama Lan **154** Adam Roberts **157** Adam Roberts **163** Clarissa Hyman **169** Carol Wilson **173** Kayleigh Rattle, credited to Marlene Viera's restaurant **177** Carol Wilson **180** Ryan Barrell, credited to Heisser Hobel Food Truck **186** Carol Wilson **191** Carol Wilson **192** Natalie Kennedy **197** Natalie Kennedy **201** Travel & Lust **203** Charlotte Jones **207** Ondina Rosch **219** Jolyon Webber **221** Kayleigh Rattle **222** Tom Jenkins **231** Sue Quinn, credited to Ragamuffin **242** Kevin Gould **247** Nada Saleh **252** Alex James, credited to Lukasz Dawidowicz, head chef at Zest JW3, London **255** Sally Prosser **265** Alex James **272** Petra Shepherd **276** Kinita Shenoy **281** Fiona Reilly **288** Fiona Reilly **290** Tessa Humphrys **295** Susanne Masters **299** Tom Jenkins **308** Judy Joo **313** Laura Barnes **319** Laura Barnes **324** Nomadic Boys **330** Luke Farrell **332** Luke Farrell **336** Luke Farrell **339** Eleanor Ross **345** Alex James, credited to Chef Jonathan Villar **348** Luke Farrell **352** Jolyon Webber **356** Mo Quiang Fang **362** Alex James **368** Lily Howes, credited to Auntie May **379** Ben Parker **391** Penn Mahuika, credited to Zaafran

INDEX

Recipes are in **bold**. Illustrations are in *italics*.

CONTRIBUTORS

Adam Roberts has run the Invisible Paris web resource (http://www.invisibleparis.net) since 2009. He is the author of *Paris CityScopes* (Reaktion Books, 2017).

Alexander James is a health, travel and lifestyle journalist who has contributed to *The Times*, *Guardian, Esquire, Marie Claire, Cosmopolitan,* lovefood.com and Channel 4. He is coauthor of *Marathons of the World* (IMM, 2016) and is launching travel video magazine: youtube.com/channeljetset (see realexjames.wordpress.com).

Anthea Gerrie is a food and travel writer who spent eight years in Los Angeles and now lives among the English vineyards of Sussex. She writes for many publications including *Food and Travel* magazine.

Arlene Kessly is a lifestyle writer and presenter. A contributor to many UK publications and local radio, markets have always featured in her weekly wanderings, both for inspiration and relaxation.

Benjamin Parker is a freelance food and travel journalist based in the UK, who until recently lived in Australia. He has written for the *New York Post* and *Tatler*, and is a regular travel contributor to *The Daily Telegraph*.

Carol Wilson is an author, journalist, restaurant reviewer and recipe developer. A member of the Guild of Food Writers, she contributes to publications in the UK, Ireland and the USA and is a judge for several food awards.

Charlotte Jones is a journalist specializing in food and travel. In 2009 she launched the website www.charlottesvveb.com, which she has used to dispel common misconceptions about Eastern Europe.

Clarissa Hyman is an award-winning food and travel writer based in the north of England. She contributes to a wide range of publications and has written five books including *The Spanish Kitchen* (Conran, 2005).

Connie Law is a London-based Kiwi who writes about her food experiences around the world on her blog (see http://connieconsumes.com/).

Eleanor Ross is a journalist and travel writer based in London. She writes mainly for the *Guardian* newspaper and spends the rest of her time exploring little-explored places around the world (see www.eleanorross.org).

Ella Buchan is a freelance travel writer. Based between London and Paso Robles, California, USA, she can often be found seeking out local dining spots and/or drinking wine with llamas.

Fiona Reilly is a writer and photographer who became obsessed with China's street food while living in Shanghai. She now divides her time between China and Australia, writing

about China's diverse cuisines for an international audience.

Graeme Taylor has an intense passion for the rich and varied food and drink landscape of Scotland. With his blog – A Scots Larder – he explores the natural larder that Scotland possesses and brings heritage recipes to life with a contemporary feel.

Isabel Hood was brought up in Mexico where she became steeped in its intensely flavoured, palate-tingling cuisine from a young age. She is the author of *Chilli and Chocolate: Stars of the Mexican Cocina* (Matador, 2008).

Jake Primley writes extensively for a wide range of magazines and partworks.

Jolyon Webber is a freelance writer and editor based in London. He has worked for the men's style and lifestyle magazine *Port*, the adventuring magazine *Avaunt* as well as the fashion titles *Seventh Man* and *Hunger*.

Judy Joo is a Korean-American, French-trained chef based in London whose recipes meld flavours from Asia, America and Europe. She is the host of Cooking Channel's *Korean Food Made Simple* and the author of *Korean Food Made Simple* (Houghton Mifflin, 2016).

Juliet Lecouffe lives in Lisbon, where she eats far too many cakes. She spends most of her time running after a badly behaved toddler, but occasionally moonlights as a French-English translator.

Kayleigh Rattle is a multimedia journalist specializing in food and travel. When not exploring the world's delicacies, she can mostly be found splitting her time between London and rural Suffolk (see kayleighrattle.com and @kayleighrattle).

Kevin Gould trained as a chef, then became a DJ, grocer, restaurateur and caterer. For the past twenty-five years he has worked as a food, wine and travel writer and photographer. He has written two food books and is currently working on writing a history of Lebanon.

Kinita Shenoy is an explorer and writer currently living in Sri Lanka. She loves cooking, writing and eating inventive cuisines (see kinitashenoy@gmail.com).

Laura Barnes is a food and travel writer from Cornwall, UK, who set her sights on the world and left to travel it. She is often found eating sushi under cherry blossoms.

Lily Howes is a journalist, writer and proud south Londoner. She spent ten months eating her way around Asia, scoffing sambol in Sri Lanka, bun cha in Hanoi and bowls of Burmese mohinga, but she's yet to brave balut (duck embryo).

Luke Farrell is a chef who trained in Singapore and Thailand. He divides his time between Bangkok and his tropical greenhouses in the UK where he grows Asian herbs for restaurants.

Maria Rieger has long experience of travelling and living abroad. Combining a personal writing style with beautiful photography on her blog www.travellingspice.com, she finds her inspiration in people, their cultures and their culinary traditions. She currently lives in Iran.

Mo Qiong Fang was born in Shanghai and still lives there. She loves food and cooking – particularly that of her native city.

Monica Schwartz is an Italian photographer, writer, chef and food stylist who lives in California, USA. She is also a world explorer, time traveller and aspiring teleporter who would love to attend Hogwarts (see www.lifeoutofbounds.com).

Nada Saleh is a food writer, nutritionist and consultant. She is the author of *Seductive Flavours of the Levant* (Robson, 2002) and *New Flavours of the Lebanese Table* (Ebury, 2007). She also contributed to *1001 Restaurants You Must Experience Before You Die* (Cassell, 2014)

Natalie Kennedy is a food and lifestyle writer based in Rome, where she regularly overindulges in gelato and/or wine. Originally from California, she has lived in Italy since 2010 with her Irish husband and Roman cat.

Nikki Spencer is a member of the Guild of Food Writers and a freelance journalist from London who specializes in food and travel. She has written for the UK's *Guardian, Independent* and *Daily Telegraph* newspapers and for many years worked for Michelin's website ViaMichelin.

Nomadic Boys is a travel blog set up by couple Stefan Arestis and Sébastien Chaneac. They have been travelling the world since 2014 after leaving their lives in London. They write about their romantic adventures, the gay scene around the world and, of course, their culinary discoveries.

Ondina Rosch trained as a photographer at London's Central Saint Martins School of Art and as a pastry chef with New York's International Culinary Center. She is passionate about design, fashion and culinary artistry.

Penn Mahuika is a media studies and sociology graduate who until recently was head chef at Auckland's iconic Federal Delicatessen. He now lives in Wellington, the city of his birth, with his young family.

Petra Shepherd is a freelance travel writer. She has visited over 100 countries and lived in Hong Kong where she edited *Eating and Drinking in Hong Kong*. She is a member of the British Guild of Travel Writers.

Ryan Barrell is a British freelance writer and food blogger based in Berlin. He can be found on Twitter @RyanBarrell, via www.thelumberjackbaker.com, or sitting in an urban coffee shop nursing an expensive latte.

Sally Prosser is a Dubai-based writer and photographer who loves seeking out authentic food in unusual places. She has lived in the Middle East for over twenty years and is author of award-winning website My Custard Pie.

Shirlee Posner is a food writer who lived in Taiwan for five years. There she was the editor of a lifestyle magazine for the international community called *Centered on Taipei* and she wrote for a number of other publications, mainly about food.

Sue Quinn is a full-time food writer and cookery book author. Her journalism and recipes have appeared in leading UK food titles including the *Guardian, Telegraph, Sunday Times, Delicious* magazine and *BBC Good Food*. Her work covers all aspects of food and cooking, with a particular emphasis on food and health.

Susanne Masters writes about food and drink as she travels around the world by plane, train and swimming (see @Ethnobotanica on Twitter and @mastersmiss on Instagram).

Tara Lee is a Canadian food and lifestyle writer who has written for local and international media, including *Best Places Vancouver, Eat Magazine, The Vancouver Sun* and CBC Radio (see Twitter and Instagram @vanglutton).

Tess Humphrys has been living in, and eating her way around, China for four years. Her favourite food experience is sampling Yangzhou fried rice at a small, family-run restaurant in the city that gave it its name.

Tom Jenkins is a British journalist, writer and editor based in Milan, Italy. He has written for the UK's *Independent* and *Telegraph Magazine, Vice* and CNN.

TRAVEL & LUST are a team dedicated to sharing the unearthed gems of boutique travel around the globe. Their business defines the key elements of boutique travel, giving readers the opportunity to become part of local life and connect with the place that they are in.

Valentine Lechevallier works in publishing in Barcelona but is originally from France. Travel-lover, enthusiastic cook and amateur food critic on the blog she cofounded, she enjoys visiting food markets around the world.

Victoria Stewart is a food and travel journalist and former food editor at the *London Evening Standard*. She specializes in stories on London and UK producers and trends (see her blog, LondonStreetFoodie.co.uk).

PICTURE CREDITS

Unless indicated, all images featured in the book are courtesy of the markets, vendors, marketing teams and contributors. Every effort has been made to credit the copyright holders of the images. We apologize in advance for any unintentional omission or errors and will insert the appropriate acknowledgement to any companies or individuals in subsequent editions of the work.

FRONT COVER Food truck ivan_baranov/iStock Monochrome stroke illustration taichi_k/iStock White painted wooden texture background Foxys_forest_manufacture/iStock **BACK COVER** clockwise from top left: 1 Boaz Rottem 2 Luke Farrell 4 Y.evy / Alamy Stock Photo 5 Carolina Connor 6 Souk El Akel **1** Boaz Rottem **6** Fiona Reilly **9** Wonderful Indonesia/Ministry of Tourism, Indonesia **10** Svetlana Feofanova / Alamy Stock Photo **15** © John von Palmer **16-17** 1 Getty Images/Rudy Sulgan 2 Go Fish/Honey of California **18-19 recipe** Michael Sider 5 Getty Images/Stuart Dee 6 Go Fish/Honey of California 7 ton koene / Alamy Stock Photo **20** 1 Megg/staring at maps 2 Svetlana Feofanova / Alamy Stock Photo 3 Wally Gobetz 4 Jean-Talon Market Crepes Breakfast, snowpea&bokchoi, https://www.flickr.com/photos/bokchoi-snowpea/4647175977/in/photolist-85DZvK, https://creativecommons.org/licenses/by/2.0/ **22-23** 1 CUESA 2 CUESA 3 CUESA 4 Kim Kulish/Corbis via Getty Images 5 CUESA 6 CUESA **24** 7 CUESA 8 CUESA 9 CUESA 10 CUESA 11 CUESA **26** Robert Landau / Alamy Stock Photo **27** Marmaduke St. John / Alamy Stock Photo **28-29** 1 Jakob N. Layman 2 Photo by Jay L. Clendenin/Los Angeles Times via Getty Images 3 Dang Nguyen 4 Photo by Jay L. Clendenin/Los Angeles Times via Getty Images **30** 5 Andrea Alonso 6 Jakob N. Layman 7 Jakob N. Layman **31 feature** Andrea Alonso **33** 4 Christian Thomas **34-35** 1 Kathy Tran **37** feature Fried shrimp and catfish, Shreveport-Bossier Convention and Tourist Bureau, https://www.flickr.com/photos/shreveportbossier/5755955226, https://creativecommons.org/licenses/by/2.0/ **38 recipe** Baton Creole **39** 1 East Side King 2 East Side King 3 East Side King 5 BBQ Revolution 6 Baton Creole **40** 1 Ninette Maumus / Alamy Stock Photo 2 age fotostock / Alamy Stock Photo **41** 3 M. Timothy O'Keefe / Alamy Stock Photo **42-43** 1 philipus / Alamy Stock Photo 2 Chad Boutte 3 Kim Welsh 4 New Orleans Convention & Visitors Bureau 5 © Werner Krug 2010 www.derkrug.at **44** 8 Kim Welsh 9 New Orleans Convention & Visitors Bureau 10 New Orleans Convention & Visitors Bureau 11 Chad Boutte 12 New Orleans Convention & Visitors Bureau **45** feature New Orleans Convention & Visitors Bureau **recipe** Janet McGowan **46-47** 1 EaterNewOrleans/© www.joshbrasted.com 2 EaterNewOrleans/© Gabrielle Geiselman 3 © Gabrielle Geiselman 4 © Gabrielle Geiselman 5 © Gabrielle Geiselman 6 EaterNewOrleans/© www.joshbrasted.com **48-49** 2 Rachel Taylor/foodlovingwino.files.wordpress.com 6 Rachel Taylor/foodlovingwino.files.wordpress.com 7 Rachel Taylor/foodlovingwino.files.wordpress.com **50-51** 1-6 Eric Craig Photography/Green City Market **52 recipe** Salvomassara / Shutterstock.com **feature** Christina Glass Gelder/Green City Market 7 Eric Craig Photography/Green City Market **54** 1 Atlantide Phototravel/ Getty Images 2 Kumar Sriskandan / Alamy Stock Photo 3 Jeff Greenberg / Alamy Stock Photo **55 recipe** Enigma / Alamy Stock Photo **60** Stacy Walsh Rosenstock / Alamy Stock Photo **61** simon leigh / Alamy Stock Photo **62** 2 Monty Stevens 3 Monty Stevens 6 Monty Stevens 8 Charles Sturges **63 feature** Charles Sturges **64-65** 3 Kate Nyland 4 Adam Kuban 6 Robyn Lee **66-67** 1-7 © John von Palmer **68-69** 8-13, **recipe, feature** © John von Palmer **70 recipe** Mr. Bing Food Truck 1 Snowday Food Truck 2 Snowday Food Truck 3-5 The Morris Truck **74-78** 1 Carolina Connor 2 Penny Koukoulas / Stockimo / Alamy Stock Photo 3 Lazyllama / Alamy Stock Photo **80-81** 1-2 Ondina Rosch/© 2011 ablogvoyage.com **82 recipe** 1-3 Ondina Rosch/© 2011 ablogvoyage.com **84** 2 Lucas de Galvez **86** 4 fitopardo.com / Getty Images **88 feature** Sergio Salvador / Getty Images 5 Anne Lewis / Alamy Stock Photo **90** 1 Charlene Collins / Getty Images 2 Marianna F 3 Jamaica Tourist Board 4 Hunter Mason 5 Alamy Stock Photo **92 feature** a454 / Shutterstock.com **recipe** Jerk Chicken Plate, Naotake Murayama, https://www.flickr.com/photos/naotakem/4239133149/in/photolist-8sDGkH-7sAEAz-7sED1N, https://creativecommons.org/licenses/by/2.0/ 6 Jamaica Tourist Board 7 Jamaica Tourist Board 8 Jen Pollack Bianco / EyeEm / Getty Images **94-95** 1 Charles O. Cecil / Alamy Stock Photo 2 Roy LANGSTAFF / Alamy Stock Photo 3 Charles O. Cecil / Alamy Stock Photo 4 D Guest Smith / Alamy Stock Photo **96 feature** Michael Wongsing / EyeEm/Getty Images **recipe** RJ Lerich / Shutterstock.com 5 Micheal DeFreitas South America / Alamy Stock Photo **98** 1 Juergen Ritterbach/Getty Images 2 Will Steeley / Alamy Stock Photo 3 Ildi.Food / Alamy Stock Photo 4 © Laurent LHOMOND **100 feature** © Laurent LHOMOND 5 Peter Langer / Getty Images 6 © Laurent LHOMOND 7 © Laurent LHOMOND **102** 1 Filipe Frazao / Shutterstock.com 2 lazyllama / Shutterstock.com **104** 1-5 © Tom Le Mesurier **106 recipe, feature,** 6-10 © Tom Le Mesurier **108** 1 © Jorge Royan / http://www.royan.com.ar / CC BY-SA 3.0 2 Y.evy / Alamy Stock Photo 4 © Jorge Royan / http://www.royan.com.ar / CC BY-SA 3.0 **110** 6 © Jorge Royan / http://www.royan.com.ar / CC BY-SA 3.0 7-9 Carolina Connor **recipe** Alexandr Vorobev / Shutterstock.com **112-116** 1 Paul Gapper / Alamy Stock Photo 2 Maxime Duhmel **118** 2 Su-Lin 4 Ruth Patrick 5 Travel Pictures / Alamy Stock Photo 6 Andrei Nekrassob / Shutterstock.com **120** 1 Austin Bush / Getty Images 2 Tuukka Ervasti/imagebank.sweden.se 3 Peter Forsberg / Alamy Stock Photo 4 Peter Erik Forsberg/Markets / Alamy Stock Photo **122** 5 Seth Lazar / Alamy Stock Photo 6 Hauke Dressler / LOOK-foto / Getty Images 7 Mauricio Abreu /Getty Images **recipe** Krzysztof Slusarczyk / Shutterstock.com **feature** CCat82 / Shutterstock.com **124** 1 Kim Petersen / Alamy Stock Photo 2 LOOK Die Bildagentur der Fotografen GmbH / Alamy Stock Photo 3 imageBROKER / Alamy Stock Photo **126** 3 Hemis / Alamy Stock Photo 4 Hemis / Alamy Stock Photo 5 Wibowo Rusli / Getty images **128** 6 Simon McGill / Getty Images 7 Niels Quist / Alamy Stock Photo 8 Niels Quist / Alamy Stock Photo **feature** Raddaele Nicolussi (www.MadGrin.com) / Getty Images **130** 1 Paul Gapper / Alamy Stock Photo **132** 1 eye35.pix / Alamy Stock Photo 5 Don Hooper / Alamy Stock Photo **recipe** Monkey Business Images / Shutterstock.com **134** 1 Elena Chaykina / Alamy Stock Photo 2 Rebecca Cole / Alamy Stock Photo **136** 5 Adrian Pope 7 Melissa Thompson **142** 8 Monica Wells / Alamy Stock Photo **144** 1 Matthew Lloyd / Contributor / Getty Images 2 Bloomberg / Contributor / Getty Images 3 Gerard Puigmal / Contributor / Getty Images 4 London Picture Library / Alamy Stock Photo **146 feature** Thom Wong 5 London Picture Library / Alamy Stock Photo 6 UrbanImages / Alamy Stock Photo 7 Gerard Puigmal / Getty Images **148** 1 Issy Croker 3 Kathy deWitt / Alamy Stock Photo 5 Kathy deWitt / Alamy Stock Photo **150** 1 Vito Arcomano France / Alamy Stock Photo 2 Photo 12 / Alamy Stock Photo 3 Norberto Lauria / Alamy Stock Photo **152** 1 HEINTZ Jean/Getty Images 5 HEINTZ Jean/Getty Images **154 recipe** ilolab / shutterstock.com 6 HEINTZ Jean/Getty Images **156** 5 Marjorier Williams **recipe** Magdanatka / shutterstock.com **158** 1 © Maxime Duhamel 4 © virginie garnier photography 6 © Cedric Daya / HTR-France / Cervia **160** 1 Matej Kastelic 2 Ros Drinkwater / Alamy Stock Photo 3 PhotoBliss / Alamy Stock Photo 4 Antonio Garcia Sanchez 5 Newscast Online Limited / Alamy Stock Photo **162** 6 RosalreneBetancourt 8 / Alamy Stock Photo 7 Lori Epstein / Getty Images 8 Jeff Greenberg 6 of 6 / Alamy Stock Photo **recipe** © YummyPixels / Alamy Stock Photo **feature** Danita Delimont / Getty Images **164** 1 Jon Hicks / Getty Images 2 AGF Srl / Alamy Stock Photo **166** 1 © V.Irin 2 Rafael Campillo /Getty Images 3 Jon Hicks / Getty Images 4 Mark Avellino /Getty Images **168** 5 Stefano Politi Markovina /Getty Images **recipe** Matteo Colombo /Getty Images **feature** John Greim / Contributor /Getty Images **170** 2 Alan Smith / Alamy Stock Photo 3 Horacio Villalobos / Contributor /Getty Images 4 Howard Harrison / Alamy Stock Photo **172** 5 Horacio Villalobos / Contributor /Getty Images 6 Horacio Villalobos / Contributor /Getty Images **feature** Time Out Market, Lisbon **174** 1 © Daria Scagliola && Stijn Brakkee, 06 - 236 81 324, daria@scagliolabrakkee.nl 2 Saskia Lighthart 3 Alice de Jong 4 Jochen Tack / Alamy Stock Photo 5 siraanamwong **176** 6 © Daria Scagliola && Stijn Brakkee, 06 236 81 324, daria@scagliolabrakkee.nl 7 S Vincent / Alamy Stock Photo 8 © Daria Scagliola && Stijn Brakkee, 06 - 236 81 324, daria@scagliolabrakkee.nl **feature** Andrew Balcombe / Alamy Stock Photo **178** 1 Sean Gallup / Staff /Getty Images 2 Chris Milne / Alamy Stock Photo 3 Sean Gallup / Staff /Getty Images 4 Chris Milne / Alamy Stock Photo **180** 5 Sean Gallup / Staff /Getty Images 6 Sean Gallup / Staff /Getty Images 7 Sean Gallup / Staff /Getty Images **184** 1 Michael Gottschalk / Contributor /Getty Images 2 dave stambooulis / Alamy Stock Photo 3 LOOK Die Bildagentur der Fotografen GmbH / Alamy Stock Photo 4 Agencja Fotograficzna Caro / Alamy Stock Photo **186 feature** Bon Appetit / Alamy Stock Photo **recipe** Das Foto darf ausschließlich bis JULI 2011 für Marketingmaßnahmen der BEWERBUNGSGESELLSCHAFT MÜNCHEN 2018 GmbH verwendet werden. Jegliche Nutzung Dritter muss mit dem Bildautor Günter Standl (www.guenterstandl.de) - (Tel.: 00491714327116) gesondert vereinbart werden. 5 Tim Graham / Contributor /Getty Images 6 INTERFOTO / Alamy Stock Photo 7 ullstein bild / Contributor /Getty Images 8 UniversalImagesGroup / Contributor /Getty Images **188** 1 Knim Hoe Ng / Stockimo / Alamy Stock Photo 2 Krzysztof Dydynski /Getty Images 4 Hackenberg-Photo-Cologne / Alamy Stock Photo **190** 6 ullstein bild / Contributor /Getty Images 7 www.peterrigaud.com 8 ullstein bild / Contributor /Getty Images **198** 1 Hubert Stadler /Getty Images 2 © Randolph Images / Alamy Stock Photo 4 Gandolfo Cannatella / shutterstock.com **200** 5 gregorylee / depositphotos 6 Randolph Images / Alamy Stock Photo 7 Travel & Lust **feature** Ian Miles-Flashpoint Pictures / Alamy Stock Photo **recipe** Gandolfo Cannatella / shutterstock.com **214** 2 Jan Wlodarczyk / Alamy Stock Photo **218 feature** David Sutherland / Alamy Stock Photo **220** 1 Gary Yeowell /Getty Images 2 Scott D Haddow 3 Boaz Rottem **recipe** Momen Khaiti / shutterstock.com **222 recipe** Duxyak 1 GEORGES GOBET / Staff / Getty Images 2 Invictus SARL / Alamy Stock Photo 3 Red Thieboudienne / Dbilakovic / https://en.wikipedia.org/wiki/Thieboudienne#/media/File:Red_Thieboudienne.JPG / CC BY-SA 4.0 4 Chrisitian Aslund /Getty Images **224** 1 Sabena Jane Blackbird / Alamy Stock Photo 2 Wendy Quinn 3 Jonathan Torgovnik / Contributor /Getty Images 4 polaris50d / shutterstock.com **226** 1 Hemis / Alamy Stock Photo 2 John Warburton-Lee Photography / Alamy Stock Photo **232** 2-3 Boaz Rottem **233** 1 dbimages / Alamy Stock Photo 2 Kayar Kayhan / Alamy Stock Photo 3 Delphotos / Alamy Stock Photo **240** 1 Boaz Rottem 2 Kevin Gould 3 Boaz Rottem 4 David Hagerman all rights reserved CC BY-NC-ND 2.0 5 Ardenstreet **242 feature** Kevin Gould 6 Boaz Rottem 7 Kevin Gould 8 Ardenstreet **250** 1-2 Boaz Rottem 3 Michael Ventura / Alamy Stock Photo 4 Dan Yeger / Alamy Stock Photo **252 feature** Y.Levy / Alamy Stock Photo 5 Didi / Alamy Stock Photo 6 Boaz Rottem 7 Boaz Rottem **254 recipe** polaris50d / shutterstock.com **256** 1 Boaz Rottem 2 Susanne Masters 3 Shirlee Posner **262** 1 Natalie Solveland / Alamy Stock Photo 2 Boaz Rottem 3 Dinodia Photos / Alamy Stock Photo **264** 1 © John Henry Claude Wil / www.superstock.com 2 © Ben Pipe - www.superstock.com 3 © Jeff Greenberg - www.superstock.com **recipe** PIFood / Alamy Stock Photo **266** 4 © Ben Pipe - www.superstock.com **268** 2 Mint / Contributorn /Getty Images 3 Mint / Contributor /Getty Images 5 UniversalImagesGroup / Contributor /Getty Images **272 recipe** Uttam Tripathy / Polti Indian Market Kitchen **274** 1 Geoff and Cherry Till **276-77** 9 Geoff and Cherry Till 10 Geoff and Cherry Till 12 Geoff and Cherry Till **278** 4 David Sanger Photography / Alamy Stock Photo **280** 8 age fotostock / Alamy Stock Photo **282** 1 Mike Kemp / Contributor /Getty Images 2 bfishadow, https://creativecommons.org/licenses/by-nd/2.0/ 3 DSC_0091, faungg, https://www.flickr.com/photos/44534236@N00/3152234191/, https://creativecommons.org/licenses/by-nd/2.0/ 4 Adam Clyde, https://creativecommons.org/licenses/by-nd/2.0/ 5 Michael Davis, https://creativecommons.org/licenses/by-nd/2.0/ **284** 1 Alex Segre / Alamy Stock Photo 2 age fotostock / Alamy Stock Photo 3 Zoonar GmbH / Alamy Stock Photo **290 recipe** Qin Xie / Alamy Stock Photo 1 Hangzhou Hefang Street, llee_wu, https://www.flickr.com/photos/13523064@N03/, https://creativecommons.org/licenses/by-nd/2.0/ 2 Wil 3 blese 4 MackyRB / Shutterstock.com **292** 1 Paul James 2 Paul James 3 Zhang Peng / Contributor /Getty Images 4 Paul James **294** 7 Paul James **feature** Paul James **296** 1 Hong Kong Tourist Board 2 Hong Kong Tourist Board 3 Hong Kong Tourist Board 4 Thomas Ruecker / Getty Images 5 Paul Rushton / Alamy stock Photo **298** 6 2013 David Wong / Getty Images 7 Hong Kong Tourist Board 8 Hong Kong Tourist Board **300** 1-6 Bruce Leong **302** 7-8 Bruce Leong **304** 1 bdimages / Alamy Stock Photo 2 Phillip Bond / Alamy Stock Photo 3 SFL Travel / Alamy Stock Photo **306** 1-3 Jean Cazals 4 dbimages / Alamy Stock Photo 5 Guitar Photographer/Shutterstock.com **308 recipe** successo images / Shutterstock.com 6 Eye Ubiquitous / Alamy Stock Photo 7 Dan Istitene / Staff / Getty Images 8 Dietrich Burgmair / Alamy Stock Photo **310** 1 Bloomberg / Contributor / Getty Images 2 Maramagnum / Getty Images 3 Nigel Killeen / Getty Images 4 Wilfred Y Wong / Getty Images **312** 1 The Asahi Shimbun / Contributor / Getty Images **recipe** Noppadol Kostsu / Alamy Stock Photo **314** 1 Tibor Bognar / Alamy Stock Photo 2 robertharding / Alamy Stock Photo 3 Vassamon Anansukkasem / Shutterstock.com **316** 1 paikong/shutterstock.com 2 Jane Rix /shutterstock.com 3 Quynh Anh Nguyen / Getty Images **318** 4 Nessa Gnatoush / Shutterstock.com 6 yaipearn / Shutterstock.com **recipe** Stuart Jenner / Shutterstock.com **320** 1 Jose Fuste Raga / Getty Images 2 Nicholas Wang 3 John S Lander / Contributor / Getty Images **322** 1 Leisa Tyler / contributor / Getty Images 2 AGF / Contributor / Getty Images 3 Anirut Rassameesritrakool / Alamy Stock Photo 4 Dave Stamboulis / Alamy Stock Photo **324** recipe Korkusung / Shutterstock.com **feature** Age Fotostock / Alamy Stock Photo 5 age Fotostock / Alamy Stock Photo 6 Hemis / Alamy Stock Photo 7 Mark Evans / Alamy Stock Photo **326** 1 Peter Adams Photography Ltd / Alamy Stock Photo 2 dave stamboulis / Alamy Stock Photo 3 Leisa Tyler / contributor / Getty Images **334** 2 Prisma by Dukas Presseagentur GmbH / Alamy Stock Photo 3 Steve Vidler / Alamy Stock photo **336 recipe** sarawutnirothon / shutterstock.com 6 501room / Shutterstock.com 7 Prisma by Dukas Presseagentur GmbH / Alamy Stock Photo **338** 1 Hemis / Alamy Stock Photo 2 Alamy Stock Photo 3 Michael Sparrow / Alamy Stock Photo **recipe** Phongthon Preuksrirat / Shutterstock.com **342** 1 Jason Langley / Alamy Stock Photo 2 Boaz Rottem 4 Boaz Rottem **344** 5-7 Boaz Rottem **recipe** Jonathan Villar **346** 1-3 Luke Farrell 4 Simon Lowthian / Alamy Stock Photo 7 Luke Farrell **348** recipe, feature, 6-10 Luke Farrell **350** 2 f11photo / Shutterstock.com 3 nanopixel / Alamy Stock Photo 4 f11photo / Shutterstock.com **352** 5 nobleIMAGES / Alamy Stock Photo 6 Dan Herrick / Alamy Stock Photo 5 nanopixel / Alamy Stock Photo **354** 2 Jayne Lloyd / Alamy Stock Photo 3 Geoff and Cherry Till 5 Geoff and Cherry Till **356 feature** Geoff and Cherry Till 6-9 Geoff and Cherry Till **358** 1 Lonely Planet / Getty Images 2 REUTERS / Alamy Stock Photo 3 REUTERS / Alamy Stock Photo **362 feature** Wonderful Indonesia/Ministry of Tourism, Indonesia 7 © Dana Irfan 2013. All rights reserved. 8 © Hanky 9 Wonderful Indonesia/Ministry of Tourism, Indonesia / © Dana Irfan 2013. All rights reserved. **364** 10 Wonderful Indonesia/Ministry of Tourism, Indonesia **366** 1-2 Wonderful Indonesia/Ministry of Tourism, Indonesia 3 REUTERS / Alamy Stock Photo 4-5 Wonderful Indonesia/ Ministry of Tourism, Indonesia **371-374** 1 © BENJAMIN PARKER / CROPSBERRY 3Sue Quinn **376** 1-5 © BENJAMIN PARKER / CROPSBERRY **378** 6-8, **recipe, feature** © BENJAMIN PARKER / CROPSBERRY **380** 1 Loop Images Ltd / Alamy Stock Photo 2 Terry Harris / Alamy Stock Photo 3 Ian Bottle / Alamy Stock Photo **382** 1 Linnet Foto 2 Daniel Boud 3 © Linnet Foto (www.linnetfoto.com) 4 Caroline McCredie

On the back cover:
A selection of images from throughout the book. See p.399 for details.

First published in the United Kingdom in 2017 by
Thames & Hudson Ltd
181A High Holborn
London WC1V 7QX

This book was designed and produced by
Quintessence
The Old Brewery, 6 Blundell Street
London N7 9BH

Project Editors	Juliet Lecouffe, Hannah Phillips
Editor	Fiona Plowman
Designer	Dean Martin
Production Manager	Anna Pauletti
Editorial Director	Ruth Patrick
Publisher	Philip Cooper

British Library Cataloguing-in-Publication Data
A catalogue record for this book is available from
the British Library

ISBN 978-0-500-51949-3

Printed in China

To find out about all our publications, please visit **www.thamesandhudson.com**
There you can subscribe to our e-newsletter, browse or download
our current catalogue, and buy and titles that are in print.